Books by David D. Wilson

A Study on the Holy Ghost
A Study on the Three Johns
The Revelation of Jesus Christ
A Study on the Warnings of Jude
A Study on the Two Peters
A Study on the Book of James
A Study on Titus and Philemon

Order your copy at:

www.ParadiseGospelPress.com

or contact us at

Paradise Gospel Press
P.O. Box 184
Paradise, Texas 76073

A Study
on the
Two Peters

Rev. David D. Wilson

PARADISE GOSPEL PRESS

A STUDY ON THE TWO PETERS, Wilson, David D.

First Edition

I Gave My Life for Thee, Frances R. Havergal, is in the Public Domain
Standing Outside, R.J. Stevens Music, LLC, is in the Public Domain

PARADISE GOSPEL PRESS

www.paradisegospelpress.com

ISBN: 978-1-946823-04-5

Table of Contents

1st Peter

2nd Peter

Bibliography

Answers

Acknowledgment

In our service of the Lord, there are many tools for us to use. We have the Bible, God's Holy Word, and then we have Bible Commentaries and studies to help enlighten the scripture to us. I know that we all do not believe exactly alike. Yet there is some good in every commentary. As I was once told about commentaries; it is like eating grapes, you eat the grape and spit out the seeds.

At this time I would like to say again as I have said at other times that I would like to give whole-hearted thanks to the authors and printers of the books and publications listed in the back of this book. Without their hard work and input, this Bible study could not have been written.

It is not my desire to write a textbook or commentary, but only to write a simple Bible study on God's Word, which can be used by those seeking a deeper understanding of the Holy Scriptures as a group or by an individual. The authors listed have a deep insight into the Holy Scriptures, and I have quoted much from some of these authors' work.

I can recommend without hesitation their work to you. I believe that the Bible teaches us that we must study to show ourselves approved unto God. Without a clear understanding of

God's Word, we fall prey to the tricks of the devil, and we cannot live a consistent Christian life. I hope and pray that this simple Bible study will help you to have a fuller understanding of God's precious Holy Word and answer some of the questions you may have.

May God bless you and lead you into the truth of His Word. Remember, only believe, for all things are possible if we will only believe. Use what God has given to you to become the man or woman that God desires you to be. Pray, study, and ask God to give you the understanding and wisdom that only He can give. Thank God for His answer and believe.

Introduction to 1st Peter

The man Peter was one of the first disciples called by Jesus. Peter's surname was Simon, thus in scripture he is called Simon, Simon Peter, Peter and Cephas. The name Peter means a stone. The Greek for Peter is Petros which means a rock or stone. The Aramaic equivalent of Peter is Cephas, so it could be said that Pater was a man with three names.

What kind of a man was Peter? What did he do? Was he large or small, loud or quiet? Before Peter met Jesus, he was a fisherman who made his living by catching fish and selling them to the public. He was in a family business with his father and his brother Andrew. Peter grew up in Bethsaida, left there and moved to Capernaum where he lived with his wife and her mother. We do not know his wife's name, or whether there were any children born to them. It is believed that his wife loved the Lord, because she accompanied Peter on some of his missionary journeys, because Paul speaks of her in this way. It is strange that Peter is the only disciple spoken of as being married.

After Peter met Jesus, everything changed. Instead of being a fisherman who caught fish, he caught men. Peter gave Jesus more trouble than any other disciple. He questioned Jesus time and time again. In Herbert W. Lockyer's book, *All the Apostles of the Bible,* on page 127, Dr. Alexander Whyte reminds us that "The four gospels are full of Peter. After the name of our Lord himself, no name comes up so often as Peter's name. No disciple speaks as often and so much as Peter. Our Lord speaks oftener to Peter than to any other of his disciples: sometimes in praise and sometimes in blame. No disciple is so pointedly reproved by our Lord as Peter, and no disciple ever ventures to reprove his Master but Peter. No other disciple ever so boldly confessed and outspokenly acknowledged and encouraged our Lord as Peter repeatedly did, and no one ever intruded, and interfered, and tempted him as repeatedly as Peter did.

"Peter's Master spoke words of approval, and praise, and even blessing to Peter the like of which he never spoke to any other man. And at the same time, and almost in the same breath, he said harder things to Peter than he ever said to any other of his twelve disciples, unless it was to Judas."

Jesus knew that if he could channel Peter's desires and zeal, Peter would be a force of power, a force that was needed to start and build the upcoming church of God. Sometimes the most rebellious individuals make the best leaders for the church of the living God. Once Peter went through the trial and realized what was at stake, he became a pillar in building the church. God gave Peter a pastor's heart, a heart that saw the lost and perishing, and caused Peter to make reaching the lost his main theme and goal.

Peter's concern caused him to write his first epistle, or letter to the churches. Satan was fighting the new-found churches. At Satan's biding there arose a persecution against the churches and the saints. Christians were being killed throughout the land, dying for the cause of Christ. Peter's warnings and his encouragement to the saints helped keep the church together and spread the Gospel message that Jesus saves. The attacks against the church mainly came from without the church. The Roman government caused Christianity to be outlawed. Christians were criminals who were arrested, put into prison, sold into slavery, and died horrible deaths at the hands of the Romans and their cohorts.

Satan soon learned that his plan to stamp out the church was a failure. The persecutions only spread the Christian movement, because everywhere Christians went to escape the persecution, they carried the gospel message, and more and more souls were being saved.

So Satan came up with a new plan to go along with the persecution. What he could not do from the outside, he would do from the inside. He found degenerate people whose hearts were easily swayed because of selfish ego and a desire for selfish gain and began to put his plan into action.

These diluted teachers and preachers began to teach and preach a perverted gospel that petted the fleshly ego and desires of men with a self-centered doctrine saying once you professed Christ as your savior, you were saved for all eternity no matter how you lived or what you did. This teaching sounds like some of the things that are being preached today. Moreover, this was only one of the false doctrines that were spreading throughout the churches.

These gnostic doctrines are still being preached today and are still leading souls away from the truth of God's Word. I heard a pastor of a huge megachurch say that he did not believe everything that's in the Bible, that he only preached the parts he believed in. This is Gnosticism, the preaching and teaching of a false perverted doctrine, that in no way can lead to the salvation of the lost. Preachers, teachers, if you truly love people, preach and teach the whole word of God. They may not like it because it gets down to where people live. Remember to tell them the truth because you love them and do not want to see them go to hell.

Chapter 1

*Peter, an apostle of Jesus Christ, to the strangers
scattered throughout Pontus, Galatia, Cappadocia, Asia,
and Bithynia,*

In this first verse, Peter tells the readers who he is. He is an apostle of Jesus Christ. What is an apostle? An apostle is **a person who had a special and very personal encounter with Jesus**. A good definition of an apostle is: **one who is sent on a mission by the Lord**. Apostles have special power and speak with an authority given by God. I believe that **there are apostles in the churches today**; men and women who are ordained by God to fill this office in our local assemblies. We know that **the disciples were witnesses of the resurrected Christ and were called apostles**. Paul also had a personal encounter with Jesus on the road to Damascus. Some say that Paul was the greatest of the apostles, for he surely had a special mission from the Lord, to preach salvation to the Gentiles.

Peter's life of following Jesus must have been glorious. To think that he was witness to the miracles that Jesus preformed; the healing of the sick, the raising of the dead, feeding the thousands

13

of people with five loaves and two fishes, all these things Peter saw with his own eyes. Peter **has his own victories and failures**, such as walking on the water to go to Jesus then sinking and crying out to Jesus for help. This was a failure, but **victory was still his as he walked back to the ship with Jesus**. Then there was the outpouring of the Holy Ghost on the day of Pentecost; is it any wonder that Peter became one of the foundation stones upon which the church was built? Peter, I am sure, was **determined to overcome his failure and to rise above his denial of Jesus**. This he did with trust and faith in Jesus.

Luke 22:31-34

> *31 And the Lord said, Simon, Simon, behold, Satan hath desired to have you, that he may sift you as wheat:*
> *32 But I have prayed for thee, that thy faith fail not: and when thou art converted, strengthen thy brethren.*
> *33 And he said unto him, Lord, I am ready to go with thee, both into prison, and to death.*
> *34 And he said, I tell thee, Peter, the cock shall not crow this day, before that thou shalt thrice deny that thou knowest me.*

Here in Luke 22, Jesus instructs Peter, after he is converted, to strengthen the brethren. To me this part of the verse, "when thou are converted," is speaking of Peter after his denial of Christ three times then going out and bitterly praying and repenting of his failure before God.

John 21:15-17

> *15 So when they had dined, Jesus saith to Simon Peter,*

Simon, son of Jonas, lovest thou me more than these? He saith unto him, Yea, Lord; thou knowest that I love thee. He saith unto him, Feed my lambs.

[16] He saith to him again the second time, Simon, son of Jonas, lovest thou me? He saith unto him, Yea, Lord; thou knowest that I love thee. He saith unto him, Feed my sheep.

[17] He saith unto him the third time, Simon, son of Jonas, lovest thou me? Peter was grieved because he said unto him the third time, Lovest thou me? And he said unto him, Lord, thou knowest all things; thou knowest that I love thee. Jesus saith unto him, Feed my sheep.

In John 21, Jesus asks three times "lovest thou me." Peter replies, "Lord you know that I love you." The first time Jesus said "feed my lambs," the second and third times Jesus said "feed my sheep." This was a message of what Peter was to do. **After Peter repented of his failures, his life was changed.**

He then came back and pulled the other disciples together to encourage them, to be the leaders that Jesus intended for them to be. The apostles were the messengers of the gospel, the founders of the Christian Church. **They were sent and anointed of God.** God used them **to spread the word of God with signs following**. They were **filled with the Holy Ghost** and **spoke with other tongues** as the Spirit gave them utterance. They **worked miracles through faith in God**.

John 14:12-14

[12] Verily, verily, I say unto you, He that believeth on me, the works that I do shall he do also; and greater works than these shall he do; because I go unto my Father.

13 And whatsoever ye shall ask in my name, that will I do, that the Father may be glorified in the Son.
14 If ye shall ask any thing in my name, I will do it.

The Word tells us in John 14, that Jesus said that *"He that believeth on me,"* shall do great works, greater even than Jesus did. That we, as the born-again children of God, can **ask in the name of Jesus for God to move, to heal, work miracles, to have His will in hearts and lives**, and according to the Word of God that **Jesus will do it all** for the glory of God and His kingdom.

This is what Jesus taught His disciples and all of the apostles. This same message transitions from the time of Christ through the ages to this present day. The message is just as powerful now as then, the meaning, the same. **We have the right to ask of Christ, believing, standing on our most holy faith, and Jesus is bound by His holy word to meet the need, as long as it brings glory and honor to God the Father.** Did you know that the only unfinished book in the Bible is the book of Acts? Because the acts of the Apostles, all true Christian believers, and the acts of the church are still going on around the world. Just as the church and true believers in Christ were persecuted in the beginning so are they being persecuted and martyred today.

Encyclopedia of Christian Martyrs states:

> Persecution of Christians is more wide spread in this century than it was in the time of the Roman Empire, and the church cannot ignore the problem. More than an estimated 160,000 believers were martyred in 1996 alone.

An example of this is Graham Staines and his sons who were burned to death by Hindu extremists in 1999.

Peter knew what manner of death he would face. Jesus told him. Jesus also told him to strengthen the brethren, to preach the word, to lead men and women to the foot of the cross where they would find their heart's desire: peace in their troubled souls, peace in the time of trouble, peace when the storms of life are raging, peace, perfect peace in Jesus. Who was Peter? He was a **steadfast rock, unshakeable, unmovable in Christ Jesus.** He was the **glue that helped hold the new-found church together.** He was the **voice of reason, when there was none.** He was the **voice of rebuke when needed,** the **voice of hope and encouragement,** he was **the rock.**

As Peter begins this letter he addresses it to the strangers that were scattered throughout Pontus, Galatia, Cappadocia, Asia, and Bithynia. Peter as he begins to write stresses that he is an apostle of Jesus Christ. This means he is **called of the Lord** and that he **speaks for the Lord here on earth.** As Peter speaks of strangers, he is not just speaking of displaced people from their homeland. Then as today, when we speak of ourselves as pilgrims and strangers, we are confessing that **this world is not our home,** that our home is in heaven where Jesus, our Lord, has prepared a place for us. We have become sojourners in this world. When we gave our hearts and lives to Jesus our savior, we became **citizens of the kingdom of heaven.**

John 14:1-3

> *¹ Let not your heart be troubled: ye believe in God, believe also in me.*
> *² In my Father's house are many mansions: if it were not so,*

I would have told you. I go to prepare a place for you.
³ And if I go and prepare a place for you, I will come again,
and receive you unto myself; that where I am, there ye may
be also.

The Word tells us that Jesus has a place prepared for us, that where He is there we might be also. We, as the blood-bought, redeemed children of God are **the blessed Bride of Christ**. To the true believer death is not the end of life, it is just the **beginning of life**. As one person related to me, death is just exhaling in this world to inhale in the presence of Jesus and God the Father, to live forever. Another example we use is to close our eyes in death here to open them in the presence of God. No one wants to die, but **to the Christian there is no fear of death**. To die is to go home.

1 Peter 1:2

Elect according to the foreknowledge of God the Father,
through sanctification of the Spirit, unto obedience and
sprinkling of the blood of Jesus Christ: Grace unto you,
and peace, be multiplied.

Verse two begins with: *Elect according to the foreknowledge of God the Father*. Who are these elect that Peter is speaking about? These elect, are those believers that, when the Spirit of the Lord dealt with their hearts and brought conviction, they **repented of their sins and asked for forgiveness, that they might be saved**. We have all heard people say, "when I decided to serve God;" the truth of the matter is **God chose us, His Spirit came to us, made us to know that we were sinners, lost and undone**. Then and only then did we make the decision to serve God or to walk away. I have heard many people say, "God chooses who will go to heaven and who will go to hell." This statement is utterly false. God's desire is that **none should perish but that all should have everlasting life.** God does not decide who will go to heaven and who will go to hell. We make that decision ourselves by our choices, by the way we choose to live and act and the things that we do. **If we do not go to heaven, we cannot blame God.** The responsibility lies squarely at our door. We can be lost and undone without God or, **we can, by repenting and accepting Jesus as our savior, become the elect of God**. (This is the elect that Peter was writing to, then and today.) As we read the words of Peter, they are just as important to us today as the day they were written. As born-again believers, we are the elect. **As Peter was writing to encourage and uplift these fellow Christians, the message is just as important for us.**

Another very important part of this verse deals with a message that the church as a whole will not teach or preach on today. That message is sanctification. What is sanctification?

Webster's New World College Dictionary states:

> to make holy, to set apart as holy; consecrate, make
> free from sin; purity

The scripture states "through sanctification of the Spirit," after we are saved, there begins an active work of the Holy Ghost. This work of the Holy Ghost is progressive all throughout our Christian lives. Now I would like to bring out that **sanctification works in two different ways in our lives**. One. there is a biblical sanctification; this is where each and every one of us must line up our lives to what the Word says, on how we are to live, what we can do and what we can't do. An example is thou shalt not bear false witness (or lie), thou shalt not steal, thou shalt not take the Lord's name in vain, thou shalt not covet, and these are examples of how we are to bring our lives in line with God's Word. This is biblical sanctification. **Then as we draw closer and closer to God, God begins to bring about a personal sanctification into our lives.** This personal sanctification is just between you and God. It is where **God talks to you, ask you to give up something or do something to see if you are willing to be obedient**.

1 Samuel 15:22

> *And Samuel said, Hath the LORD as great delight in burnt offerings and sacrifices, as in obeying the voice of the LORD? Behold, to obey is better than sacrifice, and to hearken than the fat of rams.*

In 1 Samuel 15:22, we see that **to obey is better than sacrifice**. We are tested of God to see if we will be obedient. I am convinced that there is a permissive will of God and then there is a perfect will of God for those who will be one hundred percent obedient and sold out for God. Most Christians live in the permissive will of God, but **there are those who will sell out to God and be obedient in everything God wants them to do.** How sanctified do you want to be?

God will let us draw just as close to Him as we want to be. **The apostles, the Christian martyrs, the persecuted Christians are examples of those who, through Holy Ghost sanctification, stood the tests and trials of living for God.** Are we that close to God? If the Lord tarries we may surly be put to the test. Come quickly Lord Jesus. **Peter told these early Christians to be obedient.**

Then Peter speaks of the sprinkling of the blood of Jesus Christ. Why? To the Jews the sprinkling of the blood of the sacrifice was all-important. Peter is saying something that the Christian Jews would readily understand. We who are Gentiles understand the blood as it is brought out in communion.

1 Corinthians 11:23-30

> [23] For I have received of the Lord that which also I delivered unto you, That the Lord Jesus the same night in which he was betrayed took bread:
> [24] And when he had given thanks, he brake it, and said, Take, eat: this is my body, which is broken for you: this do in remembrance of me.
> [25] After the same manner also he took the cup, when he had supped, saying, This cup is the new testament in my blood: this do ye, as oft as ye drink it, in remembrance of me.
> [26] For as often as ye eat this bread, and drink this cup, ye do shew the Lord's death till he come.
> [27] Wherefore whosoever shall eat this bread, and drink this cup of the Lord, unworthily, shall be guilty of the body and blood of the Lord.
> [28] But let a man examine himself, and so let him eat of that bread, and drink of that cup.
> [29] For he that eateth and drinketh unworthily, eateth and drinketh damnation to himself, not discerning the Lord's body.
> [30] For this cause many are weak and sickly among you, and many sleep.

To quote from *Matthew Henry's Commentary on the Whole Bible*:

They were elected also to the sprinkling of the blood

of Jesus. They were designed by God's decree to be sanctified by the spirit, and to be purified by the merit and blood of Christ. Here is a manifest allusion to the typical sprinkling of blood under the law, which language these Jewish converts understood very well. The blood of the sacrifices must not only be shed but sprinkled, to denote that the benefits designed thereby are applied and imputed to the offerers.

The Word speaks to us today and tells us **there can be no remission of sin without the shedding of the blood**, thus Jesus became the final sacrifice for our sins. There is **forgiveness through the blood of Jesus**.

Hebrews 9:22-28

> [22] *And almost all things are by the law purged with blood; and without shedding of blood is no remission.*
> [23] *It was therefore necessary that the patterns of things in the heavens should be purified with these; but the heavenly things themselves with better sacrifices than these.*
> [24] *For Christ is not entered into the holy places made with hands, which are the figures of the true; but into heaven itself, now to appear in the presence of God for us:*
> [25] *Nor yet that he should offer himself often, as the high priest entereth into the holy place every year with blood of others;*
> [26] *For then must he often have suffered since the foundation of the world: but now once in the end of the world hath he appeared to put away sin by the sacrifice of himself.*

[27] And as it is appointed unto men once to die, but after this the judgment:
[28] So Christ was once offered to bear the sins of many; and unto them that look for him shall he appear the second time without sin unto salvation.

What we do with the blood of Jesus is up to us. To some the blood of Jesus means nothing, the gospel means nothing; there is no place for the gospel or for Jesus in their lives. However, to others **the gospel is the Words of Life, the blood of Jesus that was shed to bring us back into communion with God.** Jesus has become our savior and it's all through the blood. Thank God, He loved us when we were unlovable, and redeemed us when we were unredeemable through Jesus Christ, His only begotten Son.

As Peter closes the last few words of verse two, he speaks a blessing upon those to whom he is writing. He asks for **grace and peace to be multiplied unto them** through the riches of God's love. There is a blessing that is sometimes used which I like. We used it in the church that I was saved in; the church body spoke it over anniversaries:

Numbers 6:24-26

[24] The LORD bless thee, and keep thee:
[25] The LORD make his face shine upon thee, and be gracious unto thee:
[26] The LORD lift up his countenance upon thee, and give thee peace.

1 Peter 1:3-4

[3] Blessed be the God and Father of our Lord Jesus Christ,

which according to his abundant mercy hath begotten us
again unto a lively hope by the resurrection of Jesus
Christ from the dead,
⁴ To an inheritance incorruptible, and undefiled, and that
fadeth not away, reserved in heaven for you,

As Peter begins this third verse, he starts by giving praise and glory to God the Father, the Father of our Lord and savior, Jesus Christ. We know that a Messiah, or savior was promised to us after Adam and Eve fell in the garden. The mercy of God has always been to His creation. Sometimes it may not seem so when we look at God destroying the world by a flood or raining fire and brimstone down on the cities of the plains. However, in each case **God granted mercy to those who deserved it**. It is plain that the human race does not learn from past mistakes. We continue to provoke God by giving ourselves, as a whole, over to worldly pleasure, to sin. I know that there are those who do not accept the statement that God is merciful; they look at all the tragedies that take place in the world and blame God. In storms, sometimes thousands die, and they blame God. If God was a just God, He would not let this happen. The Word tells us that **we are responsible for our soul's condition**.

God allows things to happen to Christians and sinners alike. The difference is that **a child of God knows where they will spend eternity, in the presence of a loving God**. No one really wants to die, but to a child of God we know that we are going to a better place, safe in the arms of God and His Dear Son. For you see we are not as one that hath no hope. **Our faith and hope is in Christ.** God hath begotten us again unto a lively hope by the resurrection from the dead of His Dear Son.

Hebrews 6:18-19

[18] That by two immutable things, in which it was impossible for God to lie, we might have a strong consolation, who have fled for refuge to lay hold upon the hope set before us: [19] Which hope we have as an anchor of the soul, both sure and stedfast, and which entereth into that within the veil;

We read here that we can be assured, that we can anchor our souls both sure and steadfast through faith in God. For without hope, we would be of all men most miserable. **Our faith springs forth hope**, a hope that the world scene will get better; a hope that tomorrow will be better than today; a hope, a faith, **a belief in God and His Son that we will live forever in the presence of God in a place that we call Heaven**. We must keep that faith, that hope alive. The best way for the devil to win in this battle is for God's people to give up and to have no hope. Whatever our future is, **we must maintain our hope in God**. It's the only thing that makes life bearable.

Verse four tells us what we are having faith and hope for an inheritance. What kind of inheritance? For a home that is prepared for us in Heaven.

John 14:1-4

[1] Let not your heart be troubled: ye believe in God, believe also in me.
[2] In my Father's house are many mansions: if it were not so, I would have told you. I go to prepare a place for you.
[3] And if I go and prepare a place for you, I will come again, and receive you unto myself; that where I am, there ye may

25

be also.
⁴ And whither I go ye know, and the way ye know.

Jesus tells us in John 14:1-4 that He has gone to **prepare a place for us**, that He will come again and receive us unto Himself, that **wherever He is there we will be also**. This is the hope of the church; this is our hope. We are only waiting for Jesus to come back and get us. As one person said, "I am just waiting on my ride." If thinking about our Lord's return does not stir your heart, then you need to go back and do your first works over again.

We are so blessed; just think, there is a place, Heaven, that is reserved for us. Our heavenly home is undefiled, incorruptible, and it will last forever. Again, it is <u>reserved</u> for us; **no one else can take it**. It has our name on it; it is set apart **just for you and me**. When we take long trips, we call ahead and reserve a room, a place to stay. When we get to our destination, a room is ready and waiting for us to go in. It's the same with Heaven. **Jesus has prepared for us a place, and it is reserved, meaning no one can move in and call it theirs.**

It is our inheritance as born-again children of God. In this life, we may inherit possessions but they will fade away or we die and leave them to someone else. However, in Heaven **our inheritance does not fade away**. It is eternal; it will last forever, just as **we will live forever in the presence of God**. What will our new home be like? We know very little about our heavenly home. But, what is there to know? Revelation tells us a little, but what does it matter? **We will be with Jesus and isn't that our goal, to be with the Lord?**

1 Peter 1:5

Who are kept by the power of God through faith unto

salvation ready to be revealed in the last time.

The fifth verse begins with *"Who are kept by the power of God through faith."* The child of God, we know, is kept by God's power, as long as we strive to serve God. **God keeps us by His power.** There are many today who believe in eternal security, that once you are saved, you cannot be lost, that God's power keeps you secure. I am not one who believes this doctrine; I can find no such doctrine in the Word of God. However, many try to use this verse to prove their point of eternal security. If we take scriptures out of context, we can prove anything we want, but **we must look at the whole picture and not pick and choose what we want**.

2 Peter 2:20-22

> *[20] For if after they have escaped the pollutions of the world through the knowledge of the Lord and Saviour Jesus Christ, they are again entangled therein, and overcome, the latter end is worse with them than the beginning.*
> *[21] For it had been better for them not to have known the way of righteousness, than, after they have known it, to turn from the holy commandment delivered unto them.*
> *[22] But it is happened unto them according to the true proverb, The dog is turned to his own vomit again; and the sow that was washed to her wallowing in the mire.*

Peter in these verses very clearly states that *"after they have escaped the pollutions of the world through the knowledge of the Lord and Saviour Jesus Christ,"* which is point blank saying that after a person is saved, set free of the worldly things that pollute the soul, washed in the blood of Jesus, made clean, free from their sin.

"They are again entangled therein, and overcome, the latter end is worse with them than the beginning." How much plainer can Peter say it? That **if a person backslides, goes back to the things of the world, that their soul's condition is worse than it was before they ever surrendered their life to Christ.**

Some would say that I am too nit-picky, but there are souls at stake. There are souls going into eternity believing a lie. A perfect example: I was working on a certain job, and a young woman was telling me about her troubles. I told her that she needed to start going to church and get saved, because the things she was telling me were things that a child of God would not be doing. She told me that she was saved. Whereupon I asked her what she was saved from? Her answer was this; "I don't know but my pastor told me that I was saved, so I'm alright." You may think that this is an isolated case, but I assure you that it is not. There are people all around the world that believe that they are saved because a preacher or priest told them they were. **No one can be saved without having a born-again experience, and when that happens, I assure you, you will know it, for your life will change.**

2 Peter 2:20

> *For if after they have escaped the pollutions of the world through the knowledge of the Lord and Saviour Jesus Christ, they are again entangled therein, and overcome, the latter end is worse with them than the beginning.*

Peter goes on to say to you and me that it is better never to have been saved, than to turn away from God and go back into the world of sin, after we once get saved. This scripture states **it is better for them to have never known the way of righteousness**

than to have known it and then turn away. Do not believe what the modern church world is telling you, until you seek out the truth in God's Word for yourself. People and yes, even ministers will lie to you and distort God's Word. Sin is sin, and sin goes against God's Word. There is no such thing as "once you are saved you will always be saved no matter what you do." It is not found in the Word of God. If you take scriptures out of context you can prove whatever you want, but this does not make it true. **Always check what you hear with the Word of God.**

The next part of 1 Peter 1:5 says "through faith unto salvation." So, what is faith?

Hebrews 11:1

Now faith is the substance of things hoped for, the evidence of things not seen.

Faith is the substance of things hoped for; the things that we, in prayer, ask God for believing God will answer them. Even though we do not see it happening at the present time, **we, through faith, believe that the answer from God is on its way.** This is simply the best definition that I know, however, we will look at what the dictionary has to say.

Webster's New World College Dictionary states:

1. Unquestioning belief that does not require proof or evidence
2. Unquestioning belief in God's religious tenets
3. Complete trust, confidence, or reliance

Vines Complete Expository Dictionary of Old and New Testament Words states:

1. Primarily, firm persuasion; a conviction based upon hearing

Paul exhorts that we cast off the evil that comes natural to those who walk in the world.

Faith is believing that the impossible is possible with God, that He answers our prayer as we believe Him to.

Mark 11:22-24

> [22] *And Jesus answering saith unto them, Have faith in God.* [23] *For verily I say unto you, That whosoever shall say unto this mountain, Be thou removed, and be thou cast into the sea; and shall not doubt in his heart, but shall believe that those things which he saith shall come to pass; he shall have whatsoever he saith.* [24] *Therefore I say unto you, What things soever ye desire, when ye pray, believe that ye receive them, and ye shall have them.*

In the book of Mark, Jesus tells us to have faith in God. The Word of God tells us that all things are possible, only believe. **Believing that God can and will is having faith.**

Mark 9:23

> *Jesus said unto him, If thou canst believe, all things are possible to him that believeth.*

Jesus' word stresses that we must believe, that believing is the same as having faith, and we must have faith (or we must believe; it is the same thing). We must know that **God is able to do exceedingly above all that we are able to think or ask**.

Ephesians 3:19-20

> *¹⁹ And to know the love of Christ, which passeth knowledge, that ye might be filled with all the fulness of God.*
> *²⁰ Now unto him that is able to do exceeding abundantly above all that we ask or think, according to the power that worketh in us,*

These scriptures contain a world of knowledge. All of this is done by the power that works in us, with power, faith, and believing that **God can do anything for us if we only believe**. The motto of one of the world's greatest preachers and teachers, Smith Wigglesworth, was "Only Believe." We must have faith; we must believe.

John 11:40

> *Jesus saith unto her, Said I not unto thee, that, if thou wouldest believe, thou shouldest see the glory of God?*

Jesus tells Martha that if she would believe she would see the glory of God revealed. We must have faith, we must have faith in God, for without faith, without believing and trusting in God, our lives would be hopeless. **Faith is hope, faith is believing, faith is trusting.** When we cannot see any way that what we are praying for can come to pass, nevertheless, we know that **with God all**

things are possible. In the natural, there is no hope, no possible way, but in the spiritual, there are **no limitations on what God can do**. This faith keeps us saved; **this faith brings us a "know so" salvation**, which we can know, that we know, that we know that we are saved by faith in Christ Jesus, looking and hasting to the time that our salvation will be revealed to the world, when Jesus comes and catches us away to live forever with Him in glory.

1 Peter 1:6-7

6 Wherein ye greatly rejoice, though now for a season, if need be, ye are in heaviness through manifold temptations:
7 That the trial of your faith, being much more precious than of gold that perisheth, though it be tried with fire, might be found unto praise and honour and glory at the appearing of Jesus Christ:

Verse 6 begins with, "Wherein ye greatly rejoice." Where salvation abides there is great joy, there is hope and peace of mind. **The true Christian, the child of God, has abiding peace.** Though the storms of life rage high, we are anchored to the Rock of Ages. As we keep our lives in check according to the Word of God, we will not be dismayed.

Romans 5:1-2

1 Therefore being justified by faith, we have peace with God through our Lord Jesus Christ:
2 By whom also we have access by faith into this grace wherein we stand, and rejoice in hope of the glory of God.

In Romans, God's Word tells us that we are **justified by faith through Jesus Christ our Lord**. The faith that Christians have gives us access to the very throne of God. Wherein, we bring our needs and petitions straight to Jesus our Lord. We don't have to offer sacrifices of animals. **Jesus became our supreme sacrifice** once and for all before God. Philippians 4:4 tells us to " *Rejoice in the Lord alway: and again I say, Rejoice.*" 1 Thessalonians 5:16 states, "*Rejoice evermore.*" The children of God always have a reason to rejoice, because as the song "Amazing Grace" states, "I once was lost but now I'm found, was blind but now I see." We have been **brought from a life of sin and despair** without any hope **to a life of love and peace and a hope and trust in God**.

Ephesians 2:8

> *For by grace are ye saved through faith; and that not of yourselves: it is the gift of God:*

Peter goes on to say there may be times when we will go through manifold temptations. However, **temptations, believe it or not, are for our benefit**. I have heard people ask me, why is God letting these things happen to me, and they are not satisfied when I tell them that God has a plan for our lives. That He (God) must **prepare us for what lies ahead**; that we must be seasoned for the battles that lie before us. The Word tells us that God will not let us be tempted above that we are able, and that **with every temptation God will make us a way of escape**.

However, I, like others, wish that God would not think that we could stand so much. We must learn to **trust God**, and to **thank Him for the good and the bad** that comes our way. Our faith is and will be tried **to see if we will stand the test**. Church, child of

God, we are too near our heavenly home to turn back now. In over fifty years since I was saved, I have seen many come to God, repent and get saved, then in later years backslide and walk back into the world they came out of. Then I wonder **how long before they realize they made the worst mistake of their lives, repent, and come back to God**. Some have and some have not, and those who did not repent have died in their sins without hope.

The child of God can sing that old song, "I've anchored my soul in the haven of rest, I'll sail the wide sea no more." We have **found that place of rest**, the rest wherein the weary are made to rest. Let us lift up our head for **our redemption draws nigh**. Let us show forth praise, honor, and glory to our Lord and Savior, Jesus Christ and to our Heavenly Father the Lord God almighty.

The trial of our faith, the putting of our faith to the test; it is a vital part of our Christian walk with God. Do not be misled, **the trials that we face depend upon our walk with God**. A new Christian is not tried like a seasoned soldier of the cross. When we are first saved we are like newborn babies and, like babies, we must first learn to roll over, then sit up, then crawl, stand, and walk before we can run in this spiritual race. Each trial, each test that we overcome **makes us stronger and more dependable to God**.

James 1:2-3

> [2] *My brethren, count it all joy when ye fall into divers temptations;*
> [3] *Knowing this, that the trying of your faith worketh patience.*

James tells us *"that the trying of our faith worketh patience."* The testing of our faith makes us grow in the Lord. No one likes to be tempted or to be tried, because it brings weariness or heaviness to our souls. We want the mountaintop experience, that sense of victory, but we must remember that **it is in the valley where the grass and flowers grow, and it is in the valley where we also grow**.

In *Barnes Notes on the New Testament*, we read that God often tests His children in three ways.

First, "He tries His people by prosperity."

Many a man or woman has been led away from God by personal gain. How many gospel singers have been led into the world by fame and fortune? Money and the things it can buy has turned the head of many a person. It seems like money and pride often go together. Therefore, we must **learn to control our circumstances and not let them control us**.

Second, "He tries His people in adversity."

I know we all go through trials, temptations and sometimes on every hand. We wonder, why Lord? We cry, help me, I am being overwhelmed. What am I going to do? Then we remember what the psalmist David said in Psalms.

Psalm 61:1-4:

> *[1] Hear my cry, O God; attend unto my prayer.*
> *[2] From the end of the earth will I cry unto thee, when my heart is overwhelmed: lead me to the rock that is higher than I.*
> *[3] For thou hast been a shelter for me, and a strong tower*

from the enemy.
⁴ I will abide in thy tabernacle for ever: I will trust in the
covert of thy wings. Selah.

Many times, we have to cry unto God, just as David did, *"lead me to the rock that is higher than I."* Jesus is the rock. Jesus is **our hiding place in the storm, our strong tower, our place of protection.**

Third, "He tries His people by sudden transition from one to the other."

Too many times, it seems that one trial has not ended before another trial begins. **Our only hope, our trust is in Jesus.** Jesus calmed the storm out upon the sea, and He calms our troubled hearts.

1 Peter 1:8-9

⁸ Whom having not seen, ye love; in whom, though now ye see him not, yet believing, ye rejoice with joy unspeakable and full of glory:
⁹ Receiving the end of your faith, even the salvation of your souls.

These verses go into loving someone that you have not seen. Peter, we know, saw Jesus. He walked with Him, ate with Him, saw Jesus work miracles, heal the sick and was taught by Jesus. We know that Peter loved the Lord, but is it possible to love someone you have never seen? When I met my wife, we were at a credit union supper; she sat across the table from me. I loved her at first sight, and seven weeks later we were married. We have been married for over forty-six years; I saw her beauty, I was attracted to her. However, here we are talking about loving someone that we have never seen.

We have artists' pictures of Jesus, what they think He looked like. They make Him appear so beautiful, so pleasing, but when the Bible describes Him, it states that there was no comeliness about Him that He should be desired. For two thousand years men, women, and children have surrendered their hearts to Jesus. To find a love for a man we have never seen, only heard about, what causes this bonding love? It is because we have **a personal experience with Jesus.** He takes our heart blackened by sin and **performs a change in us.** He gives us **a peace we have never known.** There springs up a love like we have never known or experienced, a love that passes all understanding, a desire to live for Jesus to worship Him, to praise Him. To go and be with Him. Words cannot explain it, but it is **a love stronger than any other love that is known.** Men, women, even children have died for Him.

Barnes Notes on the New Testament puts it this way:

> The strongest attachments which have ever existed on earth have been for this unseen Saviour. There has been a love for him stronger than that for father, or mother, or wife, or sister, or home, or country. It has been so strong, that thousands have been willing, on account of it, to bear the torture of the rack or the stake.

It is so strong that thousands die around the world each year, preferring to die rather than deny their faith in Jesus. The modern world thinks that Christians are crazy to believe in a God we cannot see, to believe in a savior we cannot touch. They do not and cannot understand, unless they experience Jesus' touch for themselves. **Once touched by Jesus' love and power, they will never be the same.**

John 20:29

> *Jesus saith unto him, Thomas, because thou hast seen me, thou hast believed: blessed are they that have not seen, and yet have believed.*

Jesus tells Thomas that because he had seen Jesus, he believed. However, *"blessed are they that have not seen, and yet have believed."* Who is Jesus speaking of? All the saints who have believed since His resurrection from the dead. Why have so many been willing to die for the faith? Because they know that Jesus has gone away to prepare for us a place that where He is there we will be also. Don't get me wrong, people don't want to die unless they are suffering from sickness or the like. But as a child of God we know that **this world is not our home**. Our home is on the other side with Jesus. Like Abraham we are looking for a **city whose builder and maker is God**. We are looking for the **day that our salvation will be consummated**, when we leave this world and **finally go home to be with the One who loved us and gave Himself for us**, Jesus Christ our Lord. Thanks be to God and Jesus.

Philippians 1:21-24

> *21 For to me to live is Christ, and to die is gain.*
> *22 But if I live in the flesh, this is the fruit of my labour: yet*

what I shall choose I wot not.
[23] For I am in a strait betwixt two, having a desire to depart,
and to be with Christ; which is far better:
[24] Nevertheless to abide in the flesh is more needful for you.

Paul here is expressing, I am sure, what Peter was feeling as well. Every true believer has a desire to go home to be with Jesus. On the other hand, every true believer has a duty to be Christ's hand extended to this lost and dying world. We are the bearers of the good news, the precious gospel of Christ. For as long as we live, **we are the ambassadors of God's kingdom on earth**. It is up to us to bring or point lost souls to Calvary, where there flows that precious fountain that washes souls and makes them clean. There is nothing on this earth which feels as good as when we meet Jesus.

I am amazed at people who will stand in line for hours, sometimes days to meet their earthly heroes, or to buy something, or see a movie that is just coming out. I can remember once at a store people lined up to buy some new electronic device. They started lining up four days before it came out to the public. They slept on the sidewalk just to be one of the first to buy this product. As I walked by them, I wondered how many of them would do that to see Jesus. God forbid, but we are living in a world where being a Christian is no longer politically correct. In addition, if you are a conservative Christian who believes the Bible means just what it says, then you are thought even less of. When the church was in its beginning, it was a reproach to be a born-again Christian. Now in these last days before Jesus comes, once again it is becoming a reproach to be a born-again Christian.

Satan has convinced the modern church world that you no longer need a born-again experience to be a Christian. So today we have churches full of people who believe they are Christians, but are not. Jesus told the man who came to Him and asked, "What must I do to be saved," that he must be born again. The modern church world wants to serve God and be Christians, but it must be on their terms. This we know cannot happen; **we serve God on His terms and by His rules, not ours**. It is easy to call yourself a Christian, but it is another thing to truly be a Christian. **Our hope, our faith, must and has to be anchored in Jesus.**

Acts 4:12

> *Neither is there salvation in any other: for there is none other name under heaven given among men, whereby we must be saved.*

Acts tells us straight forward that there is no other name given under heaven whereby that we must be saved. There is salvation only **in and through Jesus Christ our Lord**. I know that there is a movement in this world that states no religion can be exclusive. What does this mean? That the church must concede that there are other ways to go to heaven than by Jesus Christ. This trick of the devil is causing the modern church to change their beliefs. We who are born again know that this is a lie from hell. **There is no other way to go to heaven except through the shed blood of Jesus Christ.**

Romans 10:4

> *For Christ is the end of the law for righteousness to every one that believeth.*

For Christ is the end of the law for righteousness. If we

believe in Jesus Christ and serve Him, Heaven is our home. Jesus' death on the cross brought an end to the law of sacrifice, to the Old Testament law. Jesus' blood did what the blood of animals could not do.

1 Peter 1:10-12

^{10} Of which salvation the prophets have enquired and searched diligently, who prophesied of the grace that should come unto you:
^{11} Searching what, or what manner of time the Spirit of Christ which was in them did signify, when it testified beforehand the sufferings of Christ, and the glory that should follow.
^{12} Unto whom it was revealed, that not unto themselves, but unto us they did minister the things, which are now reported unto you by them that have preached the gospel unto you with the Holy Ghost sent down from heaven; which things the angels desire to look into.

In this tenth verse, we see that the prophets desired to understand the prophecies they declared under the anointing of God's Spirit. These men and women of the Old Testament, these prophets and prophetesses spoke as the Spirit of God moved upon them to do so.

2 Peter 1:21

For the prophecy came not in old time by the will of man: but holy men of God spake as they were moved by the Holy Ghost.

We can well imagine that these prophets wanted to under-stand the meaning of what God told them to say or to write down for future generations. As we read the Old Testament, we read our future, as far as God would allow at that time. These prophets desired to know about the promised Messiah. They desired to know about the grace that was to be given to the children of God, to the church. The words that the prophets spoke, they knew were great words of truth, but they could only glimpse a small part of that truth.

Jesus' birth was prophesied, so also was his death on the cross. God's grace to the Gentiles, and the Gentiles being included in with the Jews; these things went against their present-day beliefs. We can very much see their desire to know what God had in store for the future. A perfect example is our desire to know the future, what lies ahead. We have the Bible, which the prophets did not have. We search for answers in the scriptures just as they did and still no one has all the answers. Too many times we look in the wrong places. Too many people today ignore the Old Testament, which is a tragedy. God moves in strange ways. For example:

John 11:49-52

49 And one of them, named Caiaphas, being the high priest that same year, said unto them, Ye know nothing at all,
50 Nor consider that it is expedient for us, that one man should die for the people, and that the whole nation perish not.
51 And this spake he not of himself: but being high priest that year, he prophesied that Jesus should die for that nation;
52 And not for that nation only, but that also he should gather together in one the children of God that were

scattered abroad.

Here the high priest prophesied of the death of Christ and its results.

2 Peter 1:19-21

> [19] *We have also a more sure word of prophecy; whereunto ye do well that ye take heed, as unto a light that shineth in a dark place, until the day dawn, and the day star arise in your hearts:*
> [20] *Knowing this first, that no prophecy of the scripture is of any private interpretation.*
> [21] *For the prophecy came not in old time by the will of man: but holy men of God spake as they were moved by the Holy Ghost.*

Peter speaks of how the Holy Ghost moved on the Old Testament prophets to foretell of Christ and the coming church. Paul also speaks of the Old Testament prophets and their value to the plan of God. Paul spoke of how **their prophesies are for our learning, and to inspire patience and hope in our daily lives.**

Romans 15:4

> *For whatsoever things were written aforetime were written for our learning, that we through patience and comfort of the scriptures might have hope.*

1 Corinthians 10:11

> *Now all these things happened unto them for ensamples:*

and they are written for our admonition, upon whom the ends of the world are come.

These two scriptures tell us that God wants and intends for us to learn from the past. **The Old Testament, contrary to what many people believe, is not just a book of history.** It is the inspired word of God written for our benefit. These scriptures and prophesies, if we will take the time to study them, will make us see the plan of God from Genesis all the way through Revelation. I have seen and heard people who try to be scientific about the Word of God. They end up being critical about everything and are robbed of what God can and wants to reveal to them through the Old Testament scriptures. We need to understand that **the New Testament is founded upon the Old Testament scriptures and prophesies**. Look at what David wrote in Psalms, Chapter 22. How could he know what was to happen to Jesus on that dreadful day? Read it for yourself and see the future foretold.

Psalm 22:1-31

[1] My God, my God, why hast thou forsaken me? why art thou so far from helping me, and from the words of my roaring?
[2] O my God, I cry in the daytime, but thou hearest not; and in the night season, and am not silent.
[3] But thou art holy, O thou that inhabitest the praises of Israel.
[4] Our fathers trusted in thee: they trusted, and thou didst deliver them.
[5] They cried unto thee, and were delivered: they trusted in thee, and were not confounded.
[6] But I am a worm, and no man; a reproach of men, and

despised of the people.

⁷ All they that see me laugh me to scorn: they shoot out the lip, they shake the head, saying,

⁸ He trusted on the LORD that he would deliver him: let him deliver him, seeing he delighted in him.

⁹ But thou art he that took me out of the womb: thou didst make me hope when I was upon my mother's breasts.

¹⁰ I was cast upon thee from the womb: thou art my God from my mother's belly.

¹¹ Be not far from me; for trouble is near; for there is none to help.

¹² Many bulls have compassed me: strong bulls of Bashan have beset me round.

¹³ They gaped upon me with their mouths, as a ravening and a roaring lion.

¹⁴ I am poured out like water, and all my bones are out of joint: my heart is like wax; it is melted in the midst of my bowels.

¹⁵ My strength is dried up like a potsherd; and my tongue cleaveth to my jaws; and thou hast brought me into the dust of death.

¹⁶ For dogs have compassed me: the assembly of the wicked have inclosed me: they pierced my hands and my feet.

¹⁷ I may tell all my bones: they look and stare upon me. ¹⁸ They part my garments among them, and cast lots upon my vesture.

¹⁹ But be not thou far from me, O LORD: O my strength, haste thee to help me.

²⁰ Deliver my soul from the sword; my darling from the power of the dog.

²¹ Save me from the lion's mouth: for thou hast heard me

from the horns of the unicorns.

22 I will declare thy name unto my brethren: in the midst of the congregation will I praise thee.

23 Ye that fear the LORD, praise him; all ye the seed of Jacob, glorify him; and fear him, all ye the seed of Israel.

24 For he hath not despised nor abhorred the affliction of the afflicted; neither hath he hid his face from him; but when he cried unto him, he heard.

25 My praise shall be of thee in the great congregation: I will pay my vows before them that fear him.

26 The meek shall eat and be satisfied: they shall praise the LORD that seek him: your heart shall live for ever.

27 All the ends of the world shall remember and turn unto the LORD: and all the kindreds of the nations shall worship before thee.

28 For the kingdom is the LORD'S: and he is the governor among the nations.

29 All they that be fat upon earth shall eat and worship: all they that go down to the dust shall bow before him: and none can keep alive his own soul.

30 A seed shall serve him; it shall be accounted to the Lord for a generation.

31 They shall come, and shall declare his righteousness unto a people that shall be born, that he hath done this.

Isaiah 42:5-9

5 Thus saith God the LORD, he that created the heavens, and stretched them out; he that spread forth the earth, and that which cometh out of it; he that giveth breath unto the people upon it, and spirit to them that walk therein:

⁶ I the LORD have called thee in righteousness, and will hold thine hand, and will keep thee, and give thee for a covenant of the people, for a light of the Gentiles;
⁷ To open the blind eyes, to bring out the prisoners from the prison, and them that sit in darkness out of the prison house.
⁸ I am the LORD: that is my name: and my glory will I not give to another, neither my praise to graven images.
⁹ Behold, the former things are come to pass, and new things do I declare: before they spring forth I tell you of them.

Isaiah 53:1-12

¹ Who hath believed our report? and to whom is the arm of the LORD revealed?
² For he shall grow up before him as a tender plant, and as a root out of a dry ground: he hath no form nor comeliness; and when we shall see him, there is no beauty that we should desire him.
³ He is despised and rejected of men; a man of sorrows, and acquainted with grief: and we hid as it were our faces from him; he was despised, and we esteemed him not.
⁴ Surely he hath borne our griefs, and carried our sorrows: yet we did esteem him stricken, smitten of God, and afflicted.
⁵ But he was wounded for our transgressions, he was bruised for our iniquities: the chastisement of our peace was upon him; and with his stripes we are healed.
⁶ All we like sheep have gone astray; we have turned every one to his own way; and the LORD hath laid on him the iniquity of us all.
⁷ He was oppressed, and he was afflicted, yet he opened not

his mouth: he is brought as a lamb to the slaughter, and as a sheep before her shearers is dumb, so he openeth not his mouth.

[8] He was taken from prison and from judgment: and who shall declare his generation? for he was cut off out of the land of the living: for the transgression of my people was he stricken.

[9] And he made his grave with the wicked, and with the rich in his death; because he had done no violence, neither was any deceit in his mouth.

[10] Yet it pleased the LORD to bruise him; he hath put him to grief: when thou shalt make his soul an offering for sin, he shall see his seed, he shall prolong his days, and the pleasure of the LORD shall prosper in his hand.

[11] He shall see of the travail of his soul, and shall be satisfied: by his knowledge shall my righteous servant justify many; for he shall bear their iniquities.

[12] Therefore will I divide him a portion with the great, and he shall divide the spoil with the strong; because he hath poured out his soul unto death: and he was numbered with the transgressors; and he bare the sin of many, and made intercession for the transgressors.

What you have read is just a small portion of what we can find when we begin to search the scriptures of the Old Testament. You may ask why I print out the scriptures instead of just listing them. The reason is that about 95% of people will never take the time to look them up for themselves, and they are too important not to be read. Therefore, I print them because **you need to truly understand the importance of the Old Testament and how it is carried over into the New Testament**.

People who ignore the prophesies of the Old Testament are **ignoring the foundation of the church and what it cost for our salvation**. I have a big problem with preachers, teachers, and people who feel like they deserve salvation, that God ought to give salvation to them because of who they are, or because of who they think they are. There are a lot of people, some preachers and teachers, who think that they are the big frog in the pond, but they are really just a little frog making a lot of noise. The Holy Ghost anointing breaks the yoke. We have been set free from sin and bondage not because we deserved it, God forbid, but because of **the love that Christ has for us**. We are made free **through Christ's shed blood, He who died for us in our place**. The glory of God extended to lost mankind. Oh, how great a savior we have and a God whose love we do not deserve.

Finally, we see in the last part of Peter 1:12 that the angels desire to look in this salvation that man has received through Christ Jesus. From Genesis all the way through Revelation, we see that angels have and will be involved in mankind's past and future. The angels have heard and seen man at his worst and his best. They were there at the creation of this world. They saw Lucifer (Satan), rebel against God. Lucifer was cast out of heaven with one-third of their own kind.

Isaiah 14:12-15

12 How art thou fallen from heaven, O Lucifer, son of the morning! how art thou cut down to the ground, which didst weaken the nations!
13 For thou hast said in thine heart, I will ascend into heaven, I will exalt my throne above the stars of God: I will sit also upon the mount of the congregation, in the sides of

the north:

14 I will ascend above the heights of the clouds; I will be like the most High.

15 Yet thou shalt be brought down to hell, to the sides of the pit.

Revelation 12:3-4

3 And there appeared another wonder in heaven; and behold a great red dragon, having seven heads and ten horns, and seven crowns upon his heads.

4 And his tail drew the third part of the stars of heaven, and did cast them to the earth: and the dragon stood before the woman which was ready to be delivered, for to devour her child as soon as it was born.

Angels visited Abraham; they saved Lot and his daughters, Jacob dreamed of angels, and angels helped deliver the Hebrews out of Egypt. Angels are all through the Old Testament and are just as present in the New Testament. They announced the birth of John the Baptist, and they announced the birth of Jesus. They ministered to Jesus after the temptation, they were there at the resurrection, and angels were present at Christ's ascension back into heaven. Angels are present in nearly every chapter of the Book of Revelation. Angels are mentioned all through the Bible.

Psalm 8:4-9

4 What is man, that thou art mindful of him? and the son of man, that thou visitest him?

5 For thou hast made him a little lower than the angels, and hast crowned him with glory and honour.

⁶ Thou madest him to have dominion over the works of thy hands; thou hast put all things under his feet:

⁷ All sheep and oxen, yea, and the beasts of the field;

⁸ The fowl of the air, and the fish of the sea, and whatsoever passeth through the paths of the seas.

⁹ O LORD our Lord, how excellent is thy name in all the earth!

In Psalms 8:4-9 we read that man is made a little lower than the angels. So, what is so important that we have that the angels desire to look into? We know that the angels are eternal beings. They live in the presence of God, so what do we have that they desire to look into? Could it be that they desire to look into this salvation that we have through Jesus Christ? For man to enter into heaven, we must be **born again**. Our heart, our eternal soul, if you please, must be **washed clean by the blood of Jesus**. This is one experience the angels can never have. We were created **in the image of God and given a living soul**.

As for as I can understand the Word of God, angels are created beings. They are eternal, meaning they can never die. Scripture does not account for angels having souls, only man. The plan of salvation is a thing between man and God. **The only way for us to go to heaven is to be born again, is for our hearts to be changed, to be surrendered to Jesus Christ.** This changing of the heart, this personal experience with Christ, is in my opinion the very thing that they desire to look into and understand.

1 Peter 1:13-23

¹³ Wherefore gird up the loins of your mind, be sober, and

hope to the end for the grace that is to be brought unto
you at the revelation of Jesus Christ;
[14] As obedient children, not fashioning yourselves
according to the former lusts in your ignorance:
[15] But as he which hath called you is holy, so be ye holy in
all manner of conversation;
[16] Because it is written, Be ye holy; for I am holy
[17] And if ye call on the Father, who without respect of
persons judgeth according to every man's work, pass the
time of your sojourning here in fear:
[18] Forasmuch as ye know that ye were not redeemed with
corruptible things, as silver and gold, from your vain
conversation received by tradition from your fathers;
[19] But with the precious blood of Christ, as of a lamb
without blemish and without spot:
[20] Who verily was foreordained before the foundation of
the world, but was manifest in these last times for you,
[21] Who by him do believe in God, that raised him up from
the dead, and gave him glory; that your faith and hope
might be in God.
[22] Seeing ye have purified your souls in obeying the truth
through the Spirit unto unfeigned love of the brethren, see
that ye love one another with a pure heart fervently:
[23] Being born again, not of corruptible seed, but of
incorruptible, by the word of God, which liveth and
abideth for ever.

As we begin to look at these scriptures, we will be dealing with scriptures that **instruct us how to live Godly before the Lord;** how to **keep ourselves in the right path**, some instructions that if we will heed will **make serving God easier and better**. We

52

Christians too many times make things harder than they really are. Somehow, we fall into the same trap that Naaman was in as a leper. He heard from a slave, a servant girl about a prophet in Israel who could heal him of his leprosy. Naaman made the journey to Israel to see the prophet. When he got down to the prophet's house, Elisha sent out a message to Naaman to go and dip in the river Jordan seven times and he would be healed. Naaman got mad and left, and his servants asked Naaman, "If the prophet had asked for you to do something hard, would you not have done it? All He has asked is for you to dip in the river of Jordan seven times." Then Naaman conceded and dipped in the Jordan River seven times and his leprosy was healed. **Just a simple act and healing came.**

Many times, people feel like they have to earn their salvation or their healing. **We do not have to accomplish some great act to be saved or healed.** All we have to do is to receive. By simple faith, we **receive what God has for us**. We repent of our sins and receive the gift of life. We don't have to slay dragons or win great battles, simply receive. Too many times we miss the blessings, when we fail to reach out in faith to receive. The simplest way to live for Jesus is to **let Jesus live through you**; yes, there are some do's and don'ts in the Word, but when Jesus is living through us, this Christian life is not hard at all. So remember we do not have to earn our salvation. It is **freely given** to whosoever will.

Verses 13-14 states to "*gird up the loins of your mind, be sober and hope.*" The old saying that an idle mind is the devil's workshop is very true in many cases. We have to add that we must **take control of our thoughts and our imagination**. To gird up the loins of your mind literally means to **tighten up or gather up any slack or loose thoughts that might occur**. All of our mental power must be brought to bear on living a Christian life. We are to be the example to a lost and dying world. We must be **focused on Jesus**

Christ. How can we expect to lead others to Jesus if we cannot live a life that is dedicated to Jesus ourselves? We must be that example; we must show the world that serving Jesus gives us something that the world cannot give. It all starts with the girding up of our mind, focusing on one thing, **being ready for Jesus to return**. In the Old Testament in the book of Exodus, God needed the Hebrews focused on leaving Egypt. God's command was to be ready to leave.

Exodus 12:11

> *And thus shall ye eat it; with your loins girded, your shoes on your feet, and your staff in your hand; and ye shall eat it in haste: it is the LORD'S passover.*

They were to eat the Passover standing, their loins girded about them and shoes on their feet, ready to leave Egypt quickly.

Have you ever heard someone speak of another and say that they were scatterbrained? This is a good example of many so-called Christians. They have never learned to be focused on God and His Word. There are many who have been saved for years and years, yet they still **have never become rooted and grounded in God's Word**. Why? My dad used to tell me the things that you are interested in, you learn. The things you **care about you take the time to understand and explore**. So where does this leave the largest part of the Christian church? How many are **truly focused on the return of Jesus Christ for His church?**

To be ready, to be sober, not drunk. There are two kinds of being drunk; one is on strong drink. I can assure you a drunk person cannot be focused; his mind flitters from one thing to another. The second kind of drunk is to be drunk on the things of this world. Worldly pleasures, money, power, fame, drunk on whatever the world can give you, so tied up in worldly things that there is no place for God in your life. This may sound odd, but **a Christian can get so busy working for the church, trying to help everybody that needs help, that they neglect their own personal experience with Jesus**. I have heard preachers say that they were so busy trying to get the lost saved, that they neglected their own family's condition with God. We must be **focused on Jesus Christ**. We must be focused on watching and looking for the return of our Lord and Savior. There is a great danger that looms over the church world. That danger is that most churches have lost their sense of perspective. **There is no longer a driving desire to leave this world and to be at home with Jesus**.

In verse 14 it speaks of "*as obedient children not fashioning yourselves according to the former lust in your ignorance.*" Before I got saved, I patterned myself after those who were around me, I talked like the world, I did worldly things because that was all I knew. **However, the night that I found Jesus as my savior, everything changed.** Like the Bible states, the old man of sin died, and **there arose in my soul a new man in Christ Jesus**.

2 Corinthians 5:17

> *Therefore if any man be in Christ, he is a new creature: old things are passed away; behold, all things are become new.*

As Christians, God expects us to grow up to learn how we should conduct ourselves. We are the children of God; **we must be as obedient children before God**. However, at the same time, God expects us to **grow into servants that He can use**.

1 Corinthians 13:11

> *When I was a child, I spake as a child, I understood as a*

child, I thought as a child: but when I became a man, I put away childish things.

This verse speaks volumes. We must grow in our Christian experience, and we grow by **prayer, reading God's Word, and working for God**. We must progress, reach for the higher heights, go through the deep valleys, and all of this is what makes us profitable to God and His Kingdom. **Everything hinges upon one thing, us, what we want, what we reach out in faith to receive.** God will not make us serve Him.

He desires for us to serve Him, but **it all boils down to us**. What are our desires? What are our dreams, our wants, and our hopes, and where do they lie? Verses 15-16 bring us a clear picture of what God wants His people to be like. **God wants His people to be like Him**; He wants them to be **holy, separated from sin, pure in heart, and trustworthy**.

We read in *Barnes Notes on the New Testament* (Hebrews to Jude) the following:

> It is a great truth, that men everywhere will imitate the God whom they worship. They will form their character in accordance with his. They will regard what he does as right. They will attempt to rise no higher in virtue than the God whom they adore, and they will practice freely what he is supposed to do or approve. Hence, by knowing what are the characteristics of the gods which are worshipped by any people, we may form a correct estimate of the character of the people themselves; and hence, as the God who is the object of the

Christian's worship is perfectly holy, the character of his worshippers *should* also be holy.

Our purpose is to fashion ourselves in the likeness of God, to be pure, to walk in the light of the gospel, obey the rules that God has set for us, to be the image of God in love, in compassion, in pureness and fairness with all mankind. We are to be **God's hand extended to a lost and dying world**. Our prayer should be that when the world looks at us, they do not see us. They see **Jesus through us**. We need today to be praying, "Oh, God less of me and more of thee." **We sometimes act as if we have lost our way and do not know what to do or which way to go.** I have seen Christians that seemed to be in a daze, a fog. When we should be leading others, we need others to lead us. Many times, when I talk to others about God and how God wants us to be holy, they come back that there has only ever been one perfect man and His name was Jesus. They need to study the scriptures. **God will not ask us to do something that is impossible for us to do.**

Leviticus 11:44

> *For I am the LORD your God: ye shall therefore sanctify yourselves, and ye shall be holy; for I am holy: neither shall ye defile yourselves with any manner of creeping thing that creepeth upon the earth.*

Even as far back as Leviticus, God instructs the people to **be holy because He is holy**. God has not changed. What He expected from the people in Leviticus, **He also expects from us today**. Peter reinforces the call to be holy by saying, "Because it is written." **God's Word calls for holiness** from His people today, just as in the past. God does not change. So where does this leave the modern church world? I am afraid the modern church world is in a lot of hot water.

To be politically correct, the majority of the denominational church world has changed their doctrine to please man. Mankind, through their desires to live contrary to God's Word, have begun to dictate morality to the church. God forbid, but the modern church world has begun to crumble in the face of man's sinful desires and now condones man's sinful lifestyle while refusing to preach the truth of the gospel.

2 Thessalonians 2:11-12

> *[11] And for this cause God shall send them strong delusion, that they should believe a lie:*
> *[12] That they all might be damned who believed not the truth, but had pleasure in unrighteousness.*

1 Timothy 4:1-2

> *[1] Now the Spirit speaketh expressly, that in the latter times some shall depart from the faith, giving heed to seducing spirits, and doctrines of devils;*
> *[2] Speaking lies in hypocrisy; having their conscience seared with a hot iron;*

2 Timothy 4:3-4

> *[3] For the time will come when they will not endure sound doctrine; but after their own lusts shall they heap to themselves teachers, having itching ears;*

⁴ And they shall turn away their ears from the truth, and shall be turned unto fables.

The above scriptures give us a perfect picture of what is happening in the church today. It is time for every true believer to pray as never before for a revival that will shake this world to the very core. We have too many blind leaders of the blind, and they shall fall into the ditch together. Where are the true preachers of the gospel? Where are those who will **preach the truth with a passion, with a fire from God?**

I was told some time ago that there is no need today for hell, fire and brimstone preachers because the world has grown past that point. People are wiser today. They want a social gospel to soothe their minds and souls. The only problem is that **a social gospel does not teach the truth of God's Word.** A social gospel **leaves out the very thing the people need in their lives,** if they intend to make heaven their eternal home. A social gospel changes the truth into a lie, and somewhere in the near future everything is going to come to a head. **God is going to say, it is enough.**

Judgement will be exacted, and where will this social gospel leave the compromised church? There is an old song that sums up this picture. The song "Standing Outside" is found in the *Songs We Sing Complete* hymnal and goes like this:

> Standing outside the portals,
> Standing outside denied,
> Knowing that with the demons,
> Ever you shall abide;
> Never to share the beauties,
> Waiting the sanctified,
> O what an awful picture,

Standing outside.

I know that preachers today are trying to justify their actions and their reasons for their compromise, for changing of the truth of God's Word, but sad to say their reasons only satisfy themselves, not God.

Verse 17 tells us that God judges without respect of persons. He judges us **according to our works** and that we need to **sojourn here in the fear of the Lord**. Let us call on the Lord knowing that He is a righteous judge and that we must be honest before Him. We must **live and walk upright before Him**. Therefore, the question is where do we stand before God? Scripture tells us that a man needs to examine himself before God that **he may be worthy before God**.

1 Corinthians 11:28

> *But let a man examine himself, and so let him eat of that bread, and drink of that cup.*

1 Peter 1:18-21

> [18] *Forasmuch as ye know that ye were not redeemed with corruptible things, as silver and gold, from your vain conversation received by tradition from your fathers;*
> [19] *But with the precious blood of Christ, as of a lamb without blemish and without spot:*
> [20] *Who verily was foreordained before the foundation of the world, but was manifest in these last times for you,*
> [21] *Who by him do believe in God, that raised him up from the dead, and gave him glory; that your faith and hope might be in God.*

The writer begins these verses by expressing what these Christians already knew. His purpose was to bring to their remembrance what they had already learned to refresh their minds. They, just as we, from time to time need to **reflect on the price of our salvation,** on what our salvation cost. We, too many times, get carried away in the affairs of life and need that reminder to bring us back to the sure truth of God's Word. What truth, the world may say; the truth that **worldly things such as silver, gold, or precious stones do not redeem us. The shed blood of Christ redeems us.**

Titus 2:14

> *Who gave himself for us, that he might redeem us from all iniquity, and purify unto himself a peculiar people, zealous of good works.*

What, just exactly, is the meaning of the word redeemed?

Webster's New World College Dictionary states redeemed is:

1. To buy back
2. To get back; recover by paying a fee
3. To pay off
4. To set free by paying a ransom

Vincent's Word Studies on the New Testament states that redeemed means a ransom price.

To quote Dr. Williams' book, *Prevision of History*:

> To realize the magnitude and glory of this truth one must understand the Law of Redemption

according to Jewish law. Three things could be redeemed, namely, a slave, a wife, and land. To be this redeemer one must qualify first, by being a near kinsman, second by having the price to pay, and third, by being willing to pay the price.

Jesus met all of these qualifications. We were slaves to sin, Jesus is our kinsman, and Jesus paid the price for our freedom from sin. Jesus was willing to pay that price. **We are the blood bought, redeemed children of God through Christ Jesus our Lord.** The only way for a man to go to heaven, to share the spiritual things of God, is **through the blood of Jesus**.

Many have tried to buy this spiritual power like Simon Magus (Acts 8:1-24). Simon Magus offered to buy this spiritual power from Peter. Peter quickly rebuked Simon on the spot. Many try to buy the spiritual power by good works. They offer pilgrimages, they go on a fast and, as we have seen on television, they beat themselves sometimes until the blood just runs freely. Nevertheless, none of this will purchase salvation. We must come to Jesus in humbleness and honestly **ask for forgiveness** from our Lord.

People today get caught up in traditions, mostly taught by the church world. There is only virtue in one, and **His name is Jesus**. There is no power in praying to statues of dead saints or of Mary, the mother of Jesus. She was only a woman who was used of God, just like the prophets of old, or John the Baptist, or the apostles, who were only mortal flesh and blood beings who were used of God.

1 Peter 1:20-21

[20] Who verily was foreordained before the foundation of the

world, but was manifest in these last times for you,
[21] Who by him do believe in God, that raised him up from
the dead, and gave him glory; that your faith and hope
might be in God.

The plan of salvation was in place even before the world was formed, even before the world was ever made. I believe that God knew what was going to happen. I believe that **God counted the cost, Jesus dying on the cross, and thought it worthwhile**, because there would be those who would accept God. There would be those who so believed in God that they would be willing to give their lives for their belief in God. God promised them a Messiah, Jesus, His only son, and, through Jesus, multiplied millions would believe and be saved, receiving eternal life as their reward. **All this was worked out before creation was ever begun.** There was no big bang, which started creation; there was no time when man's ancestor crawled out of the Primordial Ooze or slime. **We were made in the image of God, by God. God was there with Jesus and the Holy Ghost in creation.**

All three knew the future of man, and they still thought that man was worth the effort. They knew the price was great and were still willing to go through with the plan. How great is our God and Jesus, His Son? Jesus, knowing that He would one day have to die upon the cross, was **still willing and ready** so that men might be saved. Jesus, our **redeemer**, our **savior** and our soon-coming **king**, dying on a cross, resurrected from the dead, **giving hope to the hopeless**, and promising eternal life to all born-again believers, that when we die in this life, where He is, there we might be also, at home with the God who loves us and who cares for us. The Christian faith is the **only religion whose God is not dead**. All of the other religions have gods made of wood, stone or precious metals but none of them are alive. They cannot hear or see, they cannot answer prayer. Their founders are also dead lying somewhere in a grave. How marvelous to know that **our savior is alive and well, sitting at the right hand of the Father**.

Acts 2:24

> *Whom God hath raised up, having loosed the pains of death: because it was not possible that he should be holden of it.*

Acts 3:15

> *And killed the Prince of life, whom God hath raised from the dead; whereof we are witnesses.*

Acts 3:26

> *Unto you first God, having raised up his Son Jesus, sent him to bless you, in turning away every one of you from his iniquities.*

Acts 4:10

> *Be it known unto you all, and to all the people of Israel, that by the name of Jesus Christ of Nazareth, whom ye crucified, whom God raised from the dead, even by him doth this man stand here before you whole.*

Acts 5:30-31

> *[30] The God of our fathers raised up Jesus, whom ye slew and hanged on a tree.*

31 Him hath God exalted with his right hand to be a Prince and a Saviour, for to give repentance to Israel, and forgiveness of sins.

Acts 13:29-30

29 And when they had fulfilled all that was written of him, they took him down from the tree, and laid him in a sepulchre.
30 But God raised him from the dead:

Romans 4:24-25

24 But for us also, to whom it shall be imputed, if we believe on him that raised up Jesus our Lord from the dead;
25 Who was delivered for our offences, and was raised again for our justification.

Romans 6:9

Knowing that Christ being raised from the dead dieth no more; death hath no more dominion over him.

Colossians 3:1

If ye then be risen with Christ, seek those things which are above, where Christ sitteth on the right hand of God.

Romans 8:34

Who is he that condemneth? It is Christ that died, yea

rather, that is risen again, who is even at the right hand of God, who also maketh intercession for us.

Hebrews 7:25

Wherefore he is able also to save them to the uttermost that come unto God by him, seeing he ever liveth to make intercession for them.

Search the scriptures, for in them you will find the words of life, and an **everlasting peace and hope that the world didn't give you** and the world can't take away from you.

1 Peter 1:22-25

[22] Seeing ye have purified your souls in obeying the truth through the Spirit unto unfeigned love of the brethren, see that ye love one another with a pure heart fervently: [23] Being born again, not of corruptible seed, but of incorruptible, by the word of God, which liveth and abideth for ever. [24] For all flesh is as grass, and all the glory of man as the flower of grass. The grass withereth, and the flower thereof falleth away: [25] But the word of the Lord endureth for ever. And this is the word which by the gospel is preached unto you.

There is a need among the brethren today, and it is that we love the brethren. In a world where Christians are becoming hated for their beliefs, it is time that **all true believers come together and love one another**. We do not have to all believe exactly the same thing. I have never seen two people who believe exactly the same thing. There are always some differences, but **it is time to overlook small differences**.

A wise man, Lester Roloff, said long ago, "Brethren, if we don't all stand together, I assure you we will all hang separately." Truer words were never spoken. **If the Christian churches do not pull together and stand our ground, it will not be long until there is no ground to stand on.** The enemy is slowly, systematically taking away our religious freedom to believe what the Bible teaches. They are changing the truth to a lie, and we the true believers into criminals for believing what God's Word says. We as born-again believers need to **pray as never before for heaven-sent, Holy Ghost revival, to turn our nation once again back to our Christian roots and foundation**.

Our lives are precious, but they are very, very short. Like the Word says in the 24th verse, all flesh is as grass, and grass soon withers away. Therefore, as I have already said, what we do for God, we **must do quickly**. There are lost souls that can be saved. All they need is for someone to lead them to the cross of Jesus Christ. We may be made fun of; we may be despised and rejected by the world's crowd; however, we can reach some. **Reach out, children; reach out before it is too late.** God's word will endure forever and ever; this word is the only hope that the world has. **Someone must spread the word; is that someone you?** We are all called to be witnesses; we are all called to be the hand of the Lord extended, to love the unlovable, to be kind, to show forth Christ in these last days. Let us not pull back from our duty, but be as obedient children **laboring for Christ**.

A long time ago a young lady was touched so deeply by a picture of Jesus Christ hanging upon the cross. The words under the cross said, I did this for thee. What hast thou done for me? She was so moved that she sat down and wrote a poem. The story goes that she was so deeply dissatisfied with the poem that she threw it into the fire. However, the paper came out unburned. Later, she published the poem, and today that poem is sung as a song, and it goes like this:

> I gave my life for thee
> My precious blood I shed
> That thou might ransomed be
> And quickened from the dead
> I gave, I gave, my life for thee
> What hast thou given for me?

This young lady's name was Frances Havergal. The words speak volumes. The question is still the same, what have we given to Christ our Lord?

Chapter 1 Review Questions

1. What is an Apostle?

_____

_____

2. How many times did Jesus ask Peter; "Lovest Thou ME?"

_____

_____

3. Jesus is bound by His word to meet our needs; if it brings what?

_____

_____

4. Which is the only unfinished Book of the Bible?

_____

_____

5. Who decides our fate as to where we spend eternity?

_____

_____

6. What is sanctification?

_____

_____

7. How is the best way for the devil to win the victory over the church?

_____

_____

8. Why can no one take your place in Heaven?

_____

_____

9. Is there such a thing as eternal security?

_____

_____

10. What is Faith? _____

_____

11. What causes this bonding love that Christians have for Jesus?

_____

_____

12. What was Jesus's answer to the man who asked, "What must I do to be saved?"

_____

_____

13. Acts 4:12 tells us that there is only one way through which we must be saved. What is that way?

_____

_____

14. Whatsoever things were written aforetime were written for what reason?

_____

_____

15. The New Testament is founded upon what?

_____

_____

16. What is the simplest way to live for Jesus?

_____

_____

17. What should the prayer of people today be?

_____

_____

18. How does God judge us?

_____

_____

19. What three things could be redeemed?

_____

_____

20. What three things must a redeemer be?

_____

_____

Chapter 2

1 Peter 2:1-3

¹ Wherefore laying aside all malice, and all guile, and
hypocrisies, and envies, and all evil speakings,
² As newborn babes, desire the sincere milk of the word,
that ye may grow thereby
³ If so be ye have tasted that the Lord is gracious.

Verse 1 begins by Peter telling the believer to lay aside malice, guile, hypocrisies and envies.

Webster's New World College Dictionary defines them as follows:

Malice – Active ill will, desire to harm, evil intent
Guile – Cunning, craftiness
Hypocrisies – Acting a part, pretended sanctity
Envies – Desiring to have what others have, or to be like others

Then Peter adds, "*laying aside . . . all evil speakings,*" which means that we are not to use our mouth in ungodly ways.

Romans 13:12-13

12 The night is far spent, the day is at hand: let us therefore cast off the works of darkness, and let us put on the armour of light.

13 Let us walk honestly, as in the day; not in rioting and drunkenness, not in chambering and wantonness, not in strife and envying.

Ephesians 4:22-25

22 That ye put off concerning the former conversation the old man, which is corrupt according to the deceitful lusts;

23 And be renewed in the spirit of your mind;

24 And that ye put on the new man, which after God is created in righteousness and true holiness.

25 Wherefore putting away lying, speak every man truth with his neighbour: for we are members one of another.

Colossians 3:8-10

8 But now ye also put off all these; anger, wrath, malice, blasphemy, filthy communication out of your mouth.

9 Lie not one to another, seeing that ye have put off the old man with his deeds;

10 And have put on the new man, which is renewed in knowledge after the image of him that created him:

Paul exhorts that we cast off the evil that comes natural to those who walk in the world, while in Ephesians 4 and Colossians 3, we read about putting away evil thoughts and to put on the new man through Jesus Christ. All of these scriptures stress that as Christians it is our duty as believers to **put forth a Christ-like example**. To do this we must **put off the old man and his ways and put on the new man** raised in the likeness of Christ. Peter states "lay aside" while Paul said "cast off or put away."

In Christian circles today, there is a growing belief that God does not care what we do or say, that Christ died for our sins, that He knows that we are sinners and He died for us, so everything is covered by the blood. Therefore, we can do what we want.

To quote *The Wiersbe Bible Commentary: NT:*

> It is sad when Christians have no appetite for God's Word, but must be 'fed' religious entertainment instead.

Sadly, many people go to church to be entertained. Entertained by the singing and entertained by the preaching. They desire to hear preaching that makes them feel good about themselves, but does very little to nothing for the spiritual man. **If the spiritual man is not fed, he cannot continue to be in control of a person's spiritual walk with God.** People want to live for Christ, but do not want to live the life that is required to receive God's blessings. The message being preached from most pulpits today does very little to convey the truth of God's Holy Word. **It is one thing to preach the promises of God, but another to preach what we must do to receive the promises.**

We live in an instant world; we have instant food, instant access to our bank accounts and instant communication with others around us. However, **there is no instant with God**. We must repent to be saved. We must live a godly life each and every day to receive

God's promises and God's help. We must spend time in prayer as we must read and study God's Word. We must **live the Christian life** before this ungodly world, which is something most people are not prepared to do. There is no such thing as a closet Christian. We must **lay aside the worldly life** and worldly attitudes. We must lay aside all of those things that so easily beset us or come against us.

Hebrews 12:1

> *Wherefore seeing we also are compassed about with so great a cloud of witnesses, let us lay aside every weight, and the sin which doth so easily beset us, and let us run with patience the race that is set before us,*

Make no mistake, my friend, if it is a sin before you get saved, and it would send your soul to hell, then it is still a sin after you are saved, and it will still send your soul to hell. Sin is sin, and it will condemn you before God. There is no such thing as a saved sinner. The song "Amazing Grace" says it so well: "I once was lost but now I'm found, was blind but now I see." It upsets me to hear a person say, "Well, I'm just a sinner saved by grace," when our testimony should be, I used to be a sinner but **now I am saved**; I used to be blind but **today I see**. Some say, well, you are just playing word games, but I disagree. It is like you saying, "I used to be a drunk, but I don't drink anymore." You mean what you said: I do not do it anymore. I was a sinner, but I **do not do it anymore**. I hear people say all the time, well, you have to sin every day. However, think about this, if Jesus can wash away our sins, if He has power to make us clean and He comes into our hearts to live, don't you believe **He has the power to keep us from sinning?** We read and study God's Word, and what does it say to us? It teaches us that **we don't have to sin**.

1 Corinthians 10:13

There hath no temptation taken you but such as is common to man: but God is faithful, who will not suffer you to be tempted above that ye are able; but will with the temptation also make a way to escape, that ye may be able to bear it.

Hebrews 10:2

For then would they not have ceased to be offered? because that the worshippers once purged should have had no more conscience of sins.

1 John 2:1

My little children, these things write I unto you, that ye sin not. And if any man sin, we have an advocate with the Father, Jesus Christ the righteous:

First John sums it up very well, sin not, but if we do sin, we can go before the Lord for forgiveness. The key is "**if**" we sin. It does not mean that we have a license to sin.

1 John 5:18

We know that whosoever is born of God sinneth not; but he that is begotten of God keepeth himself, and that wicked one toucheth him not.

Ezekiel 18:20

The soul that sinneth, it shall die. The son shall not bear the iniquity of the father, neither shall the father bear the iniquity of the son: the righteousness of the righteous shall be upon him, and the wickedness of the wicked shall be upon him.

We can and we must **live a life without sin**; if we cannot, then Jesus died in vain. Remember this one important thing: it is not a sin to be tempted. The sin comes when we yield to the temptation and do what the devil has tempted us with. Let us **lay aside all those things that so easily beset us** and run with patience the race that is set before us.

In verse two, Peter speaks of, "as new born babes, desire the milk of the word." What is he speaking of? He is comparing new Christians to newborn babies. Babies must be fed on their mother's milk. New Christians must be taught, read and study. We must apply ourselves to **thus says the Lord, thus says the Holy Scriptures**. It is vital that we get a good foundation as soon as possible, so that we can **stand the tests and trials** the enemy will throw at us. However, we must remember that **we cannot fight this battle ourselves**; we must let Jesus fight it through us, for there is **victory in Jesus**.

So, let us taste or experience the good things of God, for **they are truly good**: peace of mind, contentment, freedom from fear, and an overwhelming sense of wellbeing, a knowing that all is right between you and God. These are all the products of salvation, and there is much more to the child of God. We are **never alone**. Jesus is always there. We have a **constant help in the time of need**. What more could a person want, what more than to have a friend who will never leave us or forsake us? God gives us all these things; however, **there must be a foundation**. We cannot live on feelings, though feelings are great and we need them. Nevertheless, **there is much more that we must have**.

The church must supply the needs of its people spiritually. To the newborn Christian, the churches must needs be a nursery, to give them the sincere milk of the Word and to care for and nourish them so that they can **grow properly in Christ**. While to the older Christian, the church must feed them on the **meat of the Word**.

John Phillips in *Exploring the Epistles of Peter* writes:

> We smile when we hear about the little girl who had "learned" at Sunday school the text "Many are called, but few are chosen" (Matthew 22:14). When ask to quote it, she said, "Many are cold, but a few are frozen". She was, perhaps, more correct than she knew. Such is the condition of many a local church. In some churches the congregation could be described as "God's frozen people".

Is it any wonder that we see so few saved in our churches? In the modern churches, they have lost the very concept of what salvation really means. In the churches where the gospel is preached in its truth, most congregations are small, because no one wants to hear the truth because it goes against the nature of man. We will never, **unless God sends a great revival**, see multitudes saved again like in times past. If and only if the church will begin to pray for a world-shattering revival will we see multitudes saved.

I know God can and wants to send revival, but **the church must prepare for this revival**. I hear of how God is working in Muslim countries, how people are dreaming about this "man" called Jesus and are accepting Him as their personal savior and how they are getting together to worship knowing that they could be killed for doing so. No preacher came to them, no missionary from a distant land. **Jesus came to them in dreams and visions**, and they believed, while the church sits back doing nothing. People want something that is real. **Jesus is real.**

1 Peter 2:4-8

⁴ To whom coming, as unto a living stone, disallowed indeed of men, but chosen of God, and precious,
⁵ Ye also, as lively stones, are built up a spiritual house, an holy priesthood, to offer up spiritual sacrifices, acceptable to God by Jesus Christ.
⁶ Wherefore also it is contained in the scripture, Behold, I lay in Sion a chief corner stone, elect, precious: and he that believeth on him shall not be confounded.
⁷ Unto you therefore which believe he is precious: but unto them which be disobedient, the stone which the builders disallowed, the same is made the head of the corner,
⁸ And a stone of stumbling, and a rock of offence, even to them which stumble at the word, being disobedient: whereunto also they were appointed.

Verse four speaks of us coming to Jesus Christ. We come to Jesus knowing that He is the living **stone who was raised from the dead,** alive forever more, our only hope. The religious hierarchy rejected Him. Jesus was not what they were looking for. They wanted an earthly king and kingdom. He was disallowed of man but **chosen of God**. What the Jews did not understand was that Jesus was not going to build an earthly building, an earthly church.

What Jesus came to build was **a spiritual church**. Jesus is the chief cornerstone. The rest of this spiritual building **was and is being built of living stones, all saved through Jesus' blood**. We are part of this church. Each and every believer is a living stone in this spiritual house.

Wiersbe wrote this in *The Wiersbe Bible Commentary: NT:*

> Peter wrote this letter to believers living in five different provinces yet he said that they all belonged to one spiritual house. There is a unity of God's people that transcends all local and individual assemblies and fellowships. We belong to each other because we belong to Christ. This does not mean that doctrinal and denominational distinctives are wrong, because each local church must be fully persuaded by the Spirit. But it does mean that we must not permit our differences to destroy the spiritual unity we have in Christ. We ought to be mature enough to disagree without in any sense becoming disagreeable.

To this, I agree as long as the differences do not go strictly against God's Word, as some have done in recent years. We must maintain a life of **righteousness and holiness** before this lost and dying world. We cannot descend to the world's level for if we do we are of no good to the world or ourselves. The church must **lift up Christ and lift up the lost to meet Christ**. Our aim must always be to look upward to Christ and **help others along this way**. If we are not going onward and upward, then we are going backward into sin and destruction. The thing that disturbs me about the church world is how they are changing their doctrine to allow things into their churches that are contrary to God's Word. Just because they change their doctrine and try to say that sin is not sin anymore does not change the Word of God. **Sin is sin in the eyes of God.** No matter what man may say or do, they cannot change God. They can rewrite the Bible to say whatever they want it to say, but that **does not change God's Word**. God tells us in no uncertain terms that He is the same yesterday, and today, and forever, that He does not change. His Word is **forever the same**.

As we look at verses five and six, we begin to see the new order that Jesus has set into motion. **There is no longer any need for a central temple.** The temple was destroyed not long after Christ was crucified. Today there is no temple in Jerusalem, though one will be built in the last days before Jesus returns to set up His earthly reign. There is no need of a temple, because **we are the temple**. We are the living stones that this spiritual house is built of. God places each and every one of us **where He wants us to be** in the building of the house.

Then Peter brings to light a new concept. Each and every one of us are priests before God offering up spiritual sacrifices unto the Lord. There is no longer any need for a priest to offer up sacrifices for us. **We all have become priests before God.** In this new church, there are pastors, evangelists, prophets, teachers, apostles, elders, but nowhere is there any mention of a priest, because **we are the priests**.

Ephesians 4:11

> *And he gave some, apostles; and some, prophets; and some, evangelists; and some, pastors and teachers;*

The old system of the priesthood could not do what was needed. They offered up the animal sacrifices for thousands of years, but the **blood sacrifices were not enough**. There had to be a supreme sacrifice, once and for all; the final sacrifice. **Jesus became that sacrifice.** Today it is up to us to be a living witness of the power and glory of God, to spread the good news of salvation through Jesus Christ. The good news is that all men and women need to do is to **repent of their sin and accept Christ** as their savior. It sounds easy, and if that is all people had to do, there would be more people saved.

What people do not like is the fact that after you give your heart and life to Jesus, **then you must live for Him**. You must walk this Christian way **according to the Word of God**. If all we had to do was join a church or be baptized in water, the whole world would be saved. The sad fact is that it does not work that way. There is a life to be lived. There are dos and don'ts in God's Word, **things we must do and things we cannot do if we are to stay saved**. I know that the popular message is all you have to do is believe that Jesus is the Son of God to be saved. Do not be fooled with the devil's lie. Yes, we must believe, but after we believe we must **act upon what we believe**. We must count the cost we must give of ourselves. Jesus said, *"Why call ye me Lord, Lord, and do not the things which I say?"* Jesus gives us an example of what He means in Luke.

Luke 6:46-49

> [46] *And why call ye me, Lord, Lord, and do not the things which I say?*
> [47] *Whosoever cometh to me, and heareth my sayings, and doeth them, I will shew you to whom he is like:*
> [48] *He is like a man which built an house, and digged deep,*

and laid the foundation on a rock: and when the flood arose, the stream beat vehemently upon that house, and could not shake it: for it was founded upon a rock.

[49] But he that heareth, and doeth not, is like a man that without a foundation built an house upon the earth; against which the stream did beat vehemently, and immediately it fell; and the ruin of that house was great.

We can be obedient or disobedient; the choice is ours. If we choose to be disobedient then we must pay the price. Jesus is the chief cornerstone. **There is salvation in no other name given under heaven where by man can be saved.**

Acts 4:12

Neither is there salvation in any other: for there is none other name under heaven given among men, whereby we must be saved.

To those who do not believe in Him, Jesus has become a stone of stumbling. Why? Because He does not fit into their life style. Serving Jesus, accepting His word means **changing how we think, how we live and how we act**. This, most people refuse to do. They think that they are happy bowing before the gods of this world and taking what this world has to offer. They have no idea what they are passing up by not serving Jesus. **To the child of God, Jesus is life everlasting**; to the sinner, Jesus is a stumbling block that condemns them to an eternity in a devil's hell.

1 Peter 2:9-12

[9] But ye are a chosen generation, a royal priesthood, an

holy nation, a peculiar people; that ye should shew forth
the praises of him who hath called you out of darkness
into his marvellous light:
[10] Which in time past were not a people, but are now the
people of God: which had not obtained mercy, but now
have obtained mercy.
[11] Dearly beloved, I beseech you as strangers and
pilgrims, abstain from fleshly lusts, which war against the
soul;
[12] Having your conversation honest among the Gentiles:
that, whereas they speak against you as evildoers, they
may by your good works, which they shall behold, glorify
God in the day of visitation.

What God wanted and desired was to have people who would **worship Him and give Him praise and glory**. He instituted His plan from the beginning. He delivered the Hebrew people from Egypt and in Exodus 19:5-6 His propose was to begin His holy nation, His kingdom of priests.

Exodus 19:5-6

[5] Now therefore, if ye will obey my voice indeed, and keep
my covenant, then ye shall be a peculiar treasure unto me
above all people: for all the earth is mine:
[6] And ye shall be unto me a kingdom of priests, and an holy
nation. These are the words which thou shalt speak unto the
children of Israel.

Sadly, man got in the way, and God waited to begin His work. The people were not ready. They could not understand what

God desired to do. So, God instituted animal sacrifice. This, they understood, and they had the law to live by. The plan of grace would wait for three thousand years before God would send His Son. But all along the way God would give them **promises of a coming savior and of a time when man would live under grace,** a time when the **promised savior would come and establish His church** and where **all born-again believers would become a kingdom of priests, a holy nation, a peculiar people**.

What does it mean to be peculiar?

Webster's New World College Dictionary gives this definition:

[1] Particular, unique, special, a matter of peculiar interest
[2] Out of the ordinary, queer; odd, strange

Vincent's Word Studies in the New Testament states that peculiar means:

God's own possession

Vines Complete Expository Dictionary of Old and New Testament Words speaks of peculiar as:

Being possessed or owned by God

As I read these definitions, I can truly see where God's people are peculiar. We are different; we don't fit into the mold of the world. Our desires are different, our hopes are different, and our purpose in life is different. We are truly **strangers and pilgrims in**

this world looking for a city whose builder and maker is God.

Hebrews 11:10-16

> [10] *For he looked for a city which hath foundations, whose builder and maker is God.*
>
> [11] *Through faith also Sara herself received strength to conceive seed, and was delivered of a child when she was past age, because she judged him faithful who had promised.*
>
> [12] *Therefore sprang there even of one, and him as good as dead, so many as the stars of the sky in multitude, and as the sand which is by the sea shore innumerable.*
>
> [13] *These all died in faith, not having received the promises, but having seen them afar off, and were persuaded of them, and embraced them, and confessed that they were strangers and pilgrims on the earth.*
>
> [14] *For they that say such things declare plainly that they seek a country.*
>
> [15] *And truly, if they had been mindful of that country from whence they came out, they might have had opportunity to have returned.*
>
> [16] *But now they desire a better country, that is, an heavenly: wherefore God is not ashamed to be called their God: for he hath prepared for them a city.*

We, like Abraham, are just sojourning in this world. When we met Jesus and accepted Him as Lord and Savior, we became **citizens of a new country**, a country not of this world but a heavenly country where reigns righteousness. We became **heirs and joint heirs with Jesus Christ our Lord**. Before we met Jesus, we were lost, ungodly, many times rejected by those around us. But when we found Jesus real in our hearts, we then **became a people, the people of God**. We have obtained mercy though Jesus, praise the Lord. We walk not after the things of this world but **after Godly things**.

To do this we must abstain from fleshly lust, which was against the soul. In our ignorance, we ran after worldly pleasures which damned our soul to a devil's hell. But **today we are free**. Before, we did not have a choice, but **now we are free**. God's Word commands us to walk up rightly. We are to be **honest**, not defrauding our brother, speaking **words that uplift**, words that are kind and true, not downgrading or speaking slander or ill of those around us, not rendering evil for evil, and **loving our enemies as ourselves** that when they speak evil about us, by our example they are put to shame. A soft answer "turneth away wrath." We must be a **living example of Jesus Christ** to this lost world.

1 Peter 2:13-19

[13] Submit yourselves to every ordinance of man for the Lord's sake: whether it be to the king, as supreme;
[14] Or unto governors, as unto them that are sent by him for the punishment of evildoers, and for the praise of them that do well.
[15] For so is the will of God, that with well doing ye may put to silence the ignorance of foolish men:
[16] As free, and not using your liberty for a cloke of maliciousness, but as the servants of God.
[17] Honour all men. Love the brotherhood. Fear God. Honour the king.
[18] Servants, be subject to your masters with all fear; not

only to the good and gentle, but also to the froward.
¹⁹ For this is thankworthy, if a man for conscience toward
God endure grief, suffering wrongfully.

Peter writes here that we are to be subject to those in authority. We are to obey the laws that man institutes. The only exception is when the laws of man go against the laws or ordinances of God.

Barnes Notes on the New Testament:

Of course, what is here said must be understood with the limitation everywhere implied, that what is ordained by those in authority is contrary to the law of God.

The only reason for a Christian to go against the law or to disobey those who have authority over us is **when it is contrary to God's Word or law**. We must submit even to the Neros of this world. One example of God's people going against man's authority is as follows: In Daniel 3:8-23, the three Hebrews refused to bow to the image of King Nebuchadnezzar even though their punishment would be death. **They refused to go against God's law.**

Exodus 20:4-6

⁴ Thou shalt not make unto thee any graven image, or any likeness of any thing that is in heaven above, or that is in the earth beneath, or that is in the water under the earth:
⁵ Thou shalt not bow down thyself to them, nor serve them: for I the LORD thy God am a jealous God, visiting the

iniquity of the fathers upon the children unto the third and fourth generation of them that hate me;
⁶ And shewing mercy unto thousands of them that love me, and keep my commandments.

These servants, because they refused to bow down, won a great victory for God. They were **willing to die for what they believed in**. They were thrown into the fire, and in the fire they met an angel, or maybe the King was right when he said the fourth man is like the son of God. We never know how our lives affect those around us. **Your life is a witness to those in this world.** If being a Christian were against the law, would there be enough evidence to prove you guilty? Sadly, many who call themselves Christians would be proved innocent, because their lives do not measure up to God's standard.

Another example is Daniel who refused to obey the law of Darius forbidding anyone to pray to God for thirty days. True, Darius was tricked by Daniel's enemies, but the decree was given. Daniel **prayed to God anyway** knowing the punishment meant certain death. Daniel was a man of convictions; he knew what God's Word said. Daniel was taken and put into the den of lions. Just before Daniel was put in the den, the King said to Daniel, *"Thy God whom thou servest continually, he will deliver thee."* Daniel believed, and his life was such a witness that **even King Darius believed that God would deliver him**. The next morning the king went in haste to the den of lions and cried, "O Daniel, servant of the living God, is thy God able to deliver thee?" Daniel replied, "O King, live forever." **A life dedicated to God and His service brings victory in our lives, and sometimes hope and faith in the lives of others.**

Peter himself refused to obey a direct order from the

Sanhedrin. They ordered him to stop teaching and preaching in the name of Jesus. Many times, we face enemies inside and outside the church. So, what do we do? We keep on keeping on in the name of Jesus. The Word tells us **not to fear those who can kill the body**.

Matthew 10:28

> *And fear not them which kill the body, but are not able to kill the soul: but rather fear him which is able to destroy both soul and body in hell.*

Luke 12:4

> *And I say unto you my friends, Be not afraid of them that kill the body, and after that have no more that they can do.*

Martin Luther refused to obey the Pope of Rome at the Diet of Worms. The author of *Pilgrim's Progress*, John Bunyan, spent much of his life in the Bedford jail for speaking out against the church establishment and its practices. There are times when we as Christian servants of God will have to **stand and serve God rather than man**. But as a general rule, we are to obey the laws and those that have the authority over us. Thus we, by obedience, bring **glory and praise and honor to God above**.

The will of God for our lives is to **put forth a Christ-like example to a lost and dying world**. You will read this over and over in this study of 1st Peter and any other work that I write. This fifteenth verse sums up the entire message: "*that with well doing ye may put to silence the ignorance of men.*" The ignorance of this world toward God and the things of God I don't believe has ever been greater. You talk to sinners and each one has their own concept of what a Christian should be.

The largest part of the world can tell us what a Christian should be and do, when they have never studied the Word of God. I talked to a woman and she told me that she did not go to church because there were too many dos and don'ts that they had to go by. She considered herself to be spiritual, she believed in God, but she wanted to be free to live life as she wanted. She believed that she was all right and she would go to heaven when she died. This gives us a perfect example of the ignorance of this world. Being a good moral person cannot and will not take a soul to heaven. There must and has to be a **born-again experience** with Jesus Christ our Savior. Jesus tells us himself in the Word, "Ye must be born again."

John 3:3

> *Jesus answered and said unto him, Verily, verily, I say unto thee, Except a man be born again, he cannot see the kingdom of God.*

The foolishness of this world and what it believes to be Godly and Christian is amazing. It is for this reason that the church world is trying to appease the sinful world. The sinful world says that homosexual behaver is moral and right, so the church, to appease the world, changes its doctrine to promote homosexual preachers and priest and church leaders. How sad. Sometimes I wonder who is more ignorant, the world or the church for going along with the world.

Years ago, the churches had standards and convictions. But not so much anymore. How can we combat this ignorance? The only way is to **live a good Christian life before them**. Give answers when asked, a witness of God's **love and grace**. Live what we preach and teach and be the same wherever we go and to whomever we see. The world wants something real, so **be real**. Be like God, always the same, and be **kind and tender-hearted, loving the brethren as one's self.**

Verse 17 tells us to honor all men and be respectful to everyone, not looking down on people because they do not know Christ as their savior. Too many times I have heard people speak of different ones as being "holier than thou." We are not to put on airs; we are to **be as the Lord made us**. If we have respect of persons, we are no better than the world. **Show thyself friendly and have compassion.** Fear God and **live a just life for the world to see**. The best way I know to do that is to pray; Oh God, more of thee and less of me.

1 Peter 2:18-21

[18] Servants, be subject to your masters with all fear; not only to the good and gentle, but also to the froward.
[19] For this is thankworthy, if a man for conscience toward God endure grief, suffering wrongfully.
[20] For what glory is it, if, when ye be buffeted for your faults, ye shall take it patiently? but if, when ye do well, and suffer for it, ye take it patiently, this is acceptable with God.
[21] For even hereunto were ye called: because Christ also suffered for us, leaving us an example, that ye should follow his steps:

In the eighteenth verse Peter addresses the **slaves and servants who came to Christ** and became Christians. Peter stresses that though they were free from sin, that they still had a duty to perform to their masters. They were in all Christian meekness to **perform their duties to the best of their abilities**, which was their reasonable service. They were **in all Christian meekness to bear all the wrongs** that they might suffer from their masters. Many of these servants had good, kind, and gentle masters, but some were not that way. No matter good or bad, they were to put forth a Christ-like example to their masters. They were to be o**bedient, honest, and trustworthy**. If they had to endure grief or suffer wrongfully, they were to do all **for the glory of God**. *For we do not know what all God has planned for us.*

A perfect example is Joseph. God gave him dreams which made his brothers angry, and so they sold him into slavery, telling Jacob that Joseph was killed by wild beast. Joseph's brothers sold Joseph to the Ishmaelite traders who took Joseph into Egypt. There they sold Joseph to Potiphar to be a slave in his house. Even in slavery **God blessed Joseph and he rose to be the chief servant**. There his life, it would seem, took a downward trend. Accused of dishonoring Potiphar's wife, he was thrown into the prison house. There he again was **blessed of God and rose to a high position**. Joseph **never lost his faith** in his God. God again used Joseph to interpret dreams.

Then one day, Pharaoh had a dream which his magicians could not interpret. Pharaoh was told about Joseph. Pharaoh called for Joseph to be brought before him and asked Joseph the meaning of his dream, whereupon Joseph explained what was going to happen over the next fourteen years. **Joseph was made the second highest ruler in Egypt.** Joseph did not know what God's plan was for his life but he **never lost his faith**. God used all of this to save Joseph's family.

We may not understand why God does the things that He does, but **He always has a plan for our lives**. Like Joseph, we don't know what the future holds, but with faith and trust in God, whatever happens, we can have an abiding peace, and we can give the glory to God. The story of Joseph begins in Genesis chapters 37-50. It is a story of God's grace and mercy and how, if we keep our faith in God, God will **use us for His glory**. We will find in our lives that there will be times of grief and sorrow, and times of being wrongfully used. Trust in God, be patient, not rendering evil for evil, for in so doing, we become **acceptable unto God**, and isn't that our goal, to please God?

Verse 21 is a summation of the last few scriptures. We, each and every one of us, were suffering, bound by the chains of sin. We were puppets to the devil and what he wants; he pulled the strings and we danced to his tune. We could not get free. Then we heard about Jesus and His power to set the sinner free. As we called upon Jesus and accepted Him as our savior, **Jesus cut the strings of sin that bound us and set us free**. The Word tells us if the Son hath made us free, then **we are free indeed**.

John 8:36

> *If the Son therefore shall make you free, ye shall be free indeed.*

Galatians 5:1

> *Stand fast therefore in the liberty wherewith Christ hath made us free, and be not entangled again with the yoke of bondage.*

Thank God, I am free, free, free from this world of sin. Jesus Christ **is our example**. We must **walk in His footsteps** if we are to reach our heavenly home. Do you ever think about what Jesus left to come to earth, to become our savior?

John Phillips writes in *Exploring the Epistles of Peter:*

> We picture him way back before ever time began, dwelling in a light unapproachable and living in perfect harmony with God the Father and God the Holy Spirit in unimaginable glory and ever-rising tides of joy. He was uncreated, self-existing, coeternal, coequal, and coexistent with the Father and the Spirit. He was God the Son, the second person of the triune Godhead. His wisdom was infinite, his love fathomless and his power without measure or end. His nature and attributes were those of the living God. He basked in the sunshine of the Father's love in endless delight. Eternal ages rolled by without end. All was love, joy, peace, and bliss beyond all imagination or thought. Yet, he suffered for us.

What a savior we have, what a loving savior. His spirit calls to sinners, His convicting spirit that **speaks to hearts and lives to tell them that they can be free**. I do not understand how people can say no to a savior, a redeemer who wants to give them peace like they have never known. They remind me of Pharaoh. Moses went before Pharaoh and asked, "When do you want me to ask God to destroy this plague of frog from the land of Egypt?"

Exodus 8:8-10

[8] *Then Pharaoh called for Moses and Aaron, and said,*

96

Intreat the LORD, that he may take away the frogs from me, and from my people; and I will let the people go, that they may do sacrifice unto the LORD.

⁹ And Moses said unto Pharaoh, Glory over me: when shall I intreat for thee, and for thy servants, and for thy people, to destroy the frogs from thee and thy houses, that they may remain in the river only?

¹⁰ And he said, To morrow. And he said, Be it according to thy word: that thou mayest know that there is none like unto the LORD our God.

Pharaoh's answer was, "Tomorrow." Why, pray tell me, did Pharaoh want to spend one more night with the frogs. Then I think of how many times I have asked people, "Don't you want to give your heart to the Lord?" And their answer was, "No, I am not ready yet." They wanted to **spend a while longer with the frogs**. They wanted to stay a while longer **wallowing in the muck of the hog pen**. The devil tells people you can live for God when you get old; now is the time to have fun, so enjoy yourself. There is too much you need to do while you still can. Serve God when you are too old to do anything else. **The sad truth is that people believe these lies more times than not.**

1 Peter 2:22-25

²² Who did no sin, neither was guile found in his mouth:
²³ Who, when he was reviled, reviled not again; when he suffered, he threatened not; but committed himself to him that judgeth righteously:
²⁴ Who his own self bare our sins in his own body on the tree, that we, being dead to sins, should live unto

righteousness: by whose stripes ye were healed.
[25] For ye were as sheep going astray; but are now
returned unto the Shepherd and Bishop of your souls.

Verse 22 begins telling us what kind of a man Jesus was. It tells us that **Jesus did no sin**, and Peter should know. For three- to three-and-one-half years Peter walked with Jesus. He watched Jesus' life, he heard Jesus' words, he saw firsthand what kind of man Jesus was; **no one knew Jesus any better than Peter**. The words of Jesus were pure, honest and kind. If anyone had a right to be upset with people, it was Jesus, and still all He had for people was compassion, **compassion for the poor, the sick and hurting**. He could have been like many even today who feel that people don't give them the credit that they deserve, to be treated with high honor. The one thing Jesus did not want was to be considered a threat to the religious crowd. He did not come to the rich; He came to the **poor and hurting souls of man**.

The religious crowd considered Jesus a threat because **He dealt with the poor and needy**, while the religious group were too important to be bothered with the needy. He was a man that the multitudes loved. He lived and walked where they lived and walked. He healed all manner of sicknesses, He restored hearing to the deaf, He gave back sight to the blind, He fed not only the body but also the souls of men and woman. **Jesus was a sinless man in every way, as a child and as a young man.**

John Phillips wrote in *Exploring the Epistles of Peter:*

> He was without sin as a young man, as the village Carpenter, and as an itinerant Preacher. He was sinless in thought and imagination, in desire and

aspiration, and in word and deed. He was sinless when Satan found Him fasting in the wilderness. He was sinless when Satan left Him, exhausted and at the end of His physical endurance. He was sinless in his relationships with men, women, and children and sinless under the all-seeing eye of God. He was immaculate, impeccable, holy, and absolutely pleasing to God. He did not sin.

Jesus was straightforward; He told you the truth whether you wanted to hear it or not. This many times upset people; I know it does today. I make it a policy to tell people, "If you don't want to know what I think, then don't ask me, because I will tell you what I think, whether you like it or not." I sometimes truly think that people want you to lie to them, because it eases their conscience. But a lie is a lie, and nothing makes a lie right in the eyes of God.

Jesus knew the price that had to be paid for our salvation, and **He determined to pay that price**. When taken before His accusers, **they felt His peace**. When He was railed upon, He answered not a word. This made the priests even angrier, because it showed their guilt in trying to do away with Jesus. Jesus knew what the outcome was going to be. He had already spent hours in prayer committing himself to the righteous judge, His Holy Father.

The only way man could be brought back into communion with the Father was for Jesus to **become the supreme sacrifice**. When He went to that cross He **carried the weight** of sin for all mankind. The religious leaders who were supposed to be the wisest men in the land did not even know enough of the scriptures to know who Jesus was. What does the Bible say? **To search the scriptures.** There was very little searching going on. The religious group liked what was going on. They liked being looked up to and given places of honor. It reminds me of today. The religious scholars like things as they are; they don't want anybody to rock the boat. When the priests brought Jesus to Pilate, even Pilate said that **he found no fault in Jesus and would have let him go**. The priest then incited the crowd to cry for Jesus to be crucified. Pilate yielded to the crowd and had Jesus put to death. **The scriptures were fulfilled.** Jesus was **bruised for our transgressions**, and by **His stripes we are healed**.

Isaiah 53:1-12

¹ Who hath believed our report? and to whom is the arm of the LORD revealed?
² For he shall grow up before him as a tender plant, and as a root out of a dry ground: he hath no form nor comeliness; and when we shall see him, there is no beauty that we should desire him.
³ He is despised and rejected of men; a man of sorrows, and acquainted with grief: and we hid as it were our faces from him; he was despised, and we esteemed him not.
⁴ Surely he hath borne our griefs, and carried our sorrows: yet we did esteem him stricken, smitten of God, and afflicted.
⁵ But he was wounded for our transgressions, he was bruised for our iniquities: the chastisement of our peace was upon him; and with his stripes we are healed.
⁶ All we like sheep have gone astray; we have turned every one to his own way; and the LORD hath laid on him the iniquity of us all.
⁷ He was oppressed, and he was afflicted, yet he opened

*not his mouth: he is brought as a lamb to the slaughter,
and as a sheep before her shearers is dumb, so he openeth
not his mouth.*

*⁸ He was taken from prison and from judgment: and who
shall declare his generation? for he was cut off out of the
land of the living: for the transgression of my people was
he stricken.*

*⁹ And he made his grave with the wicked, and with the rich
in his death; because he had done no violence, neither was
any deceit in his mouth.*

*¹⁰ Yet it pleased the LORD to bruise him; he hath put him
to grief: when thou shalt make his soul an offering for sin,
he shall see his seed, he shall prolong his days, and the
pleasure of the LORD shall prosper in his hand.*

*¹¹ He shall see of the travail of his soul, and shall be
satisfied: by his knowledge shall my righteous servant
justify many; for he shall bear their iniquities.*

*¹² Therefore will I divide him a portion with the great, and
he shall divide the spoil with the strong; because he hath
poured out his soul unto death: and he was numbered with
the transgressors; and he bare the sin of many, and made
intercession for the transgressors.*

Isaiah says it all in this 53rd chapter. Jesus bore our sin in
His own body. He was beaten, and by the stripes that were laid
upon His back, He **purchased our healing**. Isaiah said "with his
stripes we are healed." 1st Peter says "by whose stripes ye were
healed." **Healing is ours.** It has been paid for, so accept it today.
Both Isaiah and 1st Peter 2:25 speak of sinners as lost sheep who
have gone astray. So, we can look at it this way, we who are saved
are sheep that have been brought **back into the fold**, back to the

great shepherd, **back into the arms of Jesus**.

Sheep are said to be dumb creatures. If sheep get lost, they are lost. Dogs cats and other animals, if they get lost, they can find their way home. Sheep cannot; someone must go and get them and bring them home. This is why sheep must have a shepherd, a shepherd to watch over them and to feed them and to lead them. Christ is our Shepherd, and **we are the sheep of His pastures**. Thank God for a loving shepherd, a shepherd who **gave Himself for His sheep**.

To quote from *Barnes Notes on the New Testament (Hebrews to Jude):*

> That there is something very beautiful in the expression, *"Bishop of souls."* It implies that the soul is the peculiar care of the Saviour; that it is the object of His special interest; and that it is of great value – so great that it is that which mainly deserves regard. He is the Bishop *of the soul* in a sense quite distinct from any care which He manifests for the *body. That* too, in the proper way, is the object of His care; but that has no importance compared with the soul. *Our* care is principally employed in respect to the body; the care of the Redeemer has especial reference to the soul.

There is nothing more important than the soul. Our bodies grow old and death takes us from this life. Our body is laid in the grave or disposed of in some manner. But the soul will spend eternity in heaven or hell. That depends on us and how we live. It is the Lord's will that we **spend eternity with Him**. If we will repent of our sins and ask Jesus to save us, we then become the children of God. **Jesus becomes the Bishop of our souls.** How great it is to know that we have a guardian who cares for our souls.

Chapter 2 Review Questions

1. As newborn babes what are we to desire?

   _____

   _____

2. Why do a lot of people go to church?

   _____

   _____

3. It is not a sin to be tempted. What do we have to do to sin?

   _____

   _____

4. What is the church supposed to be for the newborn Christian?

   _____

   _____

5. Jesus is quoted in the Bible as saying: Why call ye me Lord, Lord, and _____

   _____?

6. Where do we find God telling us He wants us to be a "kingdom of priests"?

   _____

   _____

7. In Ezekiel 18:20 it states that the soul that sinneth, it

   _____.

8. We are like Abraham. What we are looking for?

   _____

   _____

9. The three Hebrew children that were thrown in the fire met another man there. How did King Nebuchadnezzar describe him?

   _____

   _____

10. The scripture states: "that with well doing ye may put to silence the _____".

11. Whose image did the three Hebrew men refuse to bow down to?

   _____

   _____

12. Who was king when Daniel was put into the den of lions?

   _____

   _____

13. What did Jesus say that we must do to go to heaven?

_____

_____

14. If Jesus hath made us free then we are _____.

15. When Moses asked Pharaoh a question, what did Pharaoh

say he wanted?

_____

_____

16. Who was the Roman Governor during the time Jesus was

on the earth?

_____

_____

17. What other book and chapter of the Bible mentions healing

by Jesus' stripes?

_____

_____

18. What are we referred as, in Isaiah and 1st Peter?

_____

_____

Chapter 3

1 Peter 3:1-7

¹ Likewise, ye wives, be in subjection to your own husbands; that, if any obey not the word, they also may without the word be won by the conversation of the wives; ² While they behold your chaste conversation coupled with fear.

³ Whose adorning let it not be that outward adorning of plaiting the hair, and of wearing of gold, or of putting on of apparel;

⁴ But let it be the hidden man of the heart, in that which is not corruptible, even the ornament of a meek and quiet spirit, which is in the sight of God of great price.

⁵ For after this manner in the old time the holy women also, who trusted in God, adorned themselves, being in subjection unto their own husbands:

⁶ Even as Sara obeyed Abraham, calling him lord: whose daughters ye are, as long as ye do well, and are not afraid with any amazement.

⁷ Likewise, ye husbands, dwell with them according to knowledge, giving honour unto the wife, as unto the weaker vessel, and as being heirs together of the grace of life; that your prayers be not hindered.

As we begin to look at these verses, we can see that in this modern society, we are perhaps opening a can of worms. A big can of worms, because people do not want to live by the Word of God. So, let us look at what the Word of God has to say. *"Likewise, ye wives, be in subjection to your own husbands."* Peter and Paul both taught this same doctrine as to **how a household was to be run**.

Today we must look at the wording of the scripture and realize that over a long period of time, the whole **meaning of some words has changed**, and are continually changing. For example, if something is good, some say that it's bad, which means it's good. Makes no sense to me, but go figure. Gay used to mean happy, carefree, but today it means that you are homosexual. Their life style is anything but happy or carefree. Booty used to mean the prize won by war or pirates, but today the slang meaning is the posterior body part. I can go into some stores and ask where the soda waters are, and they do not know what I'm talking about. Sometime back I was checking out at a store. The lady handed me my bag, and I told her, thank ye muchly. She laughed and said that she had never heard that before. Things are changing all around us. Thank God, **His Word is forever the same**.

"Wives, be in subjection to your husbands" is not a popular statement to make in today's world. There are too many single parent homes today, homes without a father, even homes without a mother. The order that God has set and wants is found mostly in Christian homes where the couples are trying to live according to the Word of God and bring their children up in a Christ-like home. What the Bible is speaking of here is about a wife **whose husband is not saved**, who does not know Jesus as his savior. She, as a good wife, according to scripture, submits to her husband, and by so doing **lives a Christian life, as a witness before him**; doing so that she might **lead him to accept Jesus as his Lord and Savior**.

To quote *The Wiersbe Bible Commentary: NT:*

> A strange situation exists in society today. We have more readily available information about sex and marriage than ever before, yet we have more marital problems and divorces. Obviously, something is wrong. It is not sufficient to say that God is needed in these homes, because even many Christian marriages are falling apart.
>
> The fact that a man and a woman are both saved is no guarantee that their marriage will succeed. Marriage is something that we have to work at; success is not automatic. And when one marriage partner is not a Christian, that can make matters even more difficult.

Some of the problems that people have are their role models. When we were children, we looked to those around us to show us how we should model our lives. Children brought up in a **Godly, loving home** try to pattern their lives after their parents, most of the time. Boys want to be **like their dads**, and girls want to be **like their mothers**. But in dysfunctional homes, children get the **wrong idea as to the roles** that the parents should be playing. I talked to one man who, in his youth, went to church but backslid, got married and raised a family out of church, before he returned to church. In the years when it is so important to be a good role model, he was living an ungodly life style. Now he wonders why he can't get his children to **go to church and live for God**.

I know personally about this type of situation. My parents went to church when I was very small, then got out of church. **I don't even remember going to church when I was small.** When I was fourteen years old, the church in a nearby town was having a revival. My grandmother went to church there. She called and called asking my parents to go. Finally, they decided to go to stop Grandma from calling. That night I met Jesus and **my life has never been the same**. My parents were good moral people, but they lived a life that did not promote Christ. A few months later they **got back in church**. If this hadn't happened, I do not know in which direction my life would have gone.

It is so important to **raise our families in church**, to expose them **to the presence of God and the moving of His Spirit**. I, over the years, have seen many Christian sisters in the church that attend faithfully, but their husbands do not go. They must go alone. I admire them for the stand they take. They are **faithful to God**, believing that God **will save their husbands**. This is what Peter is talking about, that the **unbelieving spouse will be won to the Lord** by the spouse that serves God and is committed to Him. This is **witnessing at home**.

Barnes' Notes on the New Testament says:

> The conduct of the wife is to be in all respects pure; and this is to be the grand instrumentality in the conversion of her husband. A wife may be strictly chaste, and yet there may be many other things in her conduct and temper which would mar the beauty of her piety, and prevent any happy influence on the mind of her husband.

It is so important to be led by the Spirit of God. The wife submitting to her husband is God's plan for the order of marriage. The man was not made for the woman, the woman was made for the man. She was made to be his helpmate. None of this means that the man is superior or better than the woman. Neither does this mean that the woman is better than the man. It does mean that God **has established an order that He wants to be followed** in the marriage and in the home.

There cannot be two captains of a ship. Neither can there be two heads in the household. If there are two heads, then there is confusion and discontent. In nature, anything with two heads is a freak and does not live. We must **line up with the Word of God if we are to succeed**. We must be obedient to God's Word. Marriage was instituted by God, but to make a marriage work, **both parties must be committed**. Without commitment, no marriage will survive. The Bible gives us an example of a marriage that was not cared for properly. In Genesis, we read the story of Isaac and Rebekah, a marriage that started tenderly with love between this man and woman. Rebekah was barren, so Isaac prayed to the Lord for Rebekah. For a woman to be barren was a shame in those days. Rebekah conceived and bore two sons, twins. The name of the first was Esau and the second was Jacob. **Here is where problems arose, for Isaac loved Esau and Rebekah loved Jacob.**

Genesis 25:28

And Isaac loved Esau, because he did eat of his venison: but Rebekah loved Jacob.

As we read this account you can see the pit that was being dug by Isaac and Rebekah, the separation that began to come between them. Esau was favored by Isaac and Jacob was favored by Rebekah. **Think of all the years of alienation and dislike that passed between Isaac and Rebekah.** These boys grew up to manhood, each being favored by one parent. Think of the bad feelings that must have passed between them. Is it any wonder why these two, Esau and Jacob, felt the way they did? We see this in families today, way too often. People have not changed. God's will is for a family to be **loving toward one another**, each child loved the same, and the **parents showing love to each other**, reinforcing what a family should be.

Peter in the third verse goes on to speak about how a woman who professes holiness should adorn themselves.

To quote from *Barnes' Notes on the New Testament:*

> The apostle refers here to a propensity which exists in the heart of woman to seek that which would be esteemed ornamental, or that which will *appear well* in the sight of others, and commend us to them. The desire of this is laid deep in human nature, and therefore, when properly regulated, is not wrong. The only question is, what is the true and appropriate Ornament? What should be primarily sought as the right kind of adorning? The apostle does not condemn true ornament, nor does he condemn the desire to appear in such a way as to secure the esteem of others.

Religion promotes neatness, cleanliness, and a proper attention to our external appearance according to our circumstances in life, as certainly as it does to the **internal virtue of the**

soul. Peter is saying that a woman is to dress modestly.

1 Timothy 2:9-10

> [9] *In like manner also, that women adorn themselves in modest apparel, with shamefacedness and sobriety; not with broided hair, or gold, or pearls, or costly array;*
> [10] *But (which becometh women professing godliness) with good works.*

I believe that we are to represent God's kingdom. We are to **look respectful as becomes holiness**. Here I am going to get on my soap box. I cannot believe how some people dress and look when they go to church. I'm not talking about sinners who don't know better. I'm talking about people who claim to be Christians, born-again believers. To true Christians, **God's house is a very special place**. It is more special than going to an upscale restaurant or a night on the town. Yet, most people will really dress and look their best for a night out. But when it comes to going to church, they will wear any old thing. They don't seem to care. I'm going to say this, and if it makes you mad, so be it. **If you do not respect God's house enough to dress nice to dress your best, then I wonder about where you stand with God.**

To quote *The Wiersbe Bible Commentary. NT:*

> When Christian couples try to imitate the world and get their standards from Hollywood instead of from heaven, there will be trouble in the home. But if both partners will imitate Jesus Christ in his submission and obedience and his desire to serve

others, then there will be triumph and joy in the home. In Christ we see a beautiful blending of strength and tenderness and that is what it takes.

Peter goes on to speak about the wearing of gold and plaiting of the hair.

Barnes' Notes on the New Testament states:

> The wearing of gold in the hair, however, was more common among women of loose morals than among virtuous females. – Pollux iv. 153.

It cannot be said that the wearing of gold about the person is in any way wrong. But we need to **put forth a Christ-like example to others around us**. I think mostly why Peter is stressing how a woman should dress and look is because when it comes to women, men are easily led astray. In today's world, sex crimes are rampant, partly because of how women dress. Young teenage girls dress like they are twenty years old, to the shame of their parents. This is not to say that the fault is all upon the women and young girls. Men and boys are just as responsible because they yield themselves to the temptation. This is why children should be **brought up in the house of God**. It won't stop all of the sex crimes but could make a change in some people's lives.

It is what lies within the heart that **changes how we live**, how we **dress**, how we **look to the world**. Let us both, men and women, let Christ have His way in our hearts. Let us have a meek and quiet spirit before this sinful world, promoting a savior who **loves us and who wants to save the lost**. If we can do this, it is of great price to God. Peter in the fifth verse tries to get the women of that day to pattern themselves after certain women in Old Testament times, such as Sara. The Bible speaks of Sara calling Abraham lord and tells of how, **because of her love for him**, she did everything she could to be in **subjection to him and please him**. The wife is not to be a slave nor is she a servant without rights.

Colossians 3:18-19

¹⁸ *Wives, submit yourselves unto your own husbands, as it is fit in the Lord.*
¹⁹ *Husbands, love your wives, and be not bitter against them.*

Ephesians 5:24-25

²⁴ *Therefore as the church is subject unto Christ, so let the wives be to their own husbands in every thing.*
²⁵ *Husbands, love your wives, even as Christ also loved the church, and gave himself for it;*

In Colossians and Ephesians, Paul admonishes husbands to **love their wives as this is just and right before God**. Husbands are to give **honor to their wives**, as the weaker vessel. The husband is to **stand up for his wife**. I told one church where I was elected pastor that my wife and I were a package deal, that if they took one of us, they took both of us. Even in today's world of women's liberation, **wives want their husbands to protect them**.

1 Peter 3:7

Likewise, ye husbands, dwell with them according to knowledge, giving honour unto the wife, as unto the weaker vessel, and as being heirs together of the grace of life; that your prayers be not hindered.

Husbands, your wives are not your servants or slaves to wait on you hand and foot; neither are they a doormat to be walked on. Sometimes I know we complain about our wives, but remember they also have to put up with us, and that isn't easy. We are to remember that **they are heirs together with us in the grace of life**. If there is trouble and problems in the home, it hinders our prayers to God. It hinders our walk and outlook, so **walk uprightly before God**, for God is the one we have to please. Husbands, treat your wives well, and wives, be in submission to your husbands. For this is right before God. **Marriage is a partnership**; it is give and take. If you are giving in all of the time and your spouse does too, then maybe you are each giving about fifty percent. **Honor each other, love each other, care for each other and never take each other for granted**, for there will come a day if Jesus tarries, when one of you will be called home leaving the other behind. Love each other now. In 1707 Cotton Mather's wife died and he wrote this poem found in *Cotton Mather's Verse in English* by Cotton Mather, which can be found on the internet:

> Go then, my Dove, but now no longer Mine!
> Leave Earth, & now in Heavenly Glory Shine.
> Bright for they Wisdom, Goodness, Beauty here;
> Now Brighter in a more Angelick Sphaere.
> JESUS, with whom thy Soul did long to be,
> Into His Ark, and Arms, has taken thee.

John Phillips has this to say in *Exploring the Epistles of Peter:*

> Men are not to ride roughshod over their wives,

bossing and bullying them, ordering them around, letting them do heavy work beyond their strength, or making unreasonable demands upon them. We see this truth illustrated in the story of Abraham and Sarah. When Abraham hurried his wife to the kitchen to bake bread for his unexpected company, he himself dashed off to the field to find a suitable fatted calf and made arrangements for it to be dressed and cooked. Then, he himself hurried back to their living quarters to wait upon the table. This considerate behavior was doubtless observed by God and earned his blessing. No wonder Sarah called Abraham "lord"! He was a considerate husband moreover, he called her "princess", for that is the meaning of her name. Few women would find it difficult to be subject to a husband who was so courteous and considerate and who treated her like a princess.

Men, you get in return what you give. Your wives can be your closest friend and companion, or they can be your biggest adversary, depending on how you treat them. The days of women being property are long passed in most countries. Step up, take responsibly, **be the man God desires you to be**.

1 Peter 3:8-9

[8] Finally, be ye all of one mind, having compassion one of another, love as brethren, be pitiful, be courteous:
[9] Not rendering evil for evil, or railing for railing: but contrariwise blessing; knowing that ye are thereunto

called, that ye should inherit a blessing.

Peter in the eighth verse is asking everyone to **be of one mind**, having compassion for one another. Some would say that what Peter is asking is impossible. There are too many differences between Christian beliefs. Yes, there are wide doctrinal difference between denominations. **But we are all trying to go to the same place, to be with Jesus.** What has happened is that we have done like Abraham and Lot. Because of differences we have parted company and gone our own ways. But, we must remember we are still one family. We may differ in beliefs and how we are to reach our goal, but **our goal is still the same.**

Mark 10:38-40

> [38] *But Jesus said unto them, Ye know not what ye ask: can ye drink of the cup that I drink of? and be baptized with the baptism that I am baptized with?*
> [39] *And they said unto him, We can. And Jesus said unto them, Ye shall indeed drink of the cup that I drink of; and with the baptism that I am baptized withal shall ye be baptized:*
> [40] *But to sit on my right hand and on my left hand is not mine to give; but it shall be given to them for whom it is prepared.*

We must learn to disagree agreeably. There are many church doctrines that I do not agree with and believe are contrary to the Bible. But one thing I know, denominations will not save us. We are saved **by the shed blood of Jesus Christ** and nothing else. If a man or woman's heart is right with God when they die, they are bound for the presence of God. We as Christians need to show a **Christ-like love to our brethren**. Sometimes it seems like it is easier for Christians to love the sinner, than to love each other.

The Wiersbe Bible Commentary: NT tells us we must learn that:

> Unity does not mean uniformity, it means cooperation in the midst of diversity.
>
> Christians may differ on how things are to be done, but they must agree on what is to be done and why. A man criticized D.L Moody's methods of evangelism, and Moody said "Well I'm always ready for improvement. What are your methods?" The man confessed that he had none. "Then I'll stick to my own," said Moody. Whatever methods we may use, we must seek to honor Christ, win the lost, and build the church. Some methods are definitely not scriptural, but there is plenty of room for variety in the church.

We are to be one body with many members; each member has its job to preform, and when we each preform our job, the body functions properly.

1 Corinthians 12:12-27

> *[12] For as the body is one, and hath many members, and all the members of that one body, being many, are one body: so also is Christ.*
> *[13] For by one Spirit are we all baptized into one body, whether we be Jews or Gentiles, whether we be bond or free; and have been all made to drink into one Spirit.*

14 For the body is not one member, but many.

15 If the foot shall say, Because I am not the hand, I am not of the body; is it therefore not of the body?

16 And if the ear shall say, Because I am not the eye, I am not of the body; is it therefore not of the body?

17 If the whole body were an eye, where were the hearing? If the whole were hearing, where were the smelling?

18 But now hath God set the members every one of them in the body, as it hath pleased him.

19 And if they were all one member, where were the body?

20 But now are they many members, yet but one body.

21 And the eye cannot say unto the hand, I have no need of thee: nor again the head to the feet, I have no need of you.

22 Nay, much more those members of the body, which seem to be more feeble, are necessary:

23 And those members of the body, which we think to be less honourable, upon these we bestow more abundant honour; and our uncomely parts have more abundant comeliness.

24 For our comely parts have no need: but God hath tempered the body together, having given more abundant honour to that part which lacked:

25 That there should be no schism in the body; but that the members should have the same care one for another.

26 And whether one member suffer, all the members suffer with it; or one member be honoured, all the members rejoice with it.

27 Now ye are the body of Christ, and members in particular.

Whether we be Methodist, Baptist, Church of Christ, Pentecostal or any of the other denominations, our goal is the same: **to make heaven our home, to work for God, to reach the lost**

before it is too late. We are, as Peter says, to be of one mind, the mind of Christ, having **compassion or love** one for another, being **courteous** one to another, **tenderhearted**, and **not callous** in our work for the Lord. We may differ in doctrine and beliefs. But we must never let this overshadow our compassion for lost souls. The church that has lost the burden for the lost is a church that itself has become lost. The blind cannot lead the blind, for they will fall into a ditch together. We must keep our eyes **focused upon Jesus**, for it is harvest time.

John 4:35

> *Say not ye, There are yet four months, and then cometh harvest? behold, I say unto you, Lift up your eyes, and look on the fields; for they are white already to harvest.*

In verse nine, God's Word tells us **not to render evil for evil**. This world we live in has two main philosophies. Do it to others before they can do it to you, and get ready for payback, because it is going to be hell. Christians must live on a higher level than the world. Christians are said to live on one of three different levels.

1. We can, God forbid, return evil for good, wherein our Christian witness is destroyed before those who are around us.
2. We can render good for good or evil for evil, which is the natural way of living in this world. A Christian who lives on this level is really no better than the world around him, for human nature is to do the same. There are many good moral people in this world, and when they see Christians living just like they do, then what is there in

that Christian's life that the sinner should desire?

3. Then there is the level **wherein Christ walked**. The level where Christ desires for **all true believers to walk**. Where **we render good for evil**. This is the divine level, the level that Jesus walked to give us an example. We have heard it said an eye for an eye, and a tooth for a tooth, as well as it once was. **But Christ has given us a new commandment.**

Matthew 5:38-48

38 Ye have heard that it hath been said, An eye for an eye, and a tooth for a tooth:

39 But I say unto you, That ye resist not evil: but whosoever shall smite thee on thy right cheek, turn to him the other also.

40 And if any man will sue thee at the law, and take away thy coat, let him have thy cloke also.

41 And whosoever shall compel thee to go a mile, go with him twain.

42 Give to him that asketh thee, and from him that would borrow of thee turn not thou away.

43 Ye have heard that it hath been said, Thou shalt love thy neighbour, and hate thine enemy.

44 But I say unto you, Love your enemies, bless them that curse you, do good to them that hate you, and pray for them which despitefully use you, and persecute you;

45 That ye may be the children of your Father which is in heaven: for he maketh his sun to rise on the evil and on the good, and sendeth rain on the just and on the unjust.

46 For if ye love them which love you, what reward have ye?

do not even the publicans the same?
⁴⁷ And if ye salute your brethren only, what do ye more than others? do not even the publicans so?
⁴⁸ Be ye therefore perfect, even as your Father which is in heaven is perfect.

Jesus in His mercy toward us has given us the example that we should follow, not just love our fellow Christians, but **to love our enemies**. To pray for those who despitefully use you. To **do good to them that hate you**. To forgive, above all to forgive, for if we cannot forgive others, then our heavenly father will not forgive us. We should always be conscious of **what kind of an example we are giving** to those around us. Remember that our calling comes from God, and God tells us to **be perfect even as our heavenly Father which is in heaven is perfect**.

Soap box time. I hear over and over that nobody on this earth is perfect, and they can never be perfect. If this is so, then the scripture in Matthew 5:48, *"Be ye therefore perfect, even as your Father which is in heaven is perfect,"* is a lie, and God does not lie. If God tells us to be perfect, then He expects us to be perfect. Our God has never told us to do something that is impossible for us to do. **We can and must live a perfect life in the sight of God.** The book of Job tells us that Job was a perfect and upright man before God.

Job 1:1, 8, 22

¹ There was a man in the land of Uz, whose name was Job; and that man was perfect and upright, and one that feared God, and eschewed evil.
⁸ And the LORD said unto Satan, Hast thou considered my

servant Job, that there is none like him in the earth, a perfect and an upright man, one that feareth God, and escheweth evil?

²² In all this Job sinned not, nor charged God foolishly.

If Job was perfect in the sight of God, then **so can we**. To say that man has to sin every day is to go against God's Word. No, the journey is not going to be easy. There will be trials and temptations, there will be times that we feel like throwing up our hands and walking away. But we know that there is no place to quit, for if we quit we will never reach that prize that we so long for, to be at home with Jesus. Reading John Phillips' commentary, he reminds me that **anyone can be a witness for God**. The little servant girl, scripture does not give her name, who witnessed to Naaman's wife, of a prophet in Samaria who could heal her master of his leprosy. Because of her witness, God performed a miracle. She remains anonymous but **her courage to witness for her God is forever recorded in the pages of God's Word**. The last half of verse nine says, *"knowing that ye are thereunto called, that ye should inherit a blessing."* To the child of God our inheritance is to be **forever in the presence of God**. There we will be with all of those who have gone on before us. What a homecoming that will be, to see Jesus, the apostles, prophets, and all of our sainted loved ones waiting for us to join them.

1 Peter 3:10-17

¹⁰ For he that will love life, and see good days, let him refrain his tongue from evil, and his lips that they speak no guile:
¹¹ Let him eschew evil, and do good; let him seek peace,

and ensue it.
12 For the eyes of the Lord are over the righteous, and his ears are open unto their prayers: but the face of the Lord is against them that do evil.
13 And who is he that will harm you, if ye be followers of that which is good?
14 But and if ye suffer for righteousness' sake, happy are ye: and be not afraid of their terror, neither be troubled;
15 But sanctify the Lord God in your hearts: and be ready always to give an answer to every man that asketh you a reason of the hope that is in you with meekness and fear:
16 Having a good conscience; that, whereas they speak evil of you, as of evildoers, they may be ashamed that falsely accuse your good conversation in Christ.
17 For it is better, if the will of God be so, that ye suffer for well doing, than for evil doing.

Peter begins this tenth verse by quoting from Psalms 34:12-16. Though it is taken with some variation, the principle is the same.

Psalm 34:12-16

12 What man is he that desireth life, and loveth many days, that he may see good?
13 Keep thy tongue from evil, and thy lips from speaking guile.
14 Depart from evil, and do good; seek peace, and pursue it.
15 The eyes of the LORD are upon the righteous, and his ears are open unto their cry.
16 The face of the LORD is against them that do evil, to cut

off the remembrance of them from the earth.

We are told to **love others as we love ourselves**. Few people say they hate life and want to die. They may hate their situation in life but few desire to kill themselves and end it all. There are some who do take their own life because they cannot take the pressure the world puts upon them, and think the world would be a better place without them. This is an awful lie of the devil.

In *Barnes' Notes on the New Testament*, we read that there are reasons why **we should love life and want to live**.

(1) Because as already intimated, life, as such, is to be regarded as a blessing. We instinctively shrink back from death, as one of the greatest evils; we shudder at the thought of annihilation. It is not wrong to love … and we are but acting out one of the universal laws which our Creator has impressed on us, when with proper submission to his will we seek to lengthen out our days as far as possible.

(2) That we may see the works of God, and survey the wonders of his hand on earth.

(3) That we may make preparation for eternity. Man may, indeed, make preparation in a very brief period; but the longest life is not too much to examine and settle the question whether we have a well-founded hope of heaven.

(4) That we may do good to others.

Our lives should be a constant example to the lost around

us. We are, our lives are, **the only Bible that most sinners will ever read**. What kind of example are you living before the lost? Can they see in you something that is lacking in their lives? We need to **love life for those around us**, to lead them to our Lord Jesus Christ. Further, we need to **refrain our tongue from evil**. No one likes to be around a foul-mouthed person. The evil that pours out of their mouth brings them to shame, the speaking of false-hoods, profaneness, slander, obscenities, all brings them to disgrace before others and most of all, God. Refrain thyself from such works of darkness. Let thy lips speak no guile, but **let them speak praises unto the most-high God**. The scripture tells us that we are to eschew evil, to avoid the very appearance of evil, that evil be not named among the children of God.

In this world of constant evil, the Lord has **marked out a path that He desires the Christian to walk**. This path is laid out in the Holy Scripture. Read it, for in it we find God's plan for our lives. We are to be a **living example of our Lord and Master Jesus Christ**. Don't be afraid, for Jesus has already walked this path before us. All we have to do is to **walk in His footsteps**. He is waiting for us to follow Him home. But sometimes, in the difficult times, He will come and walk with us hand in hand to show us the way. Looking onto verse twelve, we read that **the eyes of the Lord are over the righteous**. What this means is that the Lord is our protector, our keeper. In one place it speaks of where the Lord gives His angels charge over us. **The Lord watches over us every moment.**

Matthew 10:29-31

> *[29] Are not two sparrows sold for a farthing? and one of them shall not fall on the ground without your Father.*

127

30 But the very hairs of your head are all numbered.
31 Fear ye not therefore, ye are of more value than many sparrows.

Matthew tells us that we are of value to the Lord, so precious are we that **even the hairs of our head are numbered**. Then people tell us that God does not care. We are **loved beyond measure**. Put your faith and trust in the Lord. He will never let you down. To the child of God, we have a 24-hour-a-day God. He never sleeps, never takes a break, and never goes on a trip. His ears are **always open to the cry of His children**. He hears our prayers when we speak aloud, and He hears our prayers when we pray within our hearts. God is **always open to the prayer of His own**. Just as God is always ready to hear and answer the prayer of His children, His face is set against those that do wickedly and walk not after the Lord.

It is said that religion makes a man look at the world differently, that life is worth the living, that it is a blessing to see the new day every morning. We don't know how long we will be allotted down here, so **let us take advantage of every day** that God gives us. Let us **lead the lost to Jesus**, pray for the sick, lift up the downtrodden, **help the helpless**. Years ago, God gave me a little saying, and we have used it in our service for God. It goes like this: **Awake, arise, there is much to do. Jesus is coming, I'm ready, how about you?**

As we take a look at verse 13, we can see that Peter was speaking in general terms. As a rule, those who live a pious life live in relative security. This is not to say that Christians have absolute security, for **many Christians suffer for their faith**. There are still places in the world where Christians are called upon to suffer, and thousands are martyred each year. But so far, as a rule, Christians who walk in the footsteps of Jesus and show forth good works and love for the lost do well.

In this modern day, we hear from the Middle East of Muslims killing Christians every day. The command is put upon them to convert, or pay a religious tax, or to be killed. Church, we need to pray as never before for the hand of God to stop this senseless killing. The scripture tells us to pray, but **we are not to be afraid of their terror,** neither are we to be troubled. The time has come to **put our most precious faith in God** and trust in the one who saved us from sin.

Barnes' Notes on the New Testament states the following:

> It is, that in our hearts we are to esteem God as a holy being, and in all our deportment to act toward him as such. The *object* of Peter in quoting the passage from Isaiah, was to lull the fears of those whom he addressed, and preserve them from any alarms in view of the persecutions to which they might be exposed; the trials which would be brought upon them by men. The sentiment of the passage then is, *that the sanctifying of the Lord God in our hearts, or proper confidence in him as a holy and righteous God, will deliver us from fear.*

Every day we face the enemy head on. He, Satan, tries our faith by putting trials and temptations in our paths. Satan does his best to convince us that the only way out of our problems is to do as he wants us to. However, there is always **another way out of the temptations of life.** For the Lord tells us that **with every temptation He will make a way of escape.**

1 Corinthians 10:13

There hath no temptation taken you but such as is common to man: but God is faithful, who will not suffer you to be tempted above that ye are able; but will with the temptation also make a way to escape, that ye may be able to bear it.

All we need to do is to seek and look for God's way of escape. As we live the Christian life there will be those who watch our lives and who want to know how we seem to get along so well. The Word commands us to **be ready and quick to give an answer** to those who ask. We should **give praise and glory to God** for His presence in our lives and that **it is only through God that we are blessed** as we are.

Verse 16 speaks of having a good conscience, why is it so important for Christians to have a good conscience.

John Phillips Commentary Series tells us:

A good conscience is essential to both a good defense in court and a good testimony before the world. As Shakespeare said, "Conscience doth make cowards of us all." It is hard to be convincing when we have an accusing conscience. Such a person is always afraid that someone will discover his guilty secret and embarrass him with it. Paul knew that the Jews had nothing on him. Neither did the Roman government. He had a clear conscience that made him as bold as a lion.

Peter knew that these things happened, because they

happened to him at Jerusalem.

There are many things in our past. Things that we committed to the Lord at salvation. **There is nothing that we can do about the past except to place it under the blood and go on for Christ and His kingdom.** When these things may be brought up, we confess to our past, explain how that we have asked the Lord to forgive us for those that we have wronged and made restitution where possible. By doing this many times, we can **put to silence the outcries of our enemies** and put them to shame. Evil doers always want someone to back them up. They want to be Mr. Big, they want to command importance, but most of the time they are afraid in their inner being, so they accuse others of trying to elevate themselves in the eyes of those around them. What lengths man will go to, to try to remove the guilt away from themselves and place guilt on someone else?

The Word says that to the Christian it is better to **suffer for doing good**, than to suffer for some evil that we may have committed. Christians, abstain from **the very appearance of evil**, let not evil once be named among you. Do the work of God, that no man may accuse you of doing evil things. Put forth a **Christ-like example** that others may see your good works and **glorify God**.

Remember we are soldiers in God's great army and in the midst of this battle we must have **confidence in our commander**, Jesus Christ. God's Word assures us that **the battle belongs to God,** and God never fails. Psalm 27:1, *"The LORD is my light and my salvation; whom shall I fear? the LORD is the strength of my life; of whom shall I be afraid?"* tells us that the Lord is our strength and **of whom shall I be afraid**. We are told to lean not upon our own understanding but **to trust in God**.

In Psalms 46:1, David wrote, "God is my refuge and strength, a very present help in trouble." David was a man who at a very early age learned to trust God. Alone in the fields with the sheep, David developed a relationship with God that **led David all through his life**. We need to develop that kind of relationship with God today. If we do, we then can say with complete confidence that **our trust is in the Lord**.

There is one thing that we must be sure of, that we are **where God wants us to be**. The devil has a counterfeit for everything God has. This is why it is so important to **know the voice of God and know the true will of God**. The enemy is a deceiver of the brethren. He is out to destroy everyone and everything that pertains to God. We must **walk upright before God**.

Proverbs 14:12

There is a way which seemeth right unto a man, but the end thereof are the ways of death.

Proverbs 16:25

There is a way that seemeth right unto a man, but the end thereof are the ways of death.

We read in Proverbs where the preacher (Solomon) sends forth the warning that we need to be aware that everything may not be like it seems. I have always been told that **if it seems too good to be true, then it usually is**. We need to be like the Word tells us to be, **wise as serpents and harmless as doves**.

Matthew 10:16

Behold, I send you forth as sheep in the midst of wolves: be ye therefore wise as serpents, and harmless as doves.

We are to put forth the gospel of Jesus Christ to this lost and dying world and tell the world that **there is a savior who loves them and died for them**. This same Jesus that went away will come again to receive His children unto himself, and where He is, **there we will be also**, and so shall we ever be with the Lord.

1 Peter 3:18-22

[18] For Christ also hath once suffered for sins, the just for the unjust, that he might bring us to God, being put to death in the flesh, but quickened by the Spirit:
[19] By which also he went and preached unto the spirits in prison;
[20] Which sometime were disobedient, when once the longsuffering of God waited in the days of Noah, while the ark was a preparing, wherein few, that is, eight souls were saved by water.
[21] The like figure whereunto even baptism doth also now save us (not the putting away of the filth of the flesh, but the answer of a good conscience toward God,) by the resurrection of Jesus Christ:
[22] Who is gone into heaven, and is on the right hand of God; angels and authorities and powers being made subject unto him.

Peter in this 18th verse is trying to bring home a very, very important point. That point is that **our savior has suffered for us**, the just for unjust, that He might **bring us to God on a personal basis**. We know that before Christ's death on the cross, the world was still under the Law of Moses. Animal sacrifice was the only way for man to approach God and His throne. But on the day that Christ died on that cross, the veil in the temple was **rent in twain** from the top to the bottom. That veil that separated man from God was **no longer there**.

From that time on we have had **direct access to the very throne room of God**. We no longer need priests to go before God for us. We can by the grace that Jesus Christ gave to us now go to God in prayer, taking our needs and petitions **straight to God**. Jesus who died for our sins, being quickened by the Spirit of God, raised from the dead, is now **alive again** and sitting at the right hand of God. There, He is making intercession for us before the father.

To quote from *Barnes' Notes on the New Testament*:

> That his death might be the means of reconciling sinners to God. It is through that death that mercy is proclaimed to the guilty; it is by that alone that God can be reconciled to men; and the fact that the Son of God loved men, and gave himself a sacrifice for them, enduring such bitter sorrows, is the most powerful appeal which can be made to mankind to induce them to return to God. There is no appeal which can be made to us more powerful than one drawn from the fact that another *suffers* on our account. We could resist the *argument* which a father, a mother, or a sister would use to reclaim us from a course of sin; but if we perceive that our conduct involves them in suffering, that fact has a power over us which no mere argument could have.

Jesus could have ended His passage here at any time. He could have gone back to heaven and said, "Father, I can't do this," but He did not. He could have said man is not worth the trouble and why should I suffer and die for him? But He did not do that. He could have refused to be put to a public trial; He could have refused to be put to a public shame dying on a cross, but He did not. He was **willing to go to the cross** carrying the sins of an ungodly world, to give you and I a chance to make heaven our home. **No greater love has ever been shone**, to such an unworthy people.

Sometimes I sit and think, why God, **why would You let Your Son die for me?** From the time of Adam to Noah there were very few people that had a relationship with God. Then after the flood Satan again raised his ugly head and man began to sin and walk in his own way. From the flood till the birth of Jesus, I know that there were multitudes that lived for God and died in the faith. From the birth of Jesus until now, I know again that multitudes have lived and died serving God.

Still I ask, oh, God, is it worth it? But I'm so glad that You paid the price for me because without You, Lord, I had no chance. Thank You, Lord, thank You, I love You so much, my heart is overwhelmed when I think of all that You have done, and are doing, and are going to do. Tears come to my eyes as I write this, **oh, how I love You, Lord, for giving to me this gift of salvation**. Glory to Your precious and Holy name. We should feel sorry for all the people is this world whose god is dead.

What good can a dead god do for you? I know that some religions have some good points in their teachings. But again, **what can a dead god do for you?** He can't heal you, he can't touch you, you cannot feel his presence or power. He is dead. **Thank God for a living savior**, one where you can feel His presence, that can touch you and heal you, one who can truly give you peace, hope, and comfort. One who, as scriptures state, will **never leave us** to the very end of life, and after death, will take our souls **to be with Him for ever and ever**. A loving savior.

1 Peter 3:19

By which also he went and preached unto the spirits in prison;

This verse is one of the most controversial verses in the Bible. Bible scholars do not agree on the meaning of this verse at all. So, no matter what position you may take, you will be told that you are wrong. Most Bible scholars believe that what the Bible says is not what the true meaning of the scripture is. I on the other hand believe that **this scripture means exactly what it says**. I do not believe that "the spirits in prison" is talking about fallen angels. I can find no basis for this belief. Scripture states that the fallen angels were cast into hell in chains of darkness there to await the coming judgement.

2 Peter 2:4

For if God spared not the angels that sinned, but cast them down to hell, and delivered them into chains of darkness, to be reserved unto judgment;

I believe that the spirits in prison are the souls of those who died before the flood.

Acts 17:29-30

29 Forasmuch then as we are the offspring of God, we ought not to think that the Godhead is like unto gold, or silver, or stone, graven by art and man's device.
30 And the times of this ignorance God winked at; but now commandeth all men every where to repent:

I believe that what this verse refers to is the time before the flood. There was no law and every man did that which was right in his own sight or eyes. But man left to himself always degrades into ungodliness. God no longer winks at the ignorance of man; that stopped with the flood when God started all over again with the eight souls of righteousness, and even then, it was not long before sin, again, begin to take control. I believe that a special dispensation was allotted to these souls, and they were placed in a special place, call it prison or paradise, **awaiting the time when there would come a savior who would lead captivity captive.**

Psalm 68:18

Thou hast ascended on high, thou hast led captivity captive: thou hast received gifts for men; yea, for the rebellious also, that the LORD God might dwell among them.

Ephesians 4:8-10

8 Wherefore he saith, When he ascended up on high, he led captivity captive, and gave gifts unto men.
9 (Now that he ascended, what is it but that he also descended first into the lower parts of the earth?
10 He that descended is the same also that ascended up far above all heavens, that he might fill all things.)

This Jesus, this savior who died for you and me, died **for the whole world**. In the days before the flood we know that God, even then, had communion with certain individuals. The Bible does not name all of them, but one it does name in particular, Enoch. Genesis states that **Enoch walked with God**, and was not for God took him. Then **God used Noah to build an ark** to save mankind from death. In the Book of Revelation 1:18, Jesus tell us that He has the keys of death and hell. He is the victor, He has won the battle, and everything is put under His feet.

John Phillips Commentary Series says this about hell:

> The Lord gives us our best description of hades in the Old Testament times and up until the time of his ascension. We learn that it was in two separate spheres divided by an impassable gulf. One side was a place of conscious torment; the other, sometimes called "Abraham's bosom" and "paradise" (Luke 23:43), was a place of conscious rest and comfort (Luke 16(19:31). The Lord himself went to hades at the time of His death, and He emptied the paradise section of hades, taking its "captives" with him to heaven (Ephesians 4:8-10). In the Old Testament the departed went down (1 Samuel 28:15) in the New Testament, they go up (2 Corinthians 12:4; Acts 1:9-11).

Luke 23:43

> *And Jesus said unto him, Verily I say unto thee, To day shalt thou be with me in paradise.*

Luke 16:19-31

19 There was a certain rich man, which was clothed in purple and fine linen, and fared sumptuously every day:

20 And there was a certain beggar named Lazarus, which was laid at his gate, full of sores,

21 And desiring to be fed with the crumbs which fell from the rich man's table: moreover the dogs came and licked his sores.

22 And it came to pass, that the beggar died, and was carried by the angels into Abraham's bosom: the rich man also died, and was buried;

23 And in hell he lift up his eyes, being in torments, and seeth Abraham afar off, and Lazarus in his bosom.

24 And he cried and said, Father Abraham, have mercy on me, and send Lazarus, that he may dip the tip of his finger in water, and cool my tongue; for I am tormented in this flame.

25 But Abraham said, Son, remember that thou in thy lifetime receivedst thy good things, and likewise Lazarus evil things: but now he is comforted, and thou art tormented.

26 And beside all this, between us and you there is a great gulf fixed: so that they which would pass from hence to you cannot; neither can they pass to us, that would come from thence.

27 Then he said, I pray thee therefore, father, that thou wouldest send him to my father's house:

28 For I have five brethren; that he may testify unto them, lest they also come into this place of torment.

29 Abraham saith unto him, They have Moses and the

prophets; let them hear them.

³⁰ And he said, Nay, father Abraham: but if one went unto them from the dead, they will repent.

³¹ And he said unto him, If they hear not Moses and the prophets, neither will they be persuaded, though one rose from the dead.

1 Samuel 28:15

And Samuel said to Saul, Why hast thou disquieted me, to bring me up? And Saul answered, I am sore distressed; for the Philistines make war against me, and God is departed from me, and answereth me no more, neither by prophets, nor by dreams: therefore I have called thee, that thou mayest make known unto me what I shall do.

2 Corinthians 12:4

How that he was caught up into paradise, and heard unspeakable words, which it is not lawful for a man to utter.

The spirits to whom the Lord made His proclamation were those "which sometimes were disobedient, when once the long suffering of God waited in the day of Noah." Whatever you believe is between you and God, but **be ready to give an answer when asked why you believe what you believe**. The end of this 20th verse states, "eight souls were saved by water." Then going into verse 21 it starts, "The like figure where unto even baptism doth also now save us." This does not mean that we are saved by water baptism. There is no power in the water. **Water baptism is a symbol of the death and resurrection of Jesus.**

What saves us is the precious blood of Jesus Christ, that blood that was shed for our sins. When we repent and ask the Lord to save us, He washes away our sins **with His precious blood**, and we have that **born-again experience with Jesus**. Water baptism is the outward show to the world that we are saved. We go down under the water, the symbol of Christ's death, and as we are raised up out of the water, it is the symbol of being **raised with Christ into the newness of life**.

To quote *John Phillips Commentary Series* again:

> We note the picture: "The like figure whereunto even baptism doth also now save us (3:21a); we note the parenthesis (not the putting away of the filth of the flesh, but the answer of a good conscience toward God)" (3:21b), and the process: "by the resurrection of Jesus Christ" (3:21c). Whatever else Peter means for us to understand by this statement, he certainly had in mind no such concept as infant baptism. An infant has no conscience, so the sprinkling of babies, which is practiced in some churches, cannot be "the answer" of the baby's "good conscience toward God." Baptismal regeneration is an idea imported into Christianity by the Roman Catholic Church and borrowed from that source by various other churches. It is the blood that saves us, not water.

Colossians 1:20

And, having made peace through the blood of his cross, by

him to reconcile all things unto himself; by him, I say, whether they be things in earth, or things in heaven.

Hebrews 9:22

And almost all things are by the law purged with blood; and without shedding of blood is no remission.

1 John 1:7

But if we walk in the light, as he is in the light, we have fellowship one with another, and the blood of Jesus Christ his Son cleanseth us from all sin.

Acts 20:28

Take heed therefore unto yourselves, and to all the flock, over the which the Holy Ghost hath made you overseers, to feed the church of God, which he hath purchased with his own blood.

Romans 3:25

Whom God hath set forth to be a propitiation through faith in his blood, to declare his righteousness for the remission of sins that are past, through the forbearance of God;

Romans 5:9

Much more then, being now justified by his blood, we shall be saved from wrath through him.

Ephesians 1:7

In whom we have redemption through his blood, the forgiveness of sins, according to the riches of his grace;

Colossians 1:14

In whom we have redemption through his blood, even the forgiveness of sins:

Revelation 1:5

And from Jesus Christ, who is the faithful witness, and the first begotten of the dead, and the prince of the kings of the earth. Unto him that loved us, and washed us from our sins in his own blood,

Today Jesus is in Heaven on the right hand of God, and **all things are now made subject to Him**.

Chapter 3 Review Questions

1. The command of God is for wives to be?

   _____

   _____

2. What does this chapter say about women wearing gold?

   _____

   _____

3. Who called her husband Lord?

   _____

4. Husbands are told to do what to their wives?

   _____

   _____

5. What does 1 Peter 3:8 tells us to be?

   _____

   _____

6. The body is made of many?

   _____

   _____

7. What is the only thing that can save us?

_____

_____

8. Where in the Bible does it state we are to be perfect in God's sight?

_____

_____

9. God said that Job was _____

_____.

10. We are called that we should inherit a _____

_____.

11. We are not to render evil for _____

_____.

12. To the one who will love life and see good days, let him refrain _____

_____.

13. What is the name of the little servant girl who witnessed to Naaman's wife? _____

_____

14. For the eyes of the Lord are over the _____

_____.

15. The very hairs of your head are_____

_____.

16. We are to always be ready to give _____

_____.

17. We are to always have a good_____

_____.

18. After Christ's death he went and preached to

_____.

19. How many souls were saved during the time of the flood?

_____

20. Where is Jesus now?

_____

_____

21. Who are the spirits that Jesus went and preached to in prison?

_____

_____

Chapter 4

¹Forasmuch then as Christ hath suffered for us in the flesh, arm yourselves likewise with the same mind: for he that hath suffered in the flesh hath ceased from sin; ²That he no longer should live the rest of his time in the flesh to the lusts of men, but to the will of God.

Peter begins by reminding these Christians that Christ had suffered for them, so that they could come into the fellowship of those who have **a personal experience with the Lord**. Further, Peter stresses the fact that their savior **suffered in the flesh** like as others. That He was not merely a far-off God, but a God who **took on the nature of man that He might be the example for those who would follow Him**. He went through suffering, torment, pain and finally death. Why death? **Because without the shedding of blood there could be no remission of sin.**

To cease from sin means that we have **given ourselves to Christ totally** and wholly and the desire to sin has **no more power over us**, thus through Jesus, **we no longer commit sin**.

Hebrews 9:22

> *And almost all things are by the law purged with blood; and*
> *without shedding of blood is no remission.*

We know as we look at this again, that the blood of animals
such as lambs (sheep), cattle, goats, doves could not be the supreme
sacrifice that was needed. Their sacrifice was not special enough to
pay the price that was needed for all mankind. The world had to
have a savior of high enough degree **to be able to cover or wash
away the sins of the world**. This does not mean, as so many
believe, that when Christ died upon the cross, the sins of the world
were forgiven. It means that when man **comes to Christ in
humbleness, repents and asks** for the forgiveness of sin, that
Christ **can and will wash away that sin** by His blood.

Peter was there at the crucifixion. It was at the trial of Jesus
that Peter denied the Lord three times. Whereupon Peter went out
and wept bitterly, asking God to forgive him of his sin, his spiritual
weakness. As Peter is here trying to prepare these Christians for the
future, what may lie ahead? **I am firmly convinced that he was
also thinking of the time when he also would go to the cross.**

2 Peter 1:14

> *Knowing that shortly I must put off this my tabernacle, even*
> *as our Lord Jesus Christ hath shewed me.*

As we read more of this scripture we find that Peter tells us
to **arm ourselves**. Not with the weapons of this world, but **with the
mind of Christ**. If we will pay the price, in time studying, praying,
seeking God's will for our lives, then we are **preparing ourselves**

for what the world may throw at us. We do not know what the future holds for the children of God. Hopefully the rapture will take place before things degrade too far, but we must, as the early Christians, **prepare for the worst and hope for the best**. Peter in the last part of this first verse tries to reassure Christians, that if they love Christ enough to suffer in the flesh, then **sin has no hold upon them**. For no man will suffer pain and torment for something that he does not truly believe to be the truth. So, Church, it is time to arm ourselves, for the battle looms ahead of us should Jesus tarry.

John Phillips Commentary Series states about Peter:

> That he no longer should live the rest of his time in the flesh to the lusts of men, but to the will of God. We are in enemy territory. We cannot expect to get through it unscathed. But we can get through it victoriously. God expects us to do just that. We are not to spend the rest of our lives giving way to our flesh or to our fears. We are to live in harmony with God's will, whatever that may be.

Man's base nature spiritually is to do evil in the sight of God. David said, "In sin did my mother conceive me." It means that he was conceived and born into a sinful world. David had a special relationship with God. God used David in many ways because David was **willing to be used of God**.

This is the same thing that the Lord wants to do with us. He wants to **use us to reach the lost and dying**. But to do this we must, and have to, **surrender our lives** to Jesus and His service. The old nature, the old man of sin, must be crucified, and in his place there must **arise the new man** in Christ Jesus. For only in

Jesus can we win this battle for our souls. The enemy does not give up. He comes at us time and time again trying to get us to once again go back into those weak and beggarly elements that condemn the soul. Let us no longer live our lives in the fleshly lusts of this world. But through Christ, let us **rise above these fleshly lusts**; let us put our minds on **winning the prize that lies before us**.

1 Corinthians 9:24

> *Know ye not that they which run in a race run all, but one receiveth the prize? So run, that ye may obtain.*

Philippians 3:14

> *I press toward the mark for the prize of the high calling of God in Christ Jesus.*

The scripture tells us to **run with patience the race that is set before us**. So let us run this race, being patient, waiting upon God to **move in our behalf to make a way** where there seems to be no way. Our God is not slack concerning His promises to us but **is long suffering**. So, **run with patience**.

Hebrew 12:1

> *Wherefore seeing we also are compassed about with so great a cloud of witnesses, let us lay aside every weight, and the sin which doth so easily beset us, and let us run with patience the race that is set before us,*

Remember, **how we live is up to us**. You cannot blame anyone for failures but yourself. Before we were saved we walked in the flesh trying to satisfy the desires of our heart. When we met Jesus and He changed our lives, **our desires changed our hopes**. Jesus did all this for us. What are you doing for Him? I find it a shame that many have walked away from Christ, gone back into the sin that they once were set free from. Then they wonder why their lives are such a failure. Without Christ in our lives, we can be nothing but a failure.

2 Peter 2:20-21

[20]For if after they have escaped the pollutions of the world through the knowledge of the Lord and Saviour Jesus Christ, they are again entangled therein, and overcome, the latter end is worse with them than the beginning.
[21]For it had been better for them not to have known the way of righteousness, than, after they have known it, to turn from the holy commandment delivered unto them.

1 Peter 4:3-4

[30]For the time past of our life may suffice us to have wrought the will of the Gentiles, when we walked in lasciviousness, lusts, excess of wine, revellings, banquetings, and abominable idolatries:
[4]Wherein they think it strange that ye run not with them to the same excess of riot, speaking evil of you:

Peter is again trying to make a point that will bring people's attention, their focus, upon where they are in Christ. I know that we are not to dwell upon the past. Why? Because as sinful as we were, there were still times when we really had fun and enjoyed ourselves. Don't get me wrong, there is pleasure in the world, mostly ungodly pleasure. So, to dwell on the past opens up a door for Satan to bring temptation before us. This being said, it is good for us at low times in our lives to look back and see where we are today.

We have traded a life of sin, a life of hopelessness, a life of longing **for a life of peace, hope, and contentment**. We have Jesus in our heart to **comfort us** in those times of trials and temptations. But most of all we have a **hope for the future**. We look for the time when **Jesus will come back and take us home**. And if we should go by the way of the grave there is no fear, for **Jesus is with us**.

Hebrew 13:5

> *Let your conversation be without covetousness; and be content with such things as ye have: for he hath said, I will never leave thee, nor forsake thee.*

Peter goes on to remind them of how they lived before salvation, before God changed their lives. How they walked in lasciviousness. "Lasciviousness" indicates a lack of restraint, indecency, wanton behavior, shamelessness. "Lust" is an overmastering desire, a desire for power, a sexual desire, to seek after those things to satisfy one's self. "Excess of wine" is drunkenness and debauchery. "Revellings" means unruly conduct and going to excess. "Banqueting" is eating and drinking to excess such as the pagan religions did.

1 Corinthians 10:14

> *Wherefore, my dearly beloved, flee from idolatry.*

"Abominable idolatries" is literally unlawful idolatries which many pagans practiced. These practices were unlawful for Jews to partake of.

Many of these Christians were Jews and many were Gentiles, but all of them were saved by the blood. They all had a past that condemned them, but when Jesus came into their lives everything changed. The world around them could not understand this change. To the Jews, their fellow Jews could not understand why they would walk away from the religion they grew up in to **follow after the teachings of a man that the priests had condemned and crucified**. How could they turn their backs on thousands of years of teachings and traditions? However, they did not know **the difference that Jesus makes in the lives of His believers**.

The pagans were just as bad as the Jew when it came to trying to understand how people they knew and worshipped with would just walk away from the pagan ways of worship and living, changing their whole lifestyle to follow the teaching of this man called Jesus. Even today those around us don't understand us. They don't understand how we can just **change from doing the worldly things we used to do to a completely different mindset**. The things we used to do, we just **don't do anymore**. So, to make up for their loss of understanding, they make jokes; oh, he got religion; just give him a little while and he or she will be back with us. Just let them get this stuff out of their system, it won't last. They have just gone a little bit crazy, calling Christians names such as "Holy Joe," "Bible Thumper," and worse, which I can't write. Until you experience this salvation, until you have an experience with this man Jesus, you will never fully understand what the Christians around you are talking about. It is a shame to know all about Jesus' life, the things He did and said, yet you have never met Him on a personal basis. **This born-again experience is the greatest thing this side of heaven.**

1 Peter 4:5-10

⁵Who shall give account to him that is ready to judge the quick and the dead.
⁶For for this cause was the gospel preached also to them that are dead, that they might be judged according to men in the flesh, but live according to God in the spirit.
⁷But the end of all things is at hand: be ye therefore sober, and watch unto prayer.
⁸And above all things have fervent charity among yourselves: for charity shall cover the multitude of sins.
⁹Use hospitality one to another without grudging.
¹⁰As every man hath received the gift, even so minister the same one to another, as good stewards of the manifold grace of God.

Verse 5 asks who will give account to him. Who is "him"? It is God that is **ready to judge the quick and the dead.** We know that all sinners alive or dead are going to give an account of the way they lived while on this earth. **Those who died in the faith or went in the rapture will be judged at the judgement seat of Christ.**

Romans 14:10

But why dost thou judge thy brother? or why dost thou set at nought thy brother? for we shall all stand before the judgment seat of Christ.

2 Corinthians 5:10

For we must all appear before the judgment seat of Christ; that every one may receive the things done in his body, according to that he hath done, whether it be good or bad.

But the sinners will stand before God's great white throne. The books will be opened, and **every sinner will be judged according to his works**.

Revelation 20:11-15

[11]And I saw a great white throne, and him that sat on it, from whose face the earth and the heaven fled away; and there was found no place for them.
[12]And I saw the dead, small and great, stand before God; and the books were opened: and another book was opened, which is the book of life: and the dead were judged out of those things which were written in the books, according to their works.
[13]And the sea gave up the dead which were in it; and death and hell delivered up the dead which were in them: and they were judged every man according to their works.
[14]And death and hell were cast into the lake of fire. This is the second death.
[15]And whosoever was not found written in the book of life was cast into the lake of fire.

No one will escape this judgement; all sinners will be there. Every knee shall bow and every tongue shall confess that **Jesus Christ is Lord**. I can assure you that there is not one soul in hell that does not believe that Jesus Christ is the savior, the Son of God. They may say they do not believe in God in this life, but after death it is an altogether different story. They know that God is real; they know that they have, like the rich man, missed the mark. And now it is too late for them. Jesus tells us a certain story about the rich man and Lazarus. Many say it is a parable, that Lazarus and the rich man never lived. As I read this story, nowhere does it say that it is a parable. I believe that **Jesus, being the Son of God, told many stories that were true, because He would know**. I believe this story is true, that it really happened.

Luke 16:19-31

19There was a certain rich man, which was clothed in purple and fine linen, and fared sumptuously every day:

20And there was a certain beggar named Lazarus, which was laid at his gate, full of sores,

21And desiring to be fed with the crumbs which fell from the rich man's table: moreover the dogs came and licked his sores.

22And it came to pass, that the beggar died, and was carried by the angels into Abraham's bosom: the rich man also died, and was buried;

23And in hell he lift up his eyes, being in torments, and seeth Abraham afar off, and Lazarus in his bosom.

24And he cried and said, Father Abraham, have mercy on me, and send Lazarus, that he may dip the tip of his finger in water, and cool my tongue; for I am tormented in this flame.

25But Abraham said, Son, remember that thou in thy lifetime receivedst thy good things, and likewise Lazarus evil things:

but now he is comforted, and thou art tormented.

26 And beside all this, between us and you there is a great gulf fixed: so that they which would pass from hence to you cannot; neither can they pass to us, that would come from thence.

27 Then he said, I pray thee therefore, father, that thou wouldest send him to my father's house:

28 For I have five brethren; that he may testify unto them, lest they also come into this place of torment.

29 Abraham saith unto him, They have Moses and the prophets; let them hear them.

30 And he said, Nay, father Abraham: but if one went unto them from the dead, they will repent.

31 And he said unto him, If they hear not Moses and the prophets, neither will they be persuaded, though one rose from the dead.

This beggar will surely be in heaven, and this rich man will surely be standing before God at the great white throne judgement. The most important question we have before us today is **will you be standing with Jesus and the saints**, or with the devil and the sinners?

This theme is continued in verse 6 and states that for this cause was the gospel preached. **Living or dead, the gospel is the same.** Some scholars believe this refers to the same scriptures used in the third chapter, verses 19-20. Others believe that it tells us that Jesus, after He died upon the cross, went and preached to all of the souls of sinners from creation to the time of His death. I don't believe this is true. They had the law and the prophets, so to me this last group of scholars are wrong.

So, you may say, what gives me the right to go against noted

Bible scholars? **The scriptures must interpret scripture**, and I can find no scripture to back up their opinion. So, my opinion, then, is just as good as theirs. I have a hard time with some Bible scholars' opinions, because scripture must be spiritually discerned, and **without a born-again experience, you cannot discern God's Word**. When I hear what some people have to say about God's Word, I think of that old country saying, you can tell that the wheel is turning, but you think the hamster is dead.

Another thought is that Peter is referring to people who are very much alive, but they are spiritually dead. I once made the statement in church that "I was glad that I didn't wake up dead." Everyone laughed but I explained to them that **every person who is not saved, wakes up dead, spiritually dead, every day**.

Let me now quote from *The Wiersbe Bible Commentary: NT:*

> We must not interpret 1 Peter 4:6 apart from the context of suffering; otherwise, we will get the idea that there is a second chance for salvation after death. Peter was reminding his readers of the Christians who had been martyred for their faith. They had been falsely judged by men, but now in the presence of God, they received their true judgement. "Them that are dead" means "them that are now dead" at the time Peter was writing. The gospel is preached only to the living (1 Peter 1:25) because there is no opportunity for salvation after death.

Hebrews 9:27

And as it is appointed unto men once to die, but after this

158

the judgment:

While we are in these human bodies (in the flesh), we are judged by human standards. One day we shall be with the Lord (in the spirit) and receive the **true and final judgement**. There is no chance of salvation after death. The decision to follow Christ **must be made while we are alive in this life**. There is no preaching to the dead. If we are not saved when we draw that last breath, then there is no salvation for our soul.

Verse 7 tells us that the end of all things is at hand. What does this mean? Peter was encouraging the people to **keep themselves in holiness before the Lord**. It was believed then as it is now that **the coming of the Lord is at hand**. We should have an expectancy. We must have a fervent hope. We must be **looking for our Lord's return every day**. If we get complacent, we could miss Jesus when He comes back for His bride, His church. There is no time to play church. We must be in prayer, we must be looking, and we must **show forth a Christ-like example today**. Tomorrow might be too late.

We read in verse 8 that we are to have a fervent charity among ourselves. Charity is not only sharing with others, but **charity means love**. We must love one another. We must **love all men, even our enemies**, those that despitefully use us, for **love covers sin**. Jesus' love for us is what took Him to Calvary. **We must have love and compassion if we are to please God.**

Verse 9 goes along with verse 8. We are to use hospitality toward one another. In the old world hospitality was a command. People were to have hospitality toward strangers as well as to each other. It was a different world in those days. They trusted and respected others. Yes, there was crime, but not like today. When I was growing up, in the country, we never locked a door, we would go on a trip for a week and not lock a door, and nothing was ever stolen or missing. People could be trusted. Peter writes to **have love, share what you have, and do it willingly** as unto the Lord Jesus Christ, not grudgingly but happily **that it be pleasing to the Lord**.

We read in verse 10 of a gift that man can receive, and it speaks of **sharing with others the gift that God has given us**. The gift of God's salvation should never be hidden away, but spread among others. As we share the good news of the gospel, hearts and lives are **given access to God's grace**. Someone – friend, man on the street, teacher, or pastor – shared with us, and that is why we are saved. The Word states that **we are to minister**. Minister here means that we are to see to the needs of others, whether by **giving to the poor**, or **praying for the sick**, to **preaching the gospel, counseling the broken-hearted, any way that we can share the gift that God has given us**.

As good stewards of the grace of God, **it is our duty to reach out to others**. Some will receive the message we bring; others will take what we have to offer, but will cast away the grace of God that we offer to them. The world has a hand-out mentality; they will take anything that is free. But they don't want any kind of counsel; they reject almost anything that has to do with religion. The mainstream thought is, "Don't tell me what I can and can't do. Don't tell me how I should live, how I should raise my family, how I should act. I will do what I want when I want, and that's all there is to it." Christians, don't give up hope. **Do good, minister where you can, pray for the lost, and let God do whatever is necessary to bring them to repentance.** Remember, some sow the seeds, another waters, and another harvests. **So share the gift that others might be saved.**

1 Peter 4:11-13

[11] If any man speak, let him speak as the oracles of God; if any man minister, let him do it as of the ability which God giveth: that God in all things may be glorified through Jesus Christ, to whom be praise and dominion for ever and ever. Amen.
[12] Beloved, think it not strange concerning the fiery trial which is to try you, as though some strange thing happened unto you:
[13] But rejoice, inasmuch as ye are partakers of Christ's sufferings; that, when his glory shall be revealed, ye may be glad also with exceeding joy.

Under the anointing Peter speaks out and tells the Christians that whatever they had to face, **do it as proven saints of God, to follow God to the very end**. I cannot imagine the turmoil that was going through the Christians' hearts at this time. Rome had made being a Christian against the law. Christians were being killed across the land. Death could be around the next corner. And here Peter was telling them to **ignore the world and what man could do to them**. They were to **spread the Word of God**. They were to speak as the oracle of God. They were to speak with **power and authority** as one sent from God. Peter's words were to use your ability, your God-given ability to minister for God. I have found that if I give God my best, which is my reasonable service, God's anointing will break the yoke. **Moreover, men, women, and children can be set free from the chains of this present world.**

If you will do your best, I can assure you **God will do the rest**. There is an old saying that when good men do nothing, evil prevails. How true this is. If we, the Christians of this world, set back and do nothing, the devil will win the day. I was reading a revealing paper today, on how the homosexual movement is preparing to hit the church, how they want the church to quit preaching that the homosexual lifestyle is a sin. That Jesus loved everybody and accepted everyone just as they were. I will say that **it's true that Jesus loved everyone**. He loved the sinners, but at the same time, **He hated the sin** that condemns their souls to hell.

A perfect example is the woman taken in the act of adultery. Her accusers wanted her stoned to death, which was the lawful penalty. But they wanted to know what Jesus had to say about it. Jesus stooped down and began to write on the ground, then told her accusers, "Let him who is without sin cast the first stone." Convection griped their hearts and they left her standing alone before Jesus. Jesus told her, "Neither do I condemn thee. Go and sin no more." And there is the point, Jesus forgave her but **told her to go and sin no more**. Jesus does not condone sin; He forgives and **tells us to do it no more**. When the homosexual comes to Jesus and He forgives them of their sin, He expects them to **change their lifestyle and sin no more**. If you live contrary to God's Word, then you are a sinner.

John 8:3-11

[3]And the scribes and Pharisees brought unto him a woman taken in adultery; and when they had set her in the midst,
[4]They say unto him, Master, this woman was taken in adultery, in the very act.
[5]Now Moses in the law commanded us, that such should be stoned: but what sayest thou?
[6]This they said, tempting him, that they might have to accuse him. But Jesus stooped down, and with his finger

wrote on the ground, as though he heard them not.

⁷So when they continued asking him, he lifted up himself, and said unto them, He that is without sin among you, let him first cast a stone at her.

⁸And again he stooped down, and wrote on the ground.

⁹And they which heard it, being convicted by their own conscience, went out one by one, beginning at the eldest, even unto the last: and Jesus was left alone, and the woman standing in the midst.

¹⁰When Jesus had lifted up himself, and saw none but the woman, he said unto her, Woman, where are those thine accusers? hath no man condemned thee?

¹¹She said, No man, Lord. And Jesus said unto her, Neither do I condemn thee: go, and sin no more.

Do all you can for God, that God may receive praise and glory. Verse 12 goes on to tell the Christians that they were to suffer persecutions as many others throughout the Roman Empire. They were not the first to suffer and would not be the last. The trials they were to face were the worst things that man could do to man. It seems that man has no end to the cruelty that he can devise. Nero was the first of ten persecuting emperors. The last of these ten would be Diocletian.

To quote *John Phillips Commentary Series:*

> Then Constantine came to the throne of the Caesars and persecution was replaced by patronage – which proved to be the ruin of the church. For its first three hundred years, the church was in the world. It was a despised and hated entity, locked in

a life-and-death struggle with a pagan society. After Constantine, however, the world was in the church, and in time, the church itself became the persecutor of those who resisted its carnality, creeds, and commands.

Church historian Andrew Miller gives us the following graphic account of the "fiery trial" that was raging even as Peter wrote.

This was the first legal persecution of the Christians; and in some of its features it stands alone in the annals of human barbarity. Inventive cruelty sought out new ways of torture to satiate the bloodthirsty Nero—the most ruthless Emperor that ever reigned. The gentle, peaceful, unoffending followers of the Lord Jesus were sewn in the skins of wild beasts, and torn by dogs; others were wrapped in a kind of dress smeared with wax, with pitch, and other combustible matter, with a stake under the chin to keep them upright, and set on fire when the day closed, that they might serve as lights in the public gardens of popular amusements. Nero lent his own gardens for these exhibitions, and gave entertainments for the people. He took an active part in the games himself; sometimes mingling with the crowd on foot, and sometimes viewing the awful spectacle from his chariot. But, accustomed as these people were to public executions and gladiatorial shows, they were moved to pity by the unexampled cruelties inflicted on the Christians. They began to see that they suffered, not for the public good, but to gratify the cruelty of one man. But fearful as their death was, it was soon over; and to them, no doubt, the happiest moment of their existence. Long, long before the lights were quenched in Nero's garden, the martyrs had found their home and rest above— in the blooming garden of God's eternal delights. This precious truth we learn from what the Savior said to the penitent thief on the cross— "Today shalt thou be with Me in Paradise." (Luke 23:43)

The Christians in verse 13 were taught that to suffer as Christ suffered was a blessing. They were to **rejoice and give God glory**. People today would say that this kind of teaching is crazy. Even in the church, people would and do agree with the world. They say, "What kind of glory can God get out of His people being hurt and tormented?" I will tell you what glory God gets. It's knowing that people love Him enough that **they are willing to suffer rather than deny His name**. These kinds of Christians are what that verse in Psalms 116:15 is all about: *"Precious in the sight of the LORD is the death of his saints."*

God rejoices when His people refuse to deny Him even at the point of death. The world today believes that when all pain and suffering have vanished will be a glorious time. But we as Christians look at things differently. We see all of the trials and tribulations as **an assurance of the might and glory of God** when Jesus returns for His saints, **a glory that we will share in**. We as Christians must know this one thing, that God is not going to replace suffering with glory, but He is going to **transform the suffering, turning it into glory**.

John 16:20-22

[20]*Verily, verily, I say unto you, That ye shall weep and*

lament, but the world shall rejoice: and ye shall be sorrowful, but your sorrow shall be turned into joy.

[21]A woman when she is in travail hath sorrow, because her hour is come: but as soon as she is delivered of the child, she remembereth no more the anguish, for joy that a man is born into the world.

[22]And ye now therefore have sorrow: but I will see you again, and your heart shall rejoice, and your joy no man taketh from you.

The Wiersbe's Bible Commentary: NT states:

Jesus used this illustration of a woman giving birth. *"The same baby that gave her pain also gave her joy."*

In birth, God does not substitute something else to relieve the mother's pain. Instead, He **uses what is there already but transforms it**. The pain was transformed into joy by the birth of the baby. The thorn in the flesh that gave Paul difficulty **also gave him power and glory**.

2 Corinthians 12:7-10

[7]And lest I should be exalted above measure through the abundance of the revelations, there was given to me a thorn in the flesh, the messenger of Satan to buffet me, lest I should be exalted above measure.

[8]For this thing I besought the Lord thrice, that it might depart from me.

[9]And he said unto me, My grace is sufficient for thee: for my

strength is made perfect in weakness. Most gladly therefore will I rather glory in my infirmities, that the power of Christ may rest upon me.

[10]Therefore I take pleasure in infirmities, in reproaches, in necessities, in persecutions, in distresses for Christ's sake: for when I am weak, then am I strong.

The cross that gave Jesus shame and pain **also brought power and glory**. We are the saved, born-again, blood-washed saints of God. Give Him praise and glory, stand the test and trial for **we are soon to go home**. We'll be at home with Jesus our Lord.

1 Peter 4:14-16

[14]If ye be reproached for the name of Christ, happy are ye; for the spirit of glory and of God resteth upon you: on their part he is evil spoken of, but on your part he is glorified.

[15]But let none of you suffer as a murderer, or as a thief, or as an evildoer, or as a busybody in other men's matters.

[16]Yet if any man suffer as a Christian, let him not be ashamed; but let him glorify God on this behalf.

This fourteenth verse really needs no explanation. It says what it means and means what it says. If we are reproached for the name of Jesus, then we are told **to rejoice and be happy**. Why? Because it means that we are **performing the task the Lord has set before us**. And if we are true to our calling then we are **honoring God and our savior, Jesus Christ**. Peter stresses over and over that the Christians would face persecution. But in that persecution they were to **rejoice and be glad**, for they would soon be going home. In a way, the church was taught to **look forward to being put to the test**. And we today should look forward to being put to the test, to being buffeted by this world for the sake of Christ. You would think that the world would embrace Christians because of our gentle, quiet, loving and kind ways, but instead they hate us. What have we done to deserve this?

Maybe it is because at one time the Catholic Church tried to rule the world. They persecuted anyone and everyone who was not Catholic, and slowly turned the world against churches. What we have in today's world is the world trying its best to transform the church into something God never meant for it to become. When the world dictates morality to the church, and Christians go along, then we cease to be of any value to God. It's time for the Christians to **stand their ground, face the reproach and wrath of the world and say no to the lies of the devil**. If the Lord tarries, true Bible-believing Christians will once again see the governments of the world persecute the saints of God.

Then in verse 15, Peter continues to exhort, in his letter to these Christians, that if they suffer, let it be for the sake of the gospel. Christians should never be guilty of murder. It was common in those days to have honor killings. For example, if someone killed your brother, then you would kill them. These type of actions are what Peter is talking about. Christians were to forgive, to **pray for those who despised them**. He goes further and warns that they were to **reject the temptations of the enemy**. They were not to kill, and they were not to be thieves, for stealing was a sin against God. Christians are servants of the most high; they were to walk before the world putting forth a life that was **acceptable to the Lord**. They were not to be evildoers or bring shame and disgrace upon the family of God. They were to **maintain the image of Christ**, not being busybodies and meddling in things that did not concern them.

We see this busybody mentality all through the modern church today. The church is full of talebearers, full of people who want to know everybody's business. People who will give you all kinds of free advice, when they don't even know what your problem may be. They are quick to tell you how you should live your life, when they can't even take care of their own. They speak when they should be quiet. They offend others, often driving them out of the church. They blame everybody but themselves. They are reckless in their speech, not caring about their fellow servants. They never do anything wrong, but everybody does them wrong. They cry on everybody's shoulder while trying to find their weak spots, so that these poor individuals can be their next victims.

Peter is doing the work of a pastor as he writes to these Christians. There are times when a pastor, a true shepherd, must step in and take total control of the situation. At times, in the spirit of love, he must reprove and rebuke, with all long suffering. If people get mad and leave the church, then so be it. **The shepherd must care for the whole flock**, not play nursemaid to a few whiners and complainers. Remember, Christ, when necessary, rebuked those who were out of line. We cannot afford to let the sheep be scattered. **Pray for our pastors, for they will stand before God and give an account of how they cared for God's children.** The Word tells us to know those who labor among us.

1 Thessalonians 5:12

And we beseech you, brethren, to know them which labour among you, and are over you in the Lord, and admonish you;

Pastors, beware, because the devil seeks to bring division into your churches, to destroy the flock of God if he can. **Ask the Lord to give you the spirit of discernment.** We must know when the devil comes in. In this time when churches are in decline, we welcome new people into our midst with open arms. But if we are not careful, if we do not have that spirit of discernment, we may be welcoming the devil himself. **Preach the truth**, preach it with passion and authority. Preach with the **anointing of the Holy Ghost and fire**, because the fire will burn out the dross. **We must be wise as serpents and harmless as doves.**

Matthew 10:16

> *Behold, I send you forth as sheep in the midst of wolves: be ye therefore wise as serpents, and harmless as doves.*

In 1 Peter 4:16, Peter tells us that under no conditions are Christians to be ashamed. We have nothing to be ashamed of and everything to be proud of.

To quote a lengthy portion from *Barnes Notes on the New Testament:*

> *Let him not be ashamed.*
> (1.) Ashamed of religion so as to refuse to suffer on account of it.
> (2.) Ashamed that he is despised and maltreated. He is to regard his religion as every way honourable, and all that fairly results from it in time and eternity as in every respect desire able. He is not to be ashamed to be called a Christian; he is not to be ashamed of the doctrines taught by his religion; he is not to be ashamed of the Saviour

whom he professes to love; he is not to be ashamed of the society and fellowship of those who are true Christians, poor and despised though they may be; he is not to be ashamed to perform any of the duties demanded by his religion; he is not to be ashamed to have his name cast out, and himself subjected to reproach and scorn. A man should be ashamed only of that which is wrong. He should glory in that which is right, whatever may be the consequences to himself. Christians now, though not subjected to open persecution, are frequently reproached by the world on account of their religion; and though the rack may not be employed, and the fires of martyrdom are not enkindled, yet it is often true that one who is a believer is called to "suffer as a Christian." He may be reviled and despised. His views may be regarded as bigoted, narrow, severe. Opprobrious epithets, on account of his opinions, may be applied to him. His former friends and companions may leave him because he has become a Christian. A wicked father, or a gay and worldly mother, may oppose a child, or a husband may revile a wife, on account of their religion.

As Christians, we are to stand for what is right and not be ashamed. How do we change a world that rejects and despises us? We do it by prayer, by **praying for a revival to be sent from God**. God can and will change things if we pray. The Lord tells us in his Word that when we will **humble ourselves and pray that God**

will be moved and come to our aid.

2 Chronicles 7:14

> *If my people, which are called by my name, shall humble themselves, and pray, and seek my face, and turn from their wicked ways; then will I hear from heaven, and will forgive their sin, and will heal their land.*

We, as I have said so many times, are under attack by the devil. Our adversary, the devil, is seeking to destroy the church from within. When men of high position in the church world, men who claim to be Christians, ministers of the gospel, when they change what they believe and go against God's Word, the results are they lead thousands, hundreds of thousands or more down the garden path, straight into the pits of hell.

A certain minister pastors a church of thousands. This minister is on television and radio daily. This man has changed what he believes in, for personal gain. He has come out and declared that homosexuality is no longer a sin. He states that the apostles were wrong and misguided; that they were ignorant and unlearned men who did not understand God's Word; that they were not moved upon by God to write the Bible; and that a large part of the Bible is wrong and full of mistakes. Brothers and sisters, we are under assault by the devil from within and from without. Let us pray as never before that the hand of God will save His Church.

When men and women get to the point that they think that they are smarter, more intelligent than God is, and when people reach the point that they do not believe in the whole Word of God, then what good is there in believing any part of it? We have reached the fulfilling of the verse that in the last days men will believe a lie and be damned.

2 Thessalonians 2:11-12

[11]And for this cause God shall send them strong delusion, that they should believe a lie:
[12]That they all might be damned who believed not the truth, but had pleasure in unrighteousness.

1 Timothy 4:1-2

[1]Now the Spirit speaketh expressly, that in the latter times some shall depart from the faith, giving heed to seducing spirits, and doctrines of devils;
[2]Speaking lies in hypocrisy; having their conscience seared with a hot iron;

2 Timothy 4:3-4

[3]For the time will come when they will not endure sound doctrine; but after their own lusts shall they heap to themselves teachers, having itching ears;
[4]And they shall turn away their ears from the truth, and shall be turned unto fables.

If the righteous scarcely be saved, where shall the sinner and ungodly appear?

1 Peter 4:18

And if the righteous scarcely be saved, where shall the ungodly and the sinner appear?

2 Peter 2:1-2

¹But there were false prophets also among the people, even as there shall be false teachers among you, who privily shall bring in damnable heresies, even denying the Lord that bought them, and bring upon themselves swift destruction. ²And many shall follow their pernicious ways; by reason of whom the way of truth shall be evil spoken of.

In all of this let us glorify God for the coming of the Lord is coming very very soon. Give God praise and glory.

1 Peter 4:17-19

¹⁷For the time is come that judgment must begin at the house of God: and if it first begin at us, what shall the end be of them that obey not the gospel of God? ¹⁸And if the righteous scarcely be saved, where shall the ungodly and the sinner appear? ¹⁹Wherefore let them that suffer according to the will of God commit the keeping of their souls to him in well doing, as unto a faithful Creator.

It is hard for people when there is all of this confusion going on in the church world of today. People say, "Who do I believe? This big preacher believes this doctrine, this other preacher says that he was wrong, and now says that the Bible is wrong. What do I do?" The answer is to believe the Word. It does not matter what man says or believes. If it does not line up with the Word of God, it is wrong. **The Word of God is the final authority.** There is a judgement day coming very soon. Sin is still sin no matter what man wants to believe. **Obey the Word; this is the only way to never die, the only way to go home to be with Jesus.**

2 Peter 2:20-22

> *²⁰For if after they have escaped the pollutions of the world through the knowledge of the Lord and Saviour Jesus Christ, they are again entangled therein, and overcome, the latter end is worse with them than the beginning.*
> *²¹For it had been better for them not to have known the way of righteousness, than, after they have known it, to turn from the holy commandment delivered unto them.*
> *²²But it is happened unto them according to the true proverb, The dog is turned to his own vomit again; and the sow that was washed to her wallowing in the mire.*

In these last days there will come scoffers, there will come those who try to turn God's Word into a lie. God's Word tells us to **ignore them and believe the truth**. We must live by the Word. Regardless of what man may say, Jesus is still the only way to heaven. Jesus is still the **only one who can give eternal life**. He is the door, and **no man can come to the Father** except through Jesus Christ. The scripture says the time is come that judgement must begin at the house of God.

1 Corinthians 11:27-29

> *²⁷Wherefore whosoever shall eat this bread, and drink this cup of the Lord, unworthily, shall be guilty of the body and*

blood of the Lord.

[28]But let a man examine himself, and so let him eat of that bread, and drink of that cup.

[29]For he that eateth and drinketh unworthily, eateth and drinketh damnation to himself, not discerning the Lord's body.

As I read this scripture in Peter, it tells me that the church must judge itself according to the scriptures. As has already been read in 1 Corinthians, the scriptures tell us to **examine ourselves in the light of God's Word**. Not what man wants to believe, not what the world wants us to believe, but **by what God's Word says**. False teachers and preachers are trying every day to pervert God's Word, to change it to suit what the world wants to believe. Sadly, they can change anything that they want, but as much as they change, they only make fools of themselves, for the Word of God is established forever, never to change.

The fool has said in his heart that there is no God, but he is a fool for a reason, because he will not accept the Word of God. **God is the same yesterday and today and forever. God does not and will not change.** Judgement must begin at the house of God. We must check and recheck to be sure that there is nothing in our hearts that will keep us from missing our Lord's return.

I was reading the other day about the pastor of the largest (if not the largest, then one of the largest) churches in the state of Texas. He has made the statement that he does not believe everything in the Bible, that the apostles Peter, Paul, and John were too narrow minded, that they were wrong to condemn people's lives. That nobody could be holy, so God has to accept all of us just as we are, and everybody is going to go the heaven. How crazy can a person be, to be so full of self-importance that they are wiser than

God and God's chosen apostles? However, we see such people all the time. It just stands out more when they are a big-name preacher.

I ministered some time ago at a meeting. A couple of months later I talked to a fellow minister that had been there. He told me that he heard me preach that night and that I had done very well. Then he said to me, "You know, I think you were a little too hard and need to weaken down your messages." This is what is happening to the churches today, everybody trying to please everyone in the church but God. So today in pleasing everybody in the church, God is left completely out of the picture. No wonder there are countless churches where no one gets saved, where God's Spirit is not allowed to move. Churches where they don't want God's presence in their services. **If we will judge ourselves, when we stand before Christ's judgement seat, there will be no marks against us.** Then, where does this leave the ungodly and the sinner? It leaves them in the hands of the living God.

Hebrews 10:31

> *It is a fearful thing to fall into the hands of the living God.*

For all of these people who know more than God's chosen ministers, pastor, prophets, apostles, all I can say is you can try and fool yourself and those who follow you. But you cannot fool God. There is coming a day when you will stand before God's great white throne for judgement, and hear Him say depart from me, for I know you not.

Luke 13:24-28

> *[24]Strive to enter in at the strait gate: for many, I say unto*

177

you, will seek to enter in, and shall not be able.

[25] When once the master of the house is risen up, and hath shut to the door, and ye begin to stand without, and to knock at the door, saying, Lord, Lord, open unto us; and he shall answer and say unto you, I know you not whence ye are:

[26] Then shall ye begin to say, We have eaten and drunk in thy presence, and thou hast taught in our streets.

[27] But he shall say, I tell you, I know you not whence ye are; depart from me, all ye workers of iniquity.

[28] There shall be weeping and gnashing of teeth, when ye shall see Abraham, and Isaac, and Jacob, and all the prophets, in the kingdom of God, and you yourselves thrust out.

Examine yourselves, unless with you it is too late. The self-righteous, the blasphemer, the backslider, the workers of sin will all stand before God on that day.

Revelation 2:11-15

[11] He that hath an ear, let him hear what the Spirit saith unto the churches; He that overcometh shall not be hurt of the second death.

[12] And to the angel of the church in Pergamos write; These things saith he which hath the sharp sword with two edges;

[13] I know thy works, and where thou dwellest, even where Satan's seat is: and thou holdest fast my name, and hast not denied my faith, even in those days wherein Antipas was my faithful martyr, who was slain among you, where Satan dwelleth.

¹⁴But I have a few things against thee, because thou hast there them that hold the doctrine of Balaam, who taught Balac to cast a stumblingblock before the children of Israel, to eat things sacrificed unto idols, and to commit fornication.
¹⁵So hast thou also them that hold the doctrine of the Nicolaitans, which thing I hate.

Revelation 21:8

But the fearful, and unbelieving, and the abominable, and murderers, and whoremongers, and sorcerers, and idolaters, and all liars, shall have their part in the lake which burneth with fire and brimstone: which is the second death.

Matthew 7:21-23

²¹Not every one that saith unto me, Lord, Lord, shall enter into the kingdom of heaven; but he that doeth the will of my Father which is in heaven.
²²Many will say to me in that day, Lord, Lord, have we not prophesied in thy name? and in thy name have cast out devils? and in thy name done many wonderful works?
²³And then will I profess unto them, I never knew you: depart from me, ye that work iniquity.

Luke 9:62

And Jesus said unto him, No man, having put his hand to

the plough, and looking back, is fit for the kingdom of God.

1 Corinthians 6:9-10

[9]Know ye not that the unrighteous shall not inherit the kingdom of God? Be not deceived: neither fornicators, nor idolaters, nor adulterers, nor effeminate, nor abusers of themselves with mankind,
[10]Nor thieves, nor covetous, nor drunkards, nor revilers, nor extortioners, shall inherit the kingdom of God.

Galatians 5:19-21

[19]Now the works of the flesh are manifest, which are these; Adultery, fornication, uncleanness, lasciviousness,
[20]Idolatry, witchcraft, hatred, variance, emulations, wrath, strife, seditions, heresies,
[21]Envyings, murders, drunkenness, revellings, and such like: of the which I tell you before, as I have also told you in time past, that they which do such things shall not inherit the kingdom of God.

Ephesians 5:5-7

[5]For this ye know, that no whoremonger, nor unclean person, nor covetous man, who is an idolater, hath any inheritance in the kingdom of Christ and of God.
[6]Let no man deceive you with vain words: for because of these things cometh the wrath of God upon the children of disobedience.
[7]Be not ye therefore partakers with them.

In the eighteenth verse, the question is, if the righteous scarcely be saved, where shall the ungodly and sinner appear? The above scriptures tell us all we need to know about where the sinner, the ungodly man, woman, boy, or girl will appear. Verse 19 exhorts us to **commit our souls to the keeping of our Lord**, our creator, our savior, our soon-coming king, Jesus Christ, the only begotten Son of God.

Chapter 4 Review Questions

1. How are we to arm ourselves?

   _____

   _____

2. What is meant by "ceased from sin"?

   _____

   _____

3. When Jesus died upon the cross, does this mean that the sins

   of the whole world were forgiven?

   _____

   _____

4. Man's base nature is to do what?

   _____

   _____

5. What is set before us that we are to win?

   _____

   _____

6. What is lasciviousness?

   _____

   _____

7. Who will be judged at the Great White Throne Judgement?

   _____

   _____

8. Do you believe the story of Lazarus is true or made up? Yes
   or no

   _____

   _____

9. Is there a chance of salvation after death?

   _____

   _____

10. Do you believe that the end of all things is at hand?

    Circle one: Yes   No

11. What does the word charity mean?

    _____

    _____

12. What is the gift in verse 10?

_____

_____

13. If any man speaks, let him speak as?

_____

_____

14. What does Peter tell us to "think it not strange"?

_____

_____

15. We are to be _____ of Christ suffering.

16. But let none of you suffer as a ?

_____

_____

17. If a man is a Christian, he is not to be?

_____

_____

18. Judgement must begin where?

_____

19. And if the righteous scarcely be _____, where

    shall the _____ and the _____ appear?

20. What are we to commit as unto a faithful Creator?

    _____

    _____

Chapter 5

We know according to scripture, **judgement begins at the house of God**. This being so, it is vital that **the house of God must above all be in order**. It needs God at the head and good spiritual leadership, or said house will fall apart. This must be a house that is **founded upon the Word,** a house that is set in order. It must have proven leadership that is established and will not run at the first sight of trouble. Leadership that will stay and fight for what is right because souls are at stake. A leader must have a vision, he must **have a burden for the lost.** He must have a loving, caring concern for the souls in his church, and **be an inspiration to them.** This is because the church will not be any more spiritual than its leader. **These leaders (elders) must be committed to those whom God has set them over.**

1 Peter 5:1-4

[1] The elders which are among you I exhort, who am also an elder, and a witness of the sufferings of Christ, and also a partaker of the glory that shall be revealed:
[2] Feed the flock of God which is among you, taking the oversight thereof, not by constraint, but willingly; not for

filthy lucre, but of a ready mind;
³ Neither as being lords over God's heritage, but being
ensamples to the flock.
⁴ And when the chief Shepherd shall appear, ye shall
receive a crown of glory that fadeth not away.

Peter begins by exhorting the elders, by pressing the point of their duty to those who were under their charge. The elder in the natural means those of age, older men who have lived a long time. However, in the church, elder means **one of spiritual maturity**. There are many older men in the church who are not qualified to be elders because of a lack of spiritual maturity. It is conceivable that a young man can and many times is qualified to be an elder of the church. Bible scholars say that **an elder is the same as a bishop or a pastor**. All three mean the same thing, an overseer, one who cares for the flock of God. Elders were not chosen lightly; their lives had to be an example to the rest of the church. They had to have spiritual maturity, **to be able to govern or oversee God's church**. Let us look at the qualifications of this office.

Titus 1:5-9

⁵ For this cause left I thee in Crete, that thou shouldest set in order the things that are wanting, and ordain elders in every city, as I had appointed thee:
⁶ If any be blameless, the husband of one wife, having faithful children not accused of riot or unruly.
⁷ For a bishop must be blameless, as the steward of God; not selfwilled, not soon angry, not given to wine, no striker, not given to filthy lucre;
⁸ But a lover of hospitality, a lover of good men, sober, just,

holy, temperate;

[9] Holding fast the faithful word as he hath been taught, that he may be able by sound doctrine both to exhort and to convince the gainsayers.

1 Timothy 3:1-7

[1] This is a true saying, If a man desire the office of a bishop, he desireth a good work.

[2] A bishop then must be blameless, the husband of one wife, vigilant, sober, of good behaviour, given to hospitality, apt to teach;

[3] Not given to wine, no striker, not greedy of filthy lucre; but patient, not a brawler, not covetous;

[4] One that ruleth well his own house, having his children in subjection with all gravity;

[5] (For if a man know not how to rule his own house, how shall he take care of the church of God?)

[6] Not a novice, lest being lifted up with pride he fall into the condemnation of the devil.

[7] Moreover he must have a good report of them which are without; lest he fall into reproach and the snare of the devil.

As we can see these men had to have **a life above reproach**. A bishop or elder had to be blameless, the husband of one wife. What this means is that **a man could not have multiple wives** (two or more). Polygamy was widely practiced at that time. The Jews and the Gentiles both practiced multiple marriages. This practice was perfectly legal in the world of that time, and it was also permitted in or legal in the eyes of God. A good example of God's permission is found in Deuteronomy.

188

Deuteronomy 25:5-10

⁵If brethren dwell together, and one of them die, and have no child, the wife of the dead shall not marry without unto a stranger: her husband's brother shall go in unto her, and take her to him to wife, and perform the duty of an husband's brother unto her.

⁶And it shall be, that the firstborn which she beareth shall succeed in the name of his brother which is dead, that his name be not put out of Israel.

⁷And if the man like not to take his brother's wife, then let his brother's wife go up to the gate unto the elders, and say, My husband's brother refuseth to raise up unto his brother a name in Israel, he will not perform the duty of my husband's brother.

⁸Then the elders of his city shall call him, and speak unto him: and if he stand to it, and say, I like not to take her,

⁹Then shall his brother's wife come unto him in the presence of the elders, and loose his shoe from off his foot, and spit in his face, and shall answer and say, So shall it be done unto that man that will not build up his brother's house.

¹⁰And his name shall be called in Israel, The house of him that hath his shoe loosed.

When a woman married and her husband died without producing any children, the woman was not to marry a stranger. She was to be taken to wife by her husband's brother which was his brotherly duty. Moreover, the first born of this union was to succeed in the name of the dead brother. **It made no difference if the living brother had no wife or one or more wives, his duty to his**

dead brother was the same. The widow became his wife by law. So polygamy was **widely practiced throughout the whole land** and in many places, and it still is to this day.

Back to the elders, an elder had to be **vigilant, sober, know how to behave himself, ready to teach, patient, given to charity, not greedy of money, not covetous a man who could manage the affairs of the church wisely and properly that the church might be without reproach.** Peter in this first verse exhorts or encourages these men (elders) to **do their duty for the church.** This is the job that they accepted when they agreed to be the elders. Notice that Peter does not command or demand this service, but exhorts or encourages his fellow servants of the Lord. Peter also calls himself an elder and goes on to say that he was an eyewitness to the suffering that Jesus Christ went through, and one glorious day he will be a partaker of the glory that is to shortly come to pass.

In the second verse, Peter tells the elders to **feed the flock, or the saints,** which is their reasonable service. I do not know what scriptures these saints had access to, but the elders were to teach or minister to the spiritual needs of the people. They used Old Testament scriptures and the letters from the apostles. Using this material, these elders had to **depend upon the Holy Ghost to fill in any blanks** that might have existed. **We never go wrong when we trust in the blessed Holy Ghost.** The elders did a good job spiritually, or the church would not be here today.

The elders were to be the protectors of the church, the overseers, **taking the oversight of the body of Christ.** They were to do this willingly and not grudgingly, not for money, but because they loved God's people and His church. The elders were overseers to look over God's people. They were not to lord themselves over God's heritage. Their lives were to be **examples for the people to follow after,** always looking for the return of the Chief Shepherd, our Lord Jesus Christ. Jesus has given us His promise that He will return for us, to take us home with Him, and there shall we ever be with Him. Jesus tells us in His Word, that in His Father's house are many mansions, and He has gone to prepare us a place there. At that time, we will receive **a crown of glory, which will never fade away**.

For one moment, **let us look at this man called Peter again**. Peter was a disciple, one of the twelve men Jesus picked. These twelve were special men, yet even one of them was overcome by the devil. They were the foundation of the coming church. They were the original foundation stones. Who, after Jesus' death on the cross, spread out carrying the gospel message to a lost and dying world? Hated by the pagan world as well as by the Jewish hierarchy, Peter, until his call, **was a fisherman** along with his brother Andrew. Peter was **in the garden with Jesus**, when Jesus prayed till the sweat was as great drops of blood. Peter was the one who **drew a sword and cut off the ear of the high priest's servant**. He was there at the **beginning of Jesus' trial** before the Chief Priest, Caiaphas. Peter was the disciple who **denied the Lord three times** and went out and wept bitterly asking God for forgiveness. He knew all about the crucifixion, for he **had seen the wounds that were placed upon Jesus' body**.

All of this Peter knew. However, he knew even more. Peter knew about the glory of God because **he was there on the Mount of Transfiguration**. He had seen the glory that shone upon Jesus' face as He was bathed in His Father's glory; there where the glory of heaven touched the earth. He was **there at the empty tomb** after Jesus had risen from the dead. He had **seen the risen Christ**. He was there **when Jesus appeared in the locked room**. He was there when Jesus was **taken up in the clouds** into heaven. He heard the angels say that this same Jesus would return in like manner, as they had seen Him go. All of this Peter had seen with his own eyes. **What Peter was telling was a lot more than just stories, because Peter was there; he was part of the story.**

Yet, in all of this, he was never more than what he was, a humble fisherman whose life Jesus had transformed into a pillar of the church. Peter never tried to be somebody, someone high and lifted up. His desire was not man's praise; his desire was to **serve his fellow man, and gain the approval of his Lord and Savior Jesus Christ**. That should be our desire, also, to **be like Jesus and to serve Him** until He returns for His bride, or He calls us home by way of the grave. Just be ready when He calls.

1 Peter 5:5-6

⁵ Likewise, ye younger, submit yourselves unto the elder. Yea, all of you be subject one to another, and be clothed with humility: for God resisteth the proud, and giveth grace to the humble.
⁶ Humble yourselves therefore under the mighty hand of God, that he may exalt you in due time:

Peter now addresses the younger members of the church on how to conduct themselves in the church. It is great to see young people taking an active part in the church. **The younger Christians are the church of tomorrow**, should the Lord tarry. Peter in verse five is stressing that **there is to be an order of conduct in the church.** Younger members should be in subjection to the older (the elders in the church). This is a two-way street, just as the younger are to submit to their elders. The elders are not to Lord it over the heads of the younger. **There must be harmony** in the church if the lost are to be reached. The elders should not dampen the zeal of the younger, but channel their zeal into a productive use in the church. At the same time, the younger Christians should not try to run the church and turn it in a different direction from what God desires.

There is an old saying, "Hire a teenager because they know everything." What this means is that they have not lived long enough to learn that they really don't know everything. It was amazing how much my dad learned from the time I was a teenager till I reached the age of twenty. Peter says, "Yea, all of you be subject one to another." There must be **harmony within the body** or the body will cease to function properly. The best way to keep the church moving forward is to **stay humble before God, to pray and put God's will and spirit first**.

Proverbs 3:34

> *Surely he scorneth the scorners: but he giveth grace unto the lowly.*

Peter quotes from Proverbs 3:24, but the quotation is changed just a little. It states: "Surely he scorneth the scorners," while Peter says "he resisteth the proud." Though the meaning is the same, it is stated differently.

The Interlinear Bible, Hebrews, Greek and English, translates like this:

> Likewise, younger ones be subject to older ones; all and to one another; being subject, humility put on, because God proud ones sets (himself) against, to humble ones but he gives grace.

This is straight from the Greek. So to keep the grace of God flowing we must **learn to be humble preferring our brother to ourselves**. Pride goes before a fall. We must battle to **keep pride in its rightful place**. I think I have said this before, but when people tell me that I preached a good message, I feel ashamed and grieved, because it's not me that preached, **it's Jesus through me that preached, and to God be the glory, not to me**. I give the glory to God because it is **from Him whom all blessings flow**. Pastors, lay members, we cannot forget, except that God fights the battle, we fight in vain. Never think, look at all that I have done, rather look and say, **look what the Lord has done**. Stay humble, stay on your knees, pray, seek God's grace and glory, and **let God have His holy way**.

All through God's Word, we find where we are to **humble ourselves before God**. In verse five we read where Peter wrote, "And be clothed with humility." The humble man is a man of great quality. **Humbleness is the opposite of pride, or being puffed up.** We are warned repeatedly not to think more highly of ourselves than we ought, told that pride goes before a fall and that **we must be willing to take any place in the service of God**. Self-important people often find themselves humiliated before others when their true importance comes out. Jesus tells us of such an example.

Luke 14:8-11

> [8]*When thou art bidden of any man to a wedding, sit not down in the highest room; lest a more honourable man than thou be bidden of him;*
> [9]*And he that bade thee and him come and say to thee, Give this man place; and thou begin with shame to take the lowest room.*

194

[10]But when thou art bidden, go and sit down in the lowest room; that when he that bade thee cometh, he may say unto thee, Friend, go up higher: then shalt thou have worship in the presence of them that sit at meat with thee.
[11]For whosoever exalteth himself shall be abased; and he that humbleth himself shall be exalted.

Quoting from *John Phillips Commentary Series:*

> Far better for us to take the humble place now, Peter affirms, and to be honored and lifted up at the Lord's return, than to strut onstage now, only to be humbled at the judgment seat of Christ.

We see so many big name preachers today that continually say, "Look what I have done." It is always, I, I, I, and they may have done great things in the world, but I am brought back to the following scripture:

Psalms 127:1

> *Except the LORD build the house, they labour in vain that build it: except the LORD keep the city, the watchman waketh but in vain.*

"Except God build the house, they labor in vain that build it." Man can build great things, and sometimes they can last for ages, but in the process of time they will all come to naught. But if **God builds it, it will last forever**. If you want to be exalted, then **learn to be humble before God and the world**.

I Peter 5:7-9

⁷Casting all your care upon him; for he careth for you.
⁸Be sober, be vigilant; because your adversary the devil,
as a roaring lion, walketh about, seeking whom he may
devour:
⁹Whom resist stedfast in the faith, knowing that the same
afflictions are accomplished in your brethren that are in
the world.

Casting all our cares upon the Lord because He cares for us is a lot easier said than done. Jesus will not fail us, but too many times we fail ourselves. The Lord's desire is that we **trust Him**, that we **put our faith in Him**. One person told me it's hard to trust the Lord when the wolf is knocking at the door. I reminded this person that there is an old saying that "the Lord helps those who help themselves." Don't sit at home and do nothing and expect the Lord to pay your bills. We have all kinds of cares: money cares, health issues, getting enough food to feed our families. We have all kinds of cares, some that we bring upon ourselves, such as only going to church when we feel like it, not paying our tithes (which is a big mistake).

I had a brother in the church that always had more month than money. I showed him in the scripture that **if we give to God what belongs to God, that the 90% would go farther than the 100%**. He said that he would put God to the test. After a few months he came to me and said, "I don't understand it; you were right. I pay my tithes and somehow, all my bills get paid, and I even have money left at the end of the month." If we show God that we care, and that we trust in Him, **God will always make a way**. When we learn that, God can be trusted with all of our problems whatever they may be, and then God shows us how much that He loves us and meets our needs **according to His riches in glory**.

Sometimes it is not easy to trust that the Lord can and will meet our needs. The hardest time most people have is with health problems. But God is **just as faithful with our health as He is with our money**. Remember, Jesus loved us when we were unlovable. **Cast your cares upon Him and watch and see how much He cares for you.**

In verse eight, **we are told to be vigilant**; to be aware of what is going on around us, sharp eyed and always on the lookout for the enemy; to be sober and not carried away with foolishness. This is not to say that Christians can't have fun or enjoyment, but don't be carried to the extreme. **When we get our eyes off Jesus, we get ourselves into trouble.** This scripture tells us that our adversary the devil goes about as a roaring lion. In another scripture, the devil is portrayed as a wolf in sheep's clothing.

Matthew 7:15

Beware of false prophets, which come to you in sheep's clothing, but inwardly they are ravening wolves.

At another time, the devil appears as an angel of light.

2 Corinthians 11:13-15

[13]For such are false apostles, deceitful workers, transforming themselves into the apostles of Christ.
[14]And no marvel; for Satan himself is transformed into an angel of light.
[15]Therefore it is no great thing if his ministers also be transformed as the ministers of righteousness; whose end

shall be according to their works.

In verse nine, Peter tells us that our only hope is to resist, resisting steadfast in the faith.

James 4:7

> *Submit yourselves therefore to God. Resist the devil, and he will flee from you.*

James in his epistle tells us that when the devil comes against us, to first **submit ourselves unto our most Holy High and lifted up God**. Once we have made sure that we are connected to God, then **resist the devil, and he will flee from us**. What the devil is really fleeing from is God within us. For we are not alone in this struggle; all of our brothers and sisters are facing the same trials as we are. Pray for one another; lift each other up in prayer, for **we are on the Lord's side**. Do not let the roaring of the devil frighten you, for **"greater is He that is in you than he that is in the world."**

I John 4:4

> *Ye are of God, little children, and have overcome them: because greater is he that is in you, than he that is in the world.*

Resist the devil, the temptations he brings, knowing that the Lord hath all power and glory. The temptations appeal to the flesh, they are pleasing to the eye, and they feel good to the touch. But they soon bite, to poison the soul. Here is a warning: if you think you can play with the world and be ok, get ready, for the world will bite you. **We must serve God because we are not**

looking at just a few years to live and it will all be over. Yes, there are just a few years to live down here, but then there is all of eternity. Where will we spend it? In the joys of heaven or the horror of hell? That decision we must make for ourselves.

I Peter 5:10-11

[10]But the God of all grace, who hath called us unto his eternal glory by Christ Jesus, after that ye have suffered a while, make you perfect, stablish, strengthen, settle you. [11]To him be glory and dominion for ever and ever. Amen.

In these closing verses, Peter is reaffirming what he has been teaching from chapter one, verse one, up to now. **God's grace is sufficient for all of our needs.** We must **put our faith in God and the moving of His Spirit**. We are saved by God's grace, **through the blood of Jesus.** This grace that saved us is also able to keep us, if we will yield ourselves to God. We are called with a holy calling. When we answer that call, we are no longer our own, for **we are bought with a price.** There may be persecutions and trials, but remember they serve a purpose and that is to **make us perfect in the sight of God.** It is to establish us, strengthen us, and to settle us in God's service.

Verse 11 says to God be the glory both now and forever, and may God have dominion (total control) forever and ever and ever. Read what Paul has to say in Romans:

Romans 8:35-39

[35]Who shall separate us from the love of Christ? shall tribulation, or distress, or persecution, or famine, or nakedness, or peril, or sword?

[36] As it is written, For thy sake we are killed all the day long; we are accounted as sheep for the slaughter.

[37] Nay, in all these things we are more than conquerors through him that loved us.

[38] For I am persuaded, that neither death, nor life, nor angels, nor principalities, nor powers, nor things present, nor things to come,

[39] Nor height, nor depth, nor any other creature, shall be able to separate us from the love of God, which is in Christ Jesus our Lord.

Nothing the devil or the world can do can separate us from the love of God. The world can kill us, but it cannot take the love of God out of our hearts. **The love of Jesus transcends all that man can do.** Praise be to God forever and ever. Amen.

1 Peter 5:12-14

[12] By Silvanus, a faithful brother unto you, as I suppose, I have written briefly, exhorting, and testifying that this is the true grace of God wherein ye stand.

[13] The church that is at Babylon, elected together with you, saluteth you; and so doth Marcus my son.

[14] Greet ye one another with a kiss of charity. Peace be with you all that are in Christ Jesus. Amen.

Peter, in closing out this epistle, makes known his fellow servant Silvanus, who would be taking these epistles to the various churches. Some say that Silvanus may even have been the one who wrote this epistle at Peter's dictation. It is even possible that this Silvanus is the same man that is called Silas in the book of Acts.

Peter said that he had briefly written this letter to **exhort and testify that this grace that they shared was the true grace of God**. Where with ye stand, stand in the grace received from Jesus Christ the Lord. In verse 13, Peter gives greeting from the church at Babylon and its elected saints, called of God. Some scholars believe that Peter was in Rome and called Rome Babylon, but it is more likely that Peter actually was in Babylon at this time. Peter goes on to say that greetings also came from Marcus, his spiritual son and coworker. This Marcus is also believed to be John Mark, so called in other letters. Verse 14 ends with Peter stating, "Greet ye one another with a kiss of charity," or love. **And, may the peace of our Lord be with you all in Christ Jesus. Amen.**

Chapter 5 Review Questions

1. To whom does Peter address this chapter?

   _____

   _____

2. Who were the elders to feed?

   _____

   _____

3. The elders were to be what to the flock?

   _____

   _____

4. Who is the chief Shepherd?

   _____

   _____

5. Likewise ye younger, _____ yourselves unto

   the elder.

6. We are to be clothed with?

   _____

   _____

7. God resists the _____ but gives grace to the

   _____ .

8. We are to cast all of our _____ upon Him

   because He does what for us?

   _____

   _____

9. The devil goes about _____ .

10. What does the devil go about seeking?

    _____

    _____

11. We are to _____ steadfastly.

12. What three ways is our adversary portrayed? List

    references to support them.

    a. _____

    b. _____

    c. _____

13. Where do you find the scripture that states "greater is he that is in you than he that is in the world"?

_____

_____

14. How are we saved?

_____

_____

15. Where was Peter when he wrote this letter?

_____

_____

16. Silvanus is thought to be the same man as?

_____

_____

17. How does Peter tell us to greet the brethren?

_____

_____

Introduction to 2nd Peter

This second epistle was written because Peter was concerned about the churches and God's people, the saints. This second letter is a warning to the churches of what the devil is doing. We must be vigilant, we must be aware of what goes on around us. And most of all, we must know those who labor among us and what they believe and teach. We are under attack. What the enemy could not do from outside, he is doing from the inside, because we have been too trusting for way too long. Like Peter lived, it is past time to just let things go by. We must take a stand for truth, for God's Word. If you truly love people, be honest with them. Warn them of where they stand before God; preach the pure truth to them. It will be a shame to see souls going to hell because you did not tell them the truth.

Be like Peter and say, "This is how it is. Repent or perish." Our only hope is in the saving grace of Jesus Christ. Jesus is the way to salvation, for there is no other way given, whereby man can be saved, but through Jesus Christ our Lord.

Chapter 1

2 Peter 1:1-2

¹ Simon Peter, a servant and an apostle of Jesus Christ, to them that have obtained like precious faith with us through the righteousness of God and our Saviour Jesus Christ:
² Grace and peace be multiplied unto you through the knowledge of God, and of Jesus our Lord,

As Peter begins this letter, he starts by telling everyone who he is. He says that he is a servant. In the time of Peter, **a servant was commonly a slave, one who served in his master's home**. Peter calls himself a servant, a slave. A slave was one who was bound by duty to serve the man or woman who bought them for the rest of their life. Peter felt this bonding with Jesus, **the feeling that he was bound to Jesus, as a slave is bound to their master**. If we look at scripture, we find out that **when we came to Jesus, we gave ourselves to Him to forever be His servants**, and that Jesus bought our salvation with His blood.

1 Corinthians 6:19-20

¹⁹ What? know ye not that your body is the temple of the Holy Ghost which is in you, which ye have of God, and ye are not your own?
²⁰ For ye are bought with a price: therefore glorify God in your body, and in your spirit, which are God's.

Scripture plainly tells us that **we are not our own because we have been bought by the blood of Jesus Christ**. Jesus paid the ransom for our souls, thus we are now the redeemed of the Lord. Jude felt the same bond to Jesus; he called himself a servant to the Lord. Paul called himself a servant of Jesus in Romans, in Philippians, in Titus, and in Philemon. Paul also called himself a prisoner of Jesus Christ. **James is another who called himself a servant.** These men freely gave themselves to servitude in the cause of Christ. This feeling **was and is not limited to the disciples and apostles**.

This same feeling is what causes men and women to go into the ministry, to become missionaries, teachers, this desire to **just be a servant of Jesus Christ**. This feeling is hard to explain; it is just an overpowering desire **to be and do whatever Jesus wants us to do**. I sit and think about Jesus and weep with such a desire to be pleasing to him. When I gave my heart to the Lord, and he came into my heart and soul, there was such a feeling, such a peace; I was made whole for the first time. **For the first time I felt complete with an overwhelming desire to be a servant to Jesus my Lord.**

Peter goes on, in this first verse, to identify those to whom he was writing, to those who **"have obtained like precious faith."** In other words, to those who had **come to Jesus and in repentance accepted Jesus as their savior**. the blood-bought, redeemed children of God. It is so humbling just to sit and think of what Jesus has done for us. All that He went through for me, who am so unworthy, yet He paid the price. I am firmly convinced **that if only one soul would have been saved, Jesus would still have gone to the cross for that one soul**, so great is His love for us. I am reminded of that old song by James Rowe, *It Is Love.*

O the precious love of Jesus,
How it thrills my ransomed soul!
More and more I'll sing its praises
While the happy ages roll.

The love of God and Jesus, His dear Son. Saints we have a gift that is **far above price and the world just passes it by**. Yes, I know that Satan has people's eyes blinded. **It is up to us to share the gospel message with them that they might see.** A very wise minister once told me to "preach the Word; many will not accept it, but there are those who will; preach the Word."

Peter, as he writes to the saints in the local churches, greets them with these words: "Grace and peace be multiplied unto you." As we live for God and spiritually grow, **we will find that God's grace and peace become more real than ever before**. Every battle, every trial makes us stronger in the Lord. As we come through these battles victorious, our faith and confidence grow in Christ. Every trial is an opportunity to gain strength through Jesus Christ. **We must learn that through the knowledge of God and Jesus there is victory.**

2 Peter 1:3

According as his divine power hath given unto us all

things that pertain unto life and godliness, through the knowledge of him that hath called us to glory and virtue:

God has a plan, and it works if we will just **follow what God has laid out**. God our Lord and Master has by His power given unto us all the things that we need to live an overcoming life. Therefore, it is up to us to use what has been given to us. At salvation, **we are empowered with God's divine spirit**. This spirit of God **gives us everything that we need to live an overcoming life**. As we study God's Word and pray every day, we add to what God gave us at salvation. **We must spiritually grow or die.** When we sit down on God, we are spiritually left behind. Without that daily spiritual infusion, it is hard to serve the Lord. **God has called us, for no man comes to God except the spirit draws him.**

John 6:44

No man can come to me, except the Father which hath sent me draw him: and I will raise him up at the last day.

Again, I say that we must **study to show ourselves approved unto God**. As I have often said, "A little knowledge can be very dangerous, so study and pray then study and pray some more."

2 Peter 1:4

Whereby are given unto us exceeding great and precious promises: that by these ye might be partakers of the divine nature, having escaped the corruption that is in the world through lust.

This verse starts by speaking of the exceeding great and precious promises. All the promises that are given to us are great; they are great **because God gives them to us**. Anything that God does is great. I know of nothing that is commonplace about God. God's Word is full of promises from Genesis to Revelation. **These promises are given for our benefit if we will use them.** However, let me interject that all of God's promises are conditional. I know that there are those who say that I am wrong, but I am not wrong. For example, **with every temptation, God will make a way of escape**.

1 Corinthians 10:13

> *There hath no temptation taken you but such as is common to man: but God is faithful, who will not suffer you to be tempted above that ye are able; but will with the temptation also make a way to escape, that ye may be able to bear it.*

Do I believe this? **I most certainly do.** However, the promise does us no good if we do not look for it. Every promise is contingent on what we do. A person is sick and needs healing. God has promised to heal His children, but to receive this promise, **we must have faith and believe that God will do what He said that He would do**. Scripture tells us that all things are possible to them that believe. **Without faith to believe, nothing can come into play.**

Mark 9:23

> *Jesus said unto him, If thou canst believe, all things are possible to him that believeth.*

Mark 11:24

Therefore I say unto you, What things soever ye desire, when ye pray, believe that ye receive them, and ye shall have them.

We must believe that God is and that He is a rewarder of those who diligently seek Him. If we were to take a survey of those who claim to be Christians, it would surprise you how many really do not believe that God answers prayer. They do not believe in the promises of God. They do not believe that Jesus Christ is the only way to heaven. Is it any wonder why God does not move in our midst anymore? **The promises are real.** God gives them to us, to help us live an overcoming life. Nevertheless, these promises **do us no good if we do not believe that God will keep His word**. We must believe to receive. There is a scripture that says ask and ye shall receive, seek and ye shall find, knock and it shall be opened unto you.

Matthew 7:7-8

[7] Ask, and it shall be given you; seek, and ye shall find; knock, and it shall be opened unto you:
[8] For every one that asketh receiveth; and he that seeketh findeth; and to him that knocketh it shall be opened.

Then, herein, is the problem. If you do not ask, how can you receive? If you do not seek then how can you find, and if you do not knock then how can it be opened unto you? **We must go to God believing that He will keep His word; as we believe so shall it be done unto us.** Just remember God knows your heart; do not try to use God for your own personal benefit. It will not work. Be honest and sincere, and above all believe, and **God will keep His promises**.

When we received salvation, **we became partakers of God's divine nature**. The old carnal, lustful nature that indwelt us died at the foot of the cross. We were raised in the newness of Christ, **a brand-new person in Christ Jesus**. *"Old things are passed away; behold, all things are become new."* We walk in the newness of life through Jesus Christ. We, according to scripture, **are to be Holy as God is Holy**. These promises of God are given to keep us in the place where God would have us to be. God's desire is for us to **stay connected to Him, just as an unborn baby is connected to its mother by the umbilical cord**. We must stay connected to the Lord. **Our umbilical cord is prayer, studying God's Word, and fasting**. This keeps us connected to God, and this is our spiritual lifeline. These promises of God are added to **give us more strength in the hard battles and trials of life**. God has promised that He would never leave us nor forsake us. It is we who walk away from God and His grace. We, if we are not careful, can be led away from God (as scripture says) by our own youthful lust. As we stay where God desires us to stay, we find **faith, hope, joy, peace, strength, love, and fellowship that the world cannot understand**. We need to seek God for knowledge, wisdom and understanding. We perish for lack of knowledge.

Hosea 4:6

> *My people are destroyed for lack of knowledge: because thou hast rejected knowledge, I will also reject thee, that thou shalt be no priest to me: seeing thou hast forgotten the law of thy God, I will also forget thy children.*

Romans 10:2-3

2 For I bear them record that they have a zeal of God, but not according to knowledge.
3 For they being ignorant of God's righteousness, and going about to establish their own righteousness, have not submitted themselves unto the righteousness of God.

Ephesians 4:18-20

18 Having the understanding darkened, being alienated from the life of God through the ignorance that is in them, because of the blindness of their heart:
19 Who being past feeling have given themselves over unto lasciviousness, to work all uncleanness with greediness.
20 But ye have not so learned Christ;

We need to understand that the promises of God are like a very great forest. We can walk among God's promises, and we can take refuge from the storms of life in the promises of God. These promises **inspire us to challenge our abilities and faith in God**. Our complete Christian life is founded upon God's promises. Salvation is a promise; Jesus tells us that **if we repent of our sins and accept Him as our savior, He will wash all our sins away and make us whole**. This is a promise from God. Salvation is a promise; healing is a promise; a victorious life in Jesus is a promise. **Our life is beset on every side by the promises of God.**

What makes Christians different from the rest of the world? It is because **we have come into contact with the divine nature of God**. Before we were saved from our sins, we were just like everyone else. Our number one goal was to satisfy self, to do

214

whatever was necessary to try to enjoy life, and to make some sense out of the world that we live in. This is the main reason why people turn to drugs, alcohol, and other perversions. They are looking for something, whatever it might be, to take their minds off their troubles and problems.

The one very important thing they forget is that the more you feed these fleshly lust and desires, the bigger and stronger they get, and the more they demand of you until you are hopelessly entrapped in the devil's web of lies and caught in the devil's snare. So let us look at this dilemma. We can make one of two choices. One, the promise of the devil is worldly pleasure for a short season then an eternity in hell. Two, **God promises us peace, love, joy, contentment and an eternity in heaven**. Which are you going to choose?

In *The Biblical Illustrator,* on 2 Peter, Rev. A. Maclaren wrote:

> Let me say, lastly, that this great text adds a Human Accompaniment of that Divine gift, "Having escaped the corruption that is in the world through lust." Corruption is initial destruction, though of course other forms of life may come from it; destruction is complete corruption. The word means both. A man either escapes from lust and evil, or he is destroyed by it. And the root of this rotting fungus "is in lust," which word, of course, is used in a much wider meaning than the fleshly since in which we employ it in modern times. It means "desire" of all sorts. The root of the world corruption is my own and my brothers' unbridled

and godless desires. So there are two states – a life plunged in putridity, or a heart touched with the Divine nature. Which is it to be? It cannot be both. A man that has got the life of God, in however feeble measure, in him, will flee away from this corruption like Lot out of Sodom. And how will he flee out of it? By subduing his own desire; not by changing position, not by shirking duty, not by withdrawing himself into unwholesome isolation from men and men's ways.

The key is in subduing our own fleshly and lustful desires. All people have desires, it is part of being human, but **the child of God determines which desires to subdue, such as worldly pleasure, personal gratification, man's acclaim, pride, and much more**. The desires that he permits are the desires to **worship, praise, and glorify God**. To be the person that God desires for us to be, to put God first in every aspect of our lives, to be a willing vessel for God's service. The world is corrupt. Only God can set us free, and being free, God then **gives us great and exceeding promises to help us to stay free in this life, free from evil and corruption, through Jesus Christ our Lord.**

2 Peter 1:5-7

> [5] And beside this, giving all diligence, add to your faith virtue; and to virtue knowledge;
> [6] And to knowledge temperance; and to temperance patience; and to patience godliness;
> [7] And to godliness brotherly kindness; and to brotherly kindness charity.

This fifth verse begins by exhorting us to give all diligence.

Webster's Dictionary says about diligence:

> 1. The quality of being diligent; constant, careful effort, perseverance. 2. Speed, haste. 3. Law of degree of attention or care expected of a person in a given situation.

This tells us to be extremely careful in our walk for the Lord. A person who is very diligent is a person who is **very self-controlled in the task set before them**. They are very **structured, attaining a precise goal**. Peter in these three verses is describing faith. We are to learn these seven goals and add them to the faith we already have. This is God's arithmetic. We are to **add to what we already have**. God is setting before us a process whereby we are to grow spiritually. As we add these seven things to our faith, **our knowledge and ability grows in our service of God**. I like what *The John Phillips Commentary* wrote:

The John Phillips Commentary Series – Exploring the Epistles of Peter

> First, *we must not only believe but also behave:* "And beside this, giving all diligence, add to your faith virtue" (1:5a). We must have a belief that behaves! This is the major theme of the epistle of James, a letter with which Peter must have been very familiar. James was a longtime colleague of Peter in the Jerusalem church. He was an austere man, not the kind of man who would be very patient with believers who stepped out of line.
>
> The phrase "beside this, giving . . ." comes from a Greek word that occurs only here. It conveys the

idea of bringing something in to be placed by the side of something else. Peter has already mentioned "like precious faith" (1:1), a faith nourished by "exceeding great and precious promises" (1:4). Faith, however, does not stand in isolation from works. Faith, Peter says, needs to have virtue brought in and placed by its side. We have already met the word for virtue (1:3). It speaks of "moral excellence." It is one of the things upon which we should meditate constantly (Phil. 4:8). The more we think about virtue, the more horrible and terrible vice will appear. The word *virtue* verbalizes for us the character of the Christian life—genuine goodness.

If we are alive in Christ Jesus then **there must be spiritual growth**. We must be **adding to our faith constantly**. We cannot stop **progressing forward**. The day we stop growing one of two things will have happened: 1. We will have been taken home. 2. We are beginning to backslide.

In the Greek way of thinking, **virtue was a way of saying excellence**. When we add excellence (or virtue) to our faith, we are **showing forth the glory of our heavenly creator**. For it is God's will that we walk in the excellence of His power before this lost and dying world. As we walk in the excellence of God's love and mercy, **we portray the love of God and His son Jesus for all the world to see**.

When we add virtue to our faith, we become **a greater witness for Christ**. After virtue, we need to **add knowledge to our faith and virtue**. As one writer once stated, faith helps us develop virtue, and virtue helps us develop knowledge. This knowledge must become a part of us, and as a part of us, **it must be ever growing in the love of God**. The kind of knowledge the Bible is talking about is knowledge that we have acquired by learning, such as **studying the Word**, and knowledge acquired by **effort and experience**. To learn we must put forth an effort. I know of no one who has ever said knowledge just came to them while they were doing nothing. **It just does not work that way.** I have seen a few people who said, "Well, if God wants one to know anything about the Bible or living a Christian life, He will just put it into my head." I have news for you: **God will not just fill your head with everything He wants you to know.**

This Christian life is built upon **faith and learning by experiences**. Each trial teaches us new things. With each storm of life that we overcome, **we learn, we gain knowledge**. Think of it this way: How can we help others who are going through trials if we have not been there ourselves? **God has never promised us a life of ease; he promised that He would never leave nor forsake us.** He will be with us every step of the way. A person who cannot learn is a person who will never prosper, and **God's desire is that we prosper in Him**.

Verse six, to faith add virtue, and to virtue add knowledge and **to knowledge we next need to add temperance**. What do we mean when we say temperance? In this passage, **it means self-control**. We are to learn from the examples given in the Scriptures.

Proverbs 16:32

> *He that is slow to anger is better than the mighty; and he that ruleth his spirit than he that taketh a city.*

Acts 24:25

> *And as he reasoned of righteousness, temperance, and*

judgment to come, Felix trembled, and answered, Go thy
way for this time; when I have a convenient season, I will
call for thee.

Romans 6:12

Let not sin therefore reign in your mortal body, that ye
should obey it in the lusts thereof.

All these scriptures deal with self-control. They deal with us, you and me, **learning how to govern our wants and our desires, learning how to say to yourself, "No, enough is enough. I do not need this."** They deal with learning to see the potential damage or harm before we get involved in the wrong thing. The person who learns self-control is a person who **takes charge of their life and future.**

In I Corinthians, the apostle Paul gives **us another example of how we should conduct or control ourselves.**

1 Corinthians 9:24-27

[24] Know ye not that they which run in a race run all, but one
receiveth the prize? So run, that ye may obtain.
[25] And every man that striveth for the mastery is temperate
in all things. Now they do it to obtain a corruptible crown;
but we an incorruptible.
[26] I therefore so run, not as uncertainly; so fight I, not as
one that beateth the air:
[27] But I keep under my body, and bring it into subjection:
lest that by any means, when I have preached to others, I
myself should be a castaway.

Paul speaks of being an athlete as an example of how Christians should live their lives. To be an athlete, a man or woman, boy or girl must learn that **to reach their goal they must train**, they must learn endurance. They must **prepare their bodies for the desired objective**. However, training their bodies is not enough. They must also **prepare their minds**. We can have a strong body, but if our minds are not prepared, then **we lack that determination that we must have to win**. Without that made-up mind, we will never be a winner.

The man or woman who has no self-control is subject to the whims of the devil. We have all seen or known of people who have no self-control. You can talk them into anything no matter how foolish. They seem to have no resistance to outside impulses or influence, and even less from inside ones. The world calls these people impulse buyers; the devil calls them easy prey. **To be temperate is to learn how to control how you react to outside and inside influences.** We must maintain mastery over all the wiles of Satan and our own selfish and evil appetites. It is like watching the television. Do you control it, or does the television control you? Do you control what you watch, or do you just watch whatever comes on? We must have control, we have to have control, or the devil will run us ragged. **The Christian who truly loves the Lord will want to control his or her life, to bring it under subjection to the law and will of God.** This life of personal and spiritual control is the only way to be truly happy and satisfied.

The next step in this spiritual journey of growth is to **add to temperance, patience**. Patience is one of the hardest things to learn and possess. I have seen Christians who have served God for many years who still have trouble showing patience. Therefore, what is patience? It is the ability to **wait for God to have His way in our hearts and lives**. The problem is that no one wants to wait upon the Lord to answer our prayers.

We live in an instant world. It seems that everything is at our fingertips. We want to talk to someone, and we just pick up the telephone and call. We have instant food. Just stick it in the microwave and in a few minutes, we can eat. People have gotten used to our instant ways of living. But, and there is always a but, **God does not work as an instant God**. Yes, sometimes in periods where we need an instant answer to prayer, God does move. As a general rule, **we have to wait upon God to answer in His own good time**. Moreover, believe it or not, it is good for us to learn that with patience, with waiting, **we are given a chance to ponder whether what we prayed for is really what we want**. We do many things in haste that we regret in leisure.

A little patience can sometimes save us a lot of problems. As we look at patience, we find that **patience is the ability to endure hardships and the trials of life**. Temperance or self-control helps us deal with the wants and pleasures of life. But patience helps us deal with the problems and the pressures of life that the devil puts on us. The age-old question is how we learn patience, and the age-old answer is still the same. **Patience can only be learned by going through trials, problems, and the pressures of life.** That is where we learn to trust God and to wait for the answers to come.

James 1:2-4

> *2 My brethren, count it all joy when ye fall into divers temptations;*
> *3 Knowing this, that the trying of your faith worketh patience.*
> *4 But let patience have her perfect work, that ye may be*

perfect and entire, wanting nothing.

James 5:7-8

[7] Be patient therefore, brethren, unto the coming of the Lord. Behold, the husbandman waiteth for the precious fruit of the earth, and hath long patience for it, until he receive the early and latter rain.
[8] Be ye also patient; stablish your hearts: for the coming of the Lord draweth nigh.

2 Timothy 2:23-26

[23] But foolish and unlearned questions avoid, knowing that they do gender strifes.
[24] And the servant of the Lord must not strive; but be gentle unto all men, apt to teach, patient,
[25] In meekness instructing those that oppose themselves; if God peradventure will give them repentance to the acknowledging of the truth;
[26] And that they may recover themselves out of the snare of the devil, who are taken captive by him at his will.

Remember Job, who still **trusted God even after the devil had taken away all that he had**. Still Job had patience and trusted God because he knew that **God had not deserted him**. Then there was Joseph who trusted God. He trusted God in the pit. He had patience, trusting God when he was sold as a slave. He did not understand but he had patience and **believed that God would one day bring him out**. He kept his trust and his patience even when he was thrown into prison. Then one day all his faith and trust, his patience, paid off. He was brought out of the prison house to stand before Pharaoh. There he **obeyed God's plan for his life**. He gave Pharaoh the meaning of his dream.

Trust and patience in God made Joseph the highest ruler in Egypt under Pharaoh. Joseph saved his family from starvation, and he saved their lives. **Joseph trusted God, and his patience brought victory and salvation to God's people.** If we will live according to God's plan, we will find that **patience pays off with dividends**.

The next step of this spiritual journey of learning and growing in God is to **add to patience, godliness**. What is the meaning of godliness? It simply means God-likeness, **to be and live in the love and likeness of God**. Today in the church, we stress that a Christian should be Christ-like. Since Jesus is the only Son of God and Jesus is God, then **to be Christ-like is to have godliness in our lives**. The person who is Christ-like is a person who lives in a right relationship with God. He is a man who lives to **show forth the love and compassion of Jesus Christ**. He walks in a right relationship with his fellow man, that the joy and love of God might be a constant witness to this lost and dying world. The man or woman who walks in godliness **lives above the petty things of life and can handle the pressures of life that try to control us**. The only one who should have control over us is Jesus, our Lord.

You talk to people about being Christ-like, having godliness in their lives, and they think you must be crazy. I sometimes get so angry at the things being preached today, preachers and teachers who stand up before their people and tell them that you cannot live a life without sin, that you have to sin every day. This is a lie straight from the pits of hell. **If God knew that we could not live as the Word says, then why did He have it put in the Bible?** I had a friend tell me that God knows that we cannot be perfect. Whereupon I asked him, "Do you not believe what the Bible says?" His reply was, "Yes, of course I do." I then asked him, "Well, what are you going to do with these scriptures?"

Matthew 5:48

Be ye therefore perfect, even as your Father which is in heaven is perfect.

Luke 6:40

The disciple is not above his master: but every one that is perfect shall be as his master.

John 17:23

I in them, and thou in me, that they may be made perfect in one; and that the world may know that thou hast sent me, and hast loved them, as thou hast loved me.

1 Corinthians 2:4-6

[4] And my speech and my preaching was not with enticing words of man's wisdom, but in demonstration of the Spirit and of power:
[5] That your faith should not stand in the wisdom of men, but in the power of God.
[6] Howbeit we speak wisdom among them that are perfect: yet not the wisdom of this world, nor of the princes of this world, that come to nought:

2 Corinthians 13:9-11

[9] For we are glad, when we are weak, and ye are strong: and this also we wish, even your perfection.
[10] Therefore I write these things being absent, lest being present I should use sharpness, according to the power which the Lord hath given me to edification, and not to destruction.
[11] Finally, brethren, farewell. Be perfect, be of good comfort, be of one mind, live in peace; and the God of love and peace shall be with you.

Ephesians 4:11-13

[11] And he gave some, apostles; and some, prophets; and some, evangelists; and some, pastors and teachers;
[12] For the perfecting of the saints, for the work of the ministry, for the edifying of the body of Christ:
[13] Till we all come in the unity of the faith, and of the knowledge of the Son of God, unto a perfect man, unto the measure of the stature of the fulness of Christ:

Philippians 3:15

Let us therefore, as many as be perfect, be thus minded: and if in any thing ye be otherwise minded, God shall reveal even this unto you.

Colossians 4:12

Epaphras, who is one of you, a servant of Christ, saluteth you, always labouring fervently for you in prayers, that ye may stand perfect and complete in all the will of God.

2 Timothy 3:16-17

[16] *All scripture is given by inspiration of God, and is profitable for doctrine, for reproof, for correction, for instruction in righteousness:*
[17] *That the man of God may be perfect, thoroughly furnished unto all good works.*

My friend's only answer to me was, "Well, I am going to have to talk to my pastor about it." You can talk about it all you want, but the Word is still the Word. **God expects us who claim to be born again, blood-bought, redeemed children of God to live by the Word.** We are to be Christ-like, to have godliness in our lives. **We must if we are to please God.**

In *The Biblical Illustrator* on 2 Peter, we read where Rev. J. Abernethy M. A. wrote the following:

The Biblical Illustrator:

The inward affections which naturally arise comprehended in godliness are first, fear, a reverence for His majesty, a serious affecting sense of all His glorious attributes, not a confounding terror and amazement. Secondly, the fear of God, as the Scriptures explains it, which is an essential part of godliness, and of the respect He claims from us, doth not exclude love. His goodness naturally excites love.

The love of God causes us, you and I, to want to pattern ourselves after the ways of God, **to be just as God-like as we possibly can**. On the other hand, the devil desires and pushes for the world to happen very quickly. Pantheism is a doctrine which identifies God and the universe as all being one manifestation, a system which embraces all religions and all gods. What Satan cannot do in one way, he tries to do in another. This is why it is so important to be just as godly or Christ-like as we can. **Godliness must hold an important part in our walk with God.**

The sixth goal we are to add to our faith is brotherly kindness. Christ taught us brotherly kindness. He taught us brotherly kindness by His very life. **Jesus had a love for everybody.** He loved the sinner, He loved the little children, He loved the sick and the lame, and **He had a compassion like the world had never seen**. A person's state in life meant nothing to Jesus, rich or poor. **He loved them all the same.** He took time to talk to the woman at the well. He stopped and asked who touched Him when the woman touched the hem of His garment. He stopped when He heard the cries of blind Bartimaeus. Jesus had compassion on people who were suffering; **He just plain loved people**. This compassion, **this love for the brethren is what the Word is telling us to add to our faith**. Love the brethren with a true love. There are many pretenders who say that they love the brethren, but it is all a pretense. And believe me, the world can surely tell. In the following scriptures we read:

Romans 12:9-10

> [9] *Let love be without dissimulation. Abhor that which is evil; cleave to that which is good.*

^{10} Be kindly affectioned one to another with brotherly love; in honour preferring one another;

Ephesians 4:31-32

^{31} Let all bitterness, and wrath, and anger, and clamour, and evil speaking, be put away from you, with all malice: ^{32} And be ye kind one to another, tenderhearted, forgiving one another, even as God for Christ's sake hath forgiven you.

Colossians 3:12-13

^{12} Put on therefore, as the elect of God, holy and beloved, bowels of mercies, kindness, humbleness of mind, meekness, longsuffering; ^{13} Forbearing one another, and forgiving one another, if any man have a quarrel against any: even as Christ forgave you, so also do ye.

As we read these scriptures, they show that **we are to pattern our lives after Jesus**. In many churches today, Jesus would be ashamed of us. There is envy and quarreling, there is bitterness and hatred in the church. What kind of example are we putting forth that would cause people to want to come to church? **A soft answer turns away wrath, and kindness can move mountains in the lives of sinners.** It does wonders for us and our attitudes.

The last of these seven steps that we are to add to our faith is charity. The charity spoken of here is love. **You can gauge love by what it does.** Love's most perfect example is the love that Jesus had. Kindness is one outward example of a true, godly love that dwells in the hearts of God's children. **The true love of God knows no boundaries.** Jesus gave His life for the lost. Yes, people say, but who would be willing to do that today?

I think of a story that I read sometime back about a missionary who was going to China. Her parents were missionaries in China, and she was born there. When the Communists took control, her parents were going to be killed, and they were going to kill her even though she was a very small child. When the soldier was going to shoot her, a Chinese man protested, and the soldier asked him if he was willing to die in her place. **He said yes and was shot right then and there, on the spot.** The little girl was taken and transported from one village to another until she was finally taken to safety. Yes, there are still people who are **willing to give their lives for others**. Missionaries risk their lives for the sake of Christ because **they love the lost and want to see them saved**.

Let's look at what John Phillips says about love.

The John Phillips Commentary Series – Exploring the Epistles of Peter:

> This kind of love is not a product of our feelings, for it does not always run parallel with our natural desires. It does not restrict itself to those for whom it entertains some common bond. It seeks the well-being of all (Rom. 15:2). It harbors ill will toward none (13:8-10). It is always alert to do other people good. It is heralded and hymned in Paul's letter to the saints at Corinth (1 Cor. 13). It is what sets Christianity apart from all of the world's religions. Once this kind of love is added to our lives, no more

things remain to be added. Love caps them all.

The seven steps of spiritual growth are the addition of God. **Add to faith virtue, and to virtue knowledge, and to knowledge temperance, and to temperance patience, and to patience brotherly kindness, and to brotherly kindness charity.** These are the seven steps in growing our spiritual lives. And as our spiritual lives grow, **so does our Christian character**. God's grace and power works on our behalf **to form us and make us into the image of Christ**. In this process there will be many trials and much tribulation. Just remember that "greater is He that is in you than he that is in the world." We, if we are willing, **can be transformed into the image of Jesus Christ, God's only Son.** Here I am speaking of being transformed by spiritual growth. Too many today do not have this spiritual growth and do not want to pay the price to get it. So they become imitations, cheap imitations, look-alikes. The only problem is that they cannot measure up. They are not real, and sooner or later the truth always comes out. **Do not pretend to be what you are not; do not claim to have what you do not possess.** The truth always has a way of coming out for everyone to see.

2 Peter 1:8

For if these things be in you, and abound, they make you that ye shall neither be barren nor unfruitful in the knowledge of our Lord Jesus Christ.

As this verse so aptly says, ". . . if these things be in you." What things? The things we have just been studying. We start by taking our faith, the faith we received at salvation. Then we begin adding to that faith the seven important lessons that we need to put forth a Christ-like life. To faith, we add virtue or excellence. Then to virtue, we add knowledge, the ability to use what God is teaching us wisely and correctly. **A man's wisdom does him very little good if he does not know how to use it.** I have seen some extremely smart people with a wealth of wisdom, but they did not know how to use the wisdom they possessed. **It takes knowledge to correctly use our stored-up wisdom.** Then to knowledge, we need to add temperance. **Temperance can best be described as self-control.** Every Christian needs to be able to control their emotions and sometimes what goes on around them. If a person cannot control what they do and say, then they stand in danger of being the devil's puppet. **Do not let the devil pull your strings. Take control.**

Then to temperance, we must add patience. A person asked me to pray that God would give them patience. In reply, I asked, "Do you know how you get patience?" They said, "No." I told them that **tribulation works patience; patience comes by going through temptations and trials**. They asked me not to pray. So to patience we need to add godliness, or to become god-like. We say Christ-like that we may **show Jesus Christ in and through us as we serve him**. So, to godliness, we add brotherly kindness, which is **to be kind to the brethren and to show forth a love to this world**.

Moreover, to brotherly kindness we add charity, **to show the love of God that works within us**. When we, as Christians, show forth a life that is complete in and through Jesus, we will not be barren or unfruitful. **We will win souls to the Lord**; we will have sheaves to lay at Jesus' feet.

2 Peter 1:9

But he that lacketh these things is blind, and cannot see afar off, and hath forgotten that he was purged from his old sins.

This verse tells us of the dangers of forgetting where we came from and of not growing in the Lord. If we lack the things that we have read about in verses seven and eight, then we stand in danger spiritually. **We must grow, we have to grow, and if we do not grow, we will spiritually go blind.** This verse says, ". . . and cannot see afar off." **When we lose sight of the finish line, we also lose our excitement, our drive to make it to the end of the race.**

Every year in Boston, Massachusetts, they run a marathon. When the race starts, thousands of people start running; as the miles add up, they start to drop out of the race. By mile marker fifteen, one half or so have dropped out of the race. **They have gone as far as they can.** Most have not trained enough and gotten their bodies in shape. **In this spiritual race, we must train spiritually, we must grow spiritually to be able to run with patience the race that is set before us.** In the Boston race, by mile twenty, even more have dropped out. As they approach mile twenty-six with the end in sight, there are still a few who just cannot go any farther. Of the twenty or so thousand who started running in the race, only a few thousand will finish. All of this is fine when running a regular race. People just do not finish, and they go home to rest. However, when running a spiritual race, **we have to finish.** To fail to finish is to **lose your soul and never make heaven your home.** This is why it is so critical that we grow in the Lord and in his Word. **To spiritually stop growing is to spiritually die.** Remember where the Lord brought you from. Remember the hopelessness and despair, the feeling of emptiness of being alone even in a crowd. Remember how you met Jesus and accepted Him as your savior and the peace you received. **Remember, always remember, never lose sight of Jesus our Lord.**

2 Peter 1:10-11

[10] Wherefore the rather, brethren, give diligence to make your calling and election sure: for if ye do these things, ye shall never fall:
[11] For so an entrance shall be ministered unto you abundantly into the everlasting kingdom of our Lord and Saviour Jesus Christ.

In this tenth verse there is a lesson that every Christian should pay strict attention to, that **we must make our calling and election sure**. Peter is trying to push the principle that we are responsible before God for our soul's condition. **If a man fails, it is his own doings that are the underlying cause.** We can sit and speculate why a person falls, but we can never know for sure, because we are not in their place. We must give diligence to our own salvation to make sure that all is right between us and God. We must, as I have said, and will say over and over, **be continually growing in the Lord.** The Christian, as the Word says, who continually grows will not fall. When we put forth the effort to serve God, then **God will bless us and help us to go forward for Him.** John Phillips in his commentary writes the following words for our consideration.

The John Phillips Commentary Series – Exploring the Epistles of Peter:

Peter began his first epistle with the great

concept that believers are elect sojourners (I Peter 1:1-2). He also gave a definitive statement about the elect – that they were "elect according to the foreknowledge of God." He expanded this concept further, when speaking of the shedding of the precious blood of Christ. He declared that the Lord Jesus was "foreordained before the foundation of the world" to be man's redeemer (I Peter 1:19-20). Election is according to foreknowledge, which, in turn, is according to God's omniscience. The sovereign choices of God in foreordination, election, and predestination are based on His omniscient knowledge of possible choices and events. Some events are divinely caused; other events are divinely permitted. God foreknew how all man would act under the various circumstances of life. He permits them to act so as part of an eternal plan. At the same time, He leaves everyone room enough to be responsible for his own behavior (Luke 22:22).

So, as you can see, **God has a foreknowledge of what is to come**. He foreknew that Jesus would be crucified and killed. But even as God permitted this to happen so that men might be saved, He still did not absolve those wicked men who participated in the death of the beloved Son. **Those men, though in the plan of God, are still held responsible.** We, you and I, are held responsible for the things we do. **We cannot blame anyone else for our actions.** There are no mitigating circumstances that we can blame for an excuse for our actions.

Peter was so concerned for the saints of God that he wrote

these letters, telling us that **we must be certain that our calling and election is sure**. The Holy Ghost deals with everyone's soul to make them aware that something is missing, and that something is God. **There are very few in the world today that have not heard the Word of God in some fashion**, whether radio, television, gospel tracts, preaching on the streets, or sign boards. Somehow, they have come into contact with the gospel message. Whether they do anything about it is up to them. We must be steadfast in reaching the lost. **We must remain steadfast in our service for the Lord.** If we have made our calling and election sure, then let us help others to do the same.

For if ye do these things, ye shall never fall. Then we read in verse eleven that if we do these things, there shall be ministered unto us **an abundant entrance into the kingdom of our Lord and savior Jesus Christ**. We are never too young or too old to serve the Lord. There lies before us a battleground to be taken for the Lord. Souls are at stake; **we must win this battle for the lost souls of mankind**. We know there are few that will be saved, but let us work to reach those few while there is still the time and the opportunity.

2 Peter 1:12

Wherefore I will not be negligent to put you always in remembrance of these things, though ye know them, and be established in the present truth.

Peter tells us that he will not be negligent in reminding the saints of who and what they are in Christ Jesus. One of the very best ways to learn is **by constantly going over the same thing**, over and over. Repetition instills knowledge into our memory.

Peter was doing what preachers are supposed to be doing today, stirring up our minds by way of remembrance, **to remind us what God's Word says**, to remember what the scripture teaches on **how we are to walk before God in righteousness and holiness**. The scripture tells us that the Holy Ghost will bring all things to our remembrance. **But the Holy Ghost cannot bring something to your remembrance that you never knew to start with.** There is no way you can remember something that you never knew. Remembering keeps us humble and pliable in God's hands.

2 Peter 1:13-15

[13] Yea, I think it meet, as long as I am in this tabernacle, to stir you up by putting you in remembrance;
[14] Knowing that shortly I must put off this my tabernacle, even as our Lord Jesus Christ hath shewed me.
[15] Moreover I will endeavour that ye may be able after my decease to have these things always in remembrance.

I think it is necessary for you, as long as I live, for me to **continually bring to your remembrance the things that you have learned**, how you are to **walk in the righteousness of God, upholding the truth of the Word**. If we abide in the truth, the truth will keep us from the lust of the world and its wickedness. We, to live for God and please Him, must **continually be in remembrance**. This we do by praying and studying the word of God daily. **Praying is where we draw spiritual strength from God, and studying is where we learn and gain the knowledge to fight the enemy by using the divine Word of God against him.** Churches, to survive, must once again **begin preaching the true Word of God**. A very painful truth is that all churches are just one generation away from extinction. Unless we reach souls for the Lord, the church of Jesus Christ is no more. **We must reach everyone we possibly can, especially the young.** We must also make it our responsibility to keep the youth that grow up within our churches, to see that they are **rooted and grounded in the Word**. God help us not to be so consumed with reaching the lost that we lose the young people of our own churches. I realize that the Great Commission tells us to go unto all the world preaching the gospel, reaching the lost for Jesus Christ, seeing souls saved, born again. And this is a great vision that every church needs. **But if we neglect the young people who are already in our churches, then we still fail.** I have been told that it is the parents' responsibility to see that their children are brought up in the ways of God, and this is true. However, **the church must also bear part of the responsibility**. The church must have good, Holy Ghost-filled Sunday school teachers and youth leaders who make it their purpose in life to work with the youth, to encourage them, to excite them in the things of God. If our teachers and youth leaders have no passion, then something is very wrong. **When we get fired up and excited, when we get passion, our excitement and passion grow and extend to others around us.** A teacher with passion reaches the hearts of students. A youth leader with passion and excitement has a youth group that is passionate, that is excited about the work of the Lord. **God, give us leaders with passion.**

In verse fourteen Peter tells us that his death was shortly to come just as Jesus had told him.

John 21:18-19

> [18] *Verily, verily, I say unto thee, When thou wast young, thou girdedst thyself, and walkedst whither thou wouldest: but*

when thou shalt be old, thou shalt stretch forth thy hands, and another shall gird thee, and carry thee whither thou wouldest not.

19 This spake he, signifying by what death he should glorify God. And when he had spoken this, he saith unto him, Follow me.

Peter knew how he was going to die. He preached of a catching away (rapture) but knew that he would never see it in his lifetime. Jesus had told him he would be crucified. **Yet Peter did not shrink from the calling upon his life.** He had failed Jesus once at the judgement hall. But he would not fail Jesus again. Tradition tell us that Peter, when he went to be crucified, asked to be crucified upside down, because he was not worthy to be crucified in the same manner as his Lord. Is this true? I like to think so. **Peter was a very humble man who purposed in his heart that he would not fail Jesus again.**

In verse fifteen Peter is telling us that he intends the words he has written **to be for a remembrance to the saints of God**. After his death, he did not want the saints to forget what he had preached and taught them. **Even in his final hours, Peter's concern was for the saints.** Oh, what love the Lord bestows in our hearts, that when in death, our desire is for others. Peter, like Paul, could say, "I have fought a good fight, I have kept the faith, and now I am going home to be with my Lord." **What can we say about Peter? We can say that he died well for our Lord.**

2 Peter 1:16-18

16 For we have not followed cunningly devised fables, when we made known unto you the power and coming of

239

our Lord Jesus Christ, but were eyewitnesses of his majesty.

[17] For he received from God the Father honour and glory, when there came such a voice to him from the excellent glory, This is my beloved Son, in whom I am well pleased.
[18] And this voice which came from heaven we heard, when we were with him in the holy mount.

As Peter writes in verse sixteen, he uses the word we. Who are the "we" that he is talking about? If we look at the scripture, it could be said that he was talking about **all the disciples that walked with Jesus every day**. And this is possible, or it could relate to the **Mount of Transfiguration where Peter, James, and John were on the Mount and beheld the glory of God** as it came upon Jesus. There also came Moses and Elijah, who talked to the Lord.

Matthew 17:1-13

[1] And after six days Jesus taketh Peter, James, and John his brother, and bringeth them up into an high mountain apart,
[2] And was transfigured before them: and his face did shine as the sun, and his raiment was white as the light.
[3] And, behold, there appeared unto them Moses and Elias talking with him.
[4] Then answered Peter, and said unto Jesus, Lord, it is good for us to be here: if thou wilt, let us make here three tabernacles; one for thee, and one for Moses, and one for Elias.
[5] While he yet spake, behold, a bright cloud overshadowed them: and behold a voice out of the cloud, which said, This

is my beloved Son, in whom I am well pleased; hear ye him.
6 And when the disciples heard it, they fell on their face, and were sore afraid.

7 And Jesus came and touched them, and said, Arise, and be not afraid.

8 And when they had lifted up their eyes, they saw no man, save Jesus only.

9 And as they came down from the mountain, Jesus charged them, saying, Tell the vision to no man, until the Son of man be risen again from the dead.

10 And his disciples asked him, saying, Why then say the scribes that Elias must first come?

11 And Jesus answered and said unto them, Elias truly shall first come, and restore all things.

12 But I say unto you, That Elias is come already, and they knew him not, but have done unto him whatsoever they listed. Likewise shall also the Son of man suffer of them. 13 Then the disciples understood that he spake unto them of John the Baptist.

Mark 9:1-10

1 And he said unto them, Verily I say unto you, That there be some of them that stand here, which shall not taste of death, till they have seen the kingdom of God come with power.

2 And after six days Jesus taketh with him Peter, and James, and John, and leadeth them up into an high mountain apart by themselves: and he was transfigured before them.

3 And his raiment became shining, exceeding white as snow; so as no fuller on earth can white them.

⁴ And there appeared unto them Elias with Moses: and they were talking with Jesus.

⁵ And Peter answered and said to Jesus, Master, it is good for us to be here: and let us make three tabernacles; one for thee, and one for Moses, and one for Elias.

⁶ For he wist not what to say; for they were sore afraid.

⁷ And there was a cloud that overshadowed them: and a voice came out of the cloud, saying, This is my beloved Son: hear him.

⁸ And suddenly, when they had looked round about, they saw no man any more, save Jesus only with themselves.

⁹ And as they came down from the mountain, he charged them that they should tell no man what things they had seen, till the Son of man were risen from the dead.

¹⁰ And they kept that saying with themselves, questioning one with another what the rising from the dead should mean.

Why did Jesus only take these three men and not all the disciples? That I cannot answer, but these three who went upon the Mount of Transfiguration with Jesus **fulfilled the very prophecy that Jesus gave in Matthew**.

Matthew 16:28

²⁸ Verily I say unto you, There be some standing here, which shall not taste of death, till they see the Son of man coming in his kingdom.

Peter, James, and John **truly saw the Son of Man in all His glory and in the power of His coming kingdom**. There they heard the voice of God speak saying, **"This is my beloved Son in whom I am well pleased."**

Peter stresses that this witness was a fact, that it was not a made-up story or fable, and that they **preached the truth and only the truth**. Other religions had to make up stories about their gods. What can a god do that is made of stone or wood? Can a stone hear, can a piece of carved wood move and answer prayers for people? The answer is no. **But the living God can and does answer prayer.** Why? Because **He is a living God**. He sees and hears and moves on our behalf as we call upon Him. I like what *The John Phillips Commentary* says.

The John Phillips Commentary Series – Exploring the Epistles of Peter:

> The amazing stories that make up so much of the gospel narratives are not fables. They certainly are not "cunningly devised" fables. The words stem from the Greek word *sophizō*, meaning "to play the sophist." Peter had a firsthand knowledge of both the facts of Christ's life and the history of the church in its early decades. He could affirm that the story of Christ's life, as handed down to us, is true. It is not some cleverly crafted story. The Virgin Birth, the immaculate life, the countless miracles, the peerless teaching, the atoning death, the burial, Resurrection, Ascension, and promised return of Christ are all sober facts. He *did* still the storm. He *did* walk upon the heaving waves. He *did* feed great multitudes with a little lad's lunch. He *did* cast out evil spirits. He *did* cleanse lepers. He *did* give sight to the blind. He *did* heal the sick. He *did* make lame

men walk. He *did* put Malchus's ear back on after he, Peter, had cut it off. He *did* rise from the dead. He *did* ascend bodily into heaven. Peter knew all of these events as an eyewitness, and Peter's witness is irrefutable. No wonder the liberals and their kind want to banish his second letter to some other century and make it the work of a forger! Well, forgers don't write Scripture any more than counterfeiters make genuine hundred-dollar bills.

Peter and the other disciples were eyewitnesses to the life and ministry of Jesus Christ. They preached what Jesus had taught them; they preached of the power of God **working in and through Jesus**. They preached that this same Jesus that was taken into heaven, for they had seen Him go, **would one day return with power to catch them away and take them home**, and that the dead who died in the Lord were to **rise first and then the living saints would be taken by Jesus into the glory of God's heavenly kingdom**. The world can laugh, mock, and say all kinds of evil things about God's people, but **that cannot keep us from going home when Jesus comes back in the rapture**. It will be the greatest mass disappearance in the history of the world. But, never fear, the world will come up with some excuse for the disappearance of God's saints.

One of the greatest fears the church should have today is **the lack of belief within the church**. Just as the Bible says, people are saying, "Where is His coming? We have heard this same preaching for years and years and nothing has changed. Where is the promise that was given? Why has it not come to pass?"

2 Peter 3:1-4

244

¹ This second epistle, beloved, I now write unto you; in both which I stir up your pure minds by way of remembrance:
² That ye may be mindful of the words which were spoken before by the holy prophets, and of the commandment of us the apostles of the Lord and Saviour:
³ Knowing this first, that there shall come in the last days scoffers, walking after their own lusts,
⁴ And saying, Where is the promise of his coming? for since the fathers fell asleep, all things continue as they were from the beginning of the creation.

And just as these scriptures say, in these last days we **can see and hear the scoffers on the radio and television**. At least ninety percent, and I would say more, of the preachers on the air today are preaching a perverted gospel. If you really listen to what they are saying, here and there you will **find small departures from the truth of God's Word**. And most of the mega churches are following this same trend. For instance, one pastor of a mega church in Houston, Texas, approves of homosexual marriages. He refuses to preach against sin. He goes so far as to say that Peter, Paul, John, James and the other Apostles should have been reprimanded for what they wrote in the Bible. That they deliberately wrote things that would hurt people's feelings. That Jesus would never do anything that would hurt someone's feelings, and He would have accepted people just as they are and not have tried to change them. What is my opinion? I think that this man (and he is not a preacher of the gospel by Christ's standards) has **lost all love and compassion for the lost souls of man**. If he loved his people, he would **warn them of their soul's condition and where they will spend eternity**. I can only conclude that the money he receives is more important to him than the souls of the people who give it. The apostles wrote what God wanted them to write. Peter heard and knew the voice of God. Peter wrote what he did because **he loved God's saints and did not want us to perish because of sin in our lives**. In the next chapter we will look at false teachers who distort the word of God.

Peter wants us to keep our eyes on **Jesus Christ, the one who has changed our lives**. There are those (and some are Bible theologians so liberal it is hard to call them theologians) who maintain that Jesus' death on the cross was only an example for us. That is a lie; **Jesus' death on the cross was to redeem us to God through Him**. Peter, like many of us, had to learn some things the hard way. We learn through every trial, every heartache, and every problem. We must ever be learning, for **through our victories we can help others**. Never, never, never, take your eyes off Jesus, because He is our help in the time of need. **He is that friend who will never leave us nor forsake us.** He will always be there.

2 Peter 1:19-21

[19] We have also a more sure word of prophecy; whereunto ye do well that ye take heed, as unto a light that shineth in a dark place, until the day dawn, and the day star arise in your hearts:
[20] Knowing this first, that no prophecy of the scripture is of any private interpretation.
[21] For the prophecy came not in old time by the will of man: but holy men of God spake as they were moved by the Holy Ghost.

As we look at what Peter is saying in this nineteenth verse, we see Peter awakening us to the fact that **there is nothing more**

sure than the Word of God. Looking back at verse sixteen, Peter is warning against people being led astray by cunningly devised fables. You and I can go into any religious bookstore and find shelves filled with books written by all manner of people. Some are good and soul-uplifting while others are trash. That may seem harsh, but **we need to be very careful what we accept as the truth**. Peter spoke of cunningly devised fables. What does that mean? It simply means that men and women take the truth of God's Word, and little by little twist and turn it to mean something different than what it really means. And sometimes **just one word added or left out can change the whole meaning of a scripture**.

To give you an example, let us look at Luke, chapter nine and verse fifty-five: *"But he turned and rebuked them, and said ye know not what manner of spirit ye are of."* What Jesus was talking about was that His disciples **did not yet fully understand that He came in love and compassion to reach the lost**, and not to bring judgement. You can say, "Well everyone understands that," but I had a pastor who would quote this verse regularly and always leave off the last word. What he was trying to push is that **people do not know what kind of spirit they are**. As God brought this to my attention, I began to look it up for myself. Then I realized that he was talking about himself. This made some of the things that he would say more understandable, such as, "When I wake up in the morning, I don't know whether I am saved or not," or, "You know, sometimes I don't know whether you are saved or not." **One word can sometimes change the whole meaning of a verse.** Let me remind you that the devil is very good at what he does. **We must beware or be lost.**

Individuals changing the Word of God to suit their own purposes has birthed all manner of cults. Be careful what you read. It is a sad fact that in today's world **people will buy and read** religious books, believing what they read is true, when they will **not open and read the Bible, God's true Holy Word**. Some, instead of preaching the true Word of God, do their best to manipulate people into believing lies, into believing a perverted gospel that has no power to save or to bring true peace to the believer. **The only true and sure word of prophecy is the Bible, God's Holy Word.** All other books shall pass away, all other teachings shall pass away, but the **pure Holy Word of God will never pass away**. It makes no difference what the world thinks or does, they **cannot change the plan of God**.

Peter calls this world a dark place, and it surely is. Without God, without God's Holy Word, and without the saints (born-again believers) **this world would be in complete and total darkness**. The scripture tells us that **the believers are the light of the world through Christ Jesus**, and that it is our job to let our light shine in the dark places of this world. This scripture reminds me of some of the very large cities around the world, cities where there is a hidden underbelly, places so evil and vile that even the police are afraid to go. Places so dark and evil that it seems that no light will ever penetrate. **But we know a light that can dispel the darkness.**

Just as missionaries spread the light to the dark continent of Africa and to other ungodly places around the world, **so must we carry the ligh**t. The light of God's Word can and will lighten the world if we will let God use us. **For we are the light.** It is up to us to **let our light shine in the darkness that men might see Jesus Christ, the world's only hope.** For Jesus is coming again. He said that He was and nothing that Satan does can stop it. **It is time that we began to look up, for our redemption draweth nigh.**

In verse twenty we read where no scripture is of any private interpretation. What does this mean? It means that **the prophecies are not to be interpreted to benefit what one person wants them**

248

to say or mean. A good rule to follow is that **scripture must interpret scripture**. Dr. Elizabeth Williams in her book *Prevision of History* wrote, "'All scripture is given by the inspiration of God' and is thereby revelation – truth communicated by God to man."

It is therefore up to us to study, to **search the Word of God to give the interpretation**. Of course, you will also find that every false teacher also claims that he is led by the spirit of God. But if you will listen to what is being said, and you know the Word, you will soon learn that his handling of God's Word will bring the truth into the light that he is false and has changed the Word of God to further his own goals and purposes. We cannot build a doctrine on one word or scripture. **We must take the whole Word of God, not individual bits and pieces as some try to do.** When we take scriptures or parts of scriptures out of context, we can prove anything we want. **But when we take the whole Word of God,** this cannot be done so easily. When the Word speaks of a "private interpretation," it refers to a person making their own interpretation to suit themselves.

Wiersbe's Bible Commentary NT:

> The word translated "private" simply means "one's own" or "its own". The suggestion is, since all scripture is inspired by the spirit it must all "hang together," and no one scripture should be divorced from the others. You can use the Bible to prove almost anything if you isolate verses from their proper context, which is exactly the approach the false teachers use. Peter stated that the witness of the apostles confirmed the witness of the prophetic word; there is one message with no contradiction.

Therefore, the only way these false teachers can "prove" their heretical doctrine is by misusing the Word of God. Isolated texts, apart from contexts become pretext.

The word of God was written to common people, not to theological professors. The writers assumed that common people could read it, understand it, and apply it, led by the same Holy Spirit who inspired it. The humble individual believer can learn about God as he reads and meditates on the Word of God; he does not need the "experts" to show him truth. However, this does not deny the ministry of teachers in the church (Ephesians 4:11), special people who have a gift for explaining and applying the scriptures. Nor does it deny the "collective wisdom" of the church as, over the ages, these doctrines have been defined and refined. Teachers and creeds have their place, but they must not usurp the authority of the word over the conscience of the individual believer."

All scripture is given by the inspiration of God. The prophecies, just as scripture, were written not of the will of man. It was written as **the Holy Ghost moved upon man to write the things that God wanted us to know and live by**. To the true believer, if we pray and seek God for the meaning of the Word, the **Holy Ghost who inspired the Word to be written can and will inspire us to discern the true meaning of said Word**. As the prophets and apostles were driven or inspired, I like the word driven because it is how I feel about doing these studies on the Word; I feel driven to write on God's Word. They were compelled; there was a feeling of **such need, such urgency to write what God wanted written**. Thank God for these men who obeyed the voice and urging of the Holy Ghost. We owe our salvation to them, because **they loved enough to give us the gospel, the precious Word of Life**.

Chapter 1 Review Questions

1. What does Peter call himself in this first verse?

_____

_____

2. In Paul's writing to Philemon Paul calls himself a?

_____

_____

3. How does Peter address those to whom he is writing?

_____

_____

4. What makes us stronger in the Lord?

_____

_____

5. What does Peter tell us that we are given in verse four?

_____

_____

6. All of God's promises are what? _____

_____

7. What is our spiritual umbilical cord?

_____

_____

8. Our whole Christian life is founded upon?

_____

_____

9. Before we were saved our number one goal was?

_____

_____

10. What is God's arithmetic? _____

_____

11. We must have a belief that? _____

_____

12. What does the word virtue mean? _____

_____

13. What does the word tell us to add to virtue?

_____

_____

14. What is the Christian life is built upon?

_____

_____

15. What does the Bible mean by temperance?

_____

_____

16. What is patience and how do we get it? _____

_____

17. List two men, in the Bible, who had great patience?

_____

_____

18. What is Pantheism? _____

_____

19. What does the word charity mean? _____

_____

Chapter 2

Before we begin with the first verse of this second chapter, we need to understand where Peter was coming from.

To quote from *Barnes Notes on the New Testament*:

> The general subject of this chapter is stated in the first verse, and it embraces these points:
>
> (1.) that it might be expected that there would be false teachers among Christians, as there were false prophets in ancient times;
>
> (2.) that they would introduce destructive errors, leading many astray; and,
>
> (3.) that they would be certainly punished. The design of the chapter is to illustrate and defend these points.

Peter will, as we study these scriptures, point out some of the **misleading characteristics and misleading doctrines to which these false teachers hold**. They will deny the Lordship of Jesus Christ, they will mislead by trickery the souls that they gain by seduction, and they will bring in all manner of indulgence, teaching that there is nothing wrong with immoral passions. As we look at the world around us, we see and hear every day of people who yield to ungodly passions. Is it any wonder the church world is in the shape it is? **Remember, for everything God has, the devil, old Satan, has a counterfeit.**

2 Corinthians 11:13-15

13 For such are false apostles, deceitful workers, transforming themselves into the apostles of Christ.
14 And no marvel; for Satan himself is transformed into an angel of light.
15 Therefore it is no great thing if his ministers also be transformed as the ministers of righteousness; whose end shall be according to their works.

From Genesis, with Eve in the garden, to Judas who betrayed Jesus, and even until now, **Satan is working hard to persuade people not to accept and serve Jesus our savior**. Paul wrote that he was concerned about people being led astray.

2 Corinthians 11:1-3

1 Would to God ye could bear with me a little in my folly: and indeed bear with me.
2 For I am jealous over you with godly jealousy: for I have espoused you to one husband, that I may present you as a chaste virgin to Christ.
3 But I fear, lest by any means, as the serpent beguiled Eve through his subtilty, so your minds should be corrupted from the simplicity that is in Christ.

We know as we read and study that the Bible warns us that there will be false Christians, counterfeit Christians, who have **a form of Godliness but deny the power thereof**.

2 Timothy 3:1-5

¹ This know also, that in the last days perilous times shall come.
² For men shall be lovers of their own selves, covetous, boasters, proud, blasphemers, disobedient to parents, unthankful, unholy,
³ Without natural affection, trucebreakers, false accusers, incontinent, fierce, despisers of those that are good,
⁴ Traitors, heady, highminded, lovers of pleasures more than lovers of God;
⁵ Having a form of godliness, but denying the power thereof: from such turn away.

Just as Satan had false prophets in the Old Testament who led people astray, **Satan has false teachers who today are doing the same thing**.

2 Peter Chapter 2:1

But there were false prophets also among the people, even as there shall be false teachers among you, who privily shall bring in damnable heresies, even denying the Lord that bought them, and bring upon themselves swift destruction.

Peter begins this first verse by bringing to mind, or

remembrance, the fact that even in the Old Testament there were false prophets among the people. You ask what a false prophet is. It is a person who **tries to smooth over people's fears by telling them what they want to hear** instead of telling them what thus sayeth the Lord. A true prophet is one who **obeys the voice of God and does whatever God tells him to do or says whatever God tells him to say regardless of the consequences to himself or to others.** There have been countless numbers of false prophets in Israel, even from the time God delivered the Hebrews out of bondage and made of them a nation. The first false prophet was Satan, when he lied to Eve in the Garden and told Eve, "Thou shalt not surely die."

The devil, the old dragon, Satan, is a liar and the father of lies. He uses everything he can to bring misfortune, mistrust, and falsehoods. His very purpose is to deceive and destroy God's people and God's plans for His people. Satan has from the beginning used God's Word to bring in lies and heresies to deceive God's people. This often happens by first questioning God's Word.

When we question things, it makes others also begin to question things. Please don't think I am telling you not to question things. Many times, that is how we learn, how we discover the world around us, by asking questions. Just remember **man always looks at things in the natural, but God works in the supernatural**. Man's logic does not always agree with the miracles of the Bible. Before long, **man's logic begins to doubt the supernatural power of God**, and people apply man's logic, which does not fit. So they, to hide their disbelief, come up with what sounds good to them. Example, the Bible is wrong, and the children of Israel did not cross the Red Sea. They crossed the sea reeds, a marshland of shallow water they could wade across. This is man's logic. **I prefer to believe the supernatural power of God, that it** happened just as the Bible, God's Word, says it happened. Some things we must accept by faith.

When we begin to question the things of God, and try to, by logic, explain them away, we have opened the door to the next step in the devil's plan to deceive God's people. What is the next step? The next step is to **outright deny that God's Word is true.** How many teachers have you heard question the things in God's Word? I can remember as a boy in school, my fourth-grade teacher told us that a whale did not swallow Jonah, because a whale was not even able to swallow something as large as a golf ball. To deny what the word of God teaches is to deny God. **We do not have the right to pick and choose what we want to believe in the Bible.** We must believe it all or none of it.

The next step, and the final one, is to begin to **insert your own words and thoughts in place of what God says and wants.** This is how heresies begin in the church. Heresies abound today, and the bigger a preacher or teacher gets, the easier it is to see how they have changed God's Word to suit themselves. We have from the very beginning had people who **try to placate those around them.** This type of person is the type that your false prophets and teachers come from. **They tell you what they think you want to hear and build from there.**

One very sad point to bring out here is this: In nearly all these cases, the false teachers **are not people who are just innocently ignorant of what God's Word says.** These are people who have made a pact with the devil to deliberately deceive people for their own misguided purposes. These false prophets and false teachers speak words **so sweet that it seems honey drips from their lips.** They offer knowledge and wisdom, but **it is not God's wisdom.** It is a man's wisdom, the natural logic of this world, which is opposite of God's wisdom.

A person who is just innocently ignorant when shown the error of his or her belief will change and accept instruction, **because their heart is sincerely desiring to know the truth and to obey the truth**. The false teacher on the other hand will not receive instruction but will get angry at those who point out their wrong ideas and beliefs. There are so many false teachers in the church it is hard for pastors to invite speakers to come and speak. Where pastors used to try and find those who would really help their churches and uplift the congregation, they now try to find those who will not hurt or damage the church and its people. It is unbelievable the shift that has taken place in the last forty to fifty years.

I am not saying there is no hope, because **there is hope**. But we must **pray, pray, pray for the church and pray for a revival to sweep this world around**. We need to pray for a revival that will bring the hearts of the people back to God one more time before the rapture of the church. **The church not only has to be on the watch for false teachers from within, but it also must contend with false teachings from occults and other false religions.**

Some of these groups are (1) the Jehovah's Witness. They teach that there is no trinity or Godhead; they deny the very deity of our Lord and Savior Jesus Christ. They also deny the resurrection of Jesus from the dead. In addition, they deny that hell is an everlasting place of torment for lost souls, and that only one hundred and forty-four thousand souls will go into heaven to be with God.

The second group that we will look at is (2) the Mormons. They believe the same lie that Satan told Eve in the garden. Satan in beguiling Eve told her that she and Adam would become as gods if they would only eat of the forbidden fruit. Too late, Adam and

Eve found out Satan had lied to them. The damage was already done. They had sinned and would face God's judgement.

Many people find themselves today in this very same place. They have believed Satan's lie, and now they are **reaping the rewards of their foolish decisions**. Again, Satan is a liar and the father of lies; **do not believe what he has to say**, for it only leads to destruction. Every time man has believed and followed what Satan says, it has brought him only sorrow, suffering, and pain. If it sounds too good to be true then it usually is. Test the waters, **probe the spirits see if they be of God**. In talking to some Mormons, they believe that after they die, a man and his wife or wives will go off to populate some planet and be the God over that planet. They also believe they can be baptized for dead friends and family so they can go to heaven. They believe the Book of Mormon is more important than the Bible. One thing I do like about them is their teaching on family values.

The next religion we will look at is (3) the Muslim religion, which claims to be a peaceful religion, but that is a lie. They are a **religion of hatred to anyone who is not of the Muslim faith**. Their hatred of non-Muslims causes them to do unspeakable things to the nonbeliever (those who do not believe in the Muslim faith). We have seen and heard on the radio and TV news channels of ethnic groups (including Christians) being killed because of not believing the Muslim faith. Men, women, and even small children have been beheaded, shot, hung or beaten to death. They seem to have no humanity about them when it comes to their misguided faith. I am not saying that all Muslims feel this way, but many do. According to their faith it is all right to kill their daughters if they keep company with a boy who is not Muslim. They have **no respect for women, and their women have no rights**. This religion, which traces its roots all the way back to Abraham and claims to worship the God of Abraham, has **no love or compassion for other human beings unless they totally submit to the Muslim religion**. They have no mercy, no compassion, yet they claim to serve a compassionate and loving God and claim to follow his teachings. This, we can see by their actions, is a lie.

The next one we look at is (4) Romanism, or the Catholic Church. The Catholic Church has been taken in by a large number of heresies. One of the main ones is the worship of Mary. They put Mary on an equal basis with our Lord Jesus. **Mary was just a natural woman who was used of God, just like the prophets of old.** She holds no special position or place in the kingdom of God; she is and always was just a natural woman. **Mary is not, nor ever will be, equal to Jesus and should not be worshiped or prayed to.** Neither should any of the church's elected saints be worshiped or prayed to. Other beliefs that are wrong: (1) the Pope is without sin, (2) the belief in purgatory, (3) priests can forgive sin – only Jesus can do that, and (4) Mary is the queen of heaven, so ordained by the Catholic Church.

The belief that there is a queen of heaven started in paganism with Seminaries, wife of Nimrod and queen of Babylon. From Babylon the belief of polytheism spread throughout the world. Polytheism is the belief in many gods. The statue of a goddess holding her divine child also started in Babylon with Seminaries holding Dammuze. (In the Hebrew, he is called Tammuz.) In Egypt the goddess and son were Isis and Horus, plus there are many, many more who were worshiped and had statues of them holding their children. This is one more way that heresies have come into the Catholic Church. **Mary holding the Christ child and being ordained the queen of heaven is just one of a long list of goddesses being worshiped today.** Am I saying that Catholics are not saved? No, I am not saying that a Catholic is not saved. It is my belief that **as long as a person's heart is right with God at the point of death, that person will go to heaven to be with the Lord no matter their religion**.

However, it is very important that we remember this one thing, that church membership does not and will not save you, and neither will water baptism. **There must be a born-again experience that takes place in your heart and life, for without it there is no salvation, and that experience only comes through Jesus Christ and no other.**

There are many false religions in the world today, and there are many cults in the Christian church. **Any church or group that does not preach and teach against sin is very, very wrong.** The beginning of falsehood starts little by little, changing the scripture to suit themselves and what they perceive or want to be the truth. I know of preachers and teachers who will tell you that they do not believe everything in the Bible. From these people run away, for they are wrong, wrong, wrong. **Remember, Satan, that old devil, will come in as an angel of light to deceive and destroy the souls of man.**

To quote from the *Wiersbe Bible Commentary NT:*

> But counterfeits are nothing new. Satan is the "great imitator" (2 Corinthians 11:13-15), and he has been hard at work ever since he deceived Eve in the garden. (Genesis 3:1-7; I Corinthians 11:1-4). He has false Christians (Matthew 13:38; John 8:44), a false gospel (Galatians 1:6-9), and even a false righteousness (Romans 9:30 and Romans 10:4). One day he will present to the world a false Christ (2 Thessalonians 2).

The only way to spot a counterfeit is to be on the watch, and even then, **without the Holy Ghost to reveal them to us, many will trick and deceive us**. Church, we are in an all-out war with the devil, and the victory can only be won **through Jesus Christ and the Holy Ghost**. As the disciples and apostles died and passed off the scene, Peter was afraid of what might happen to the churches, and so he wrote these two epistles. His hope was that men and women would **read them, take them to heart, and be watchful of the church and of each** other lest they be led astray. I may be going over ground that we have already covered but **learn this lesson**. It may save you from destruction.

A person who is a false teacher or preacher will give himself or herself away. These false teachers are not saved. They may have been saved at one time but are now backslidden, lost and undone, away from God. As these counterfeit teachers go about their work of leading souls away from God, listen and you will find **they deny much more of God's Word than they agree with**. These counterfeit teachers deny the virgin birth. They do their best to deny the deity of Jesus Christ, because if they can, **they can destroy the church and the body of Jesus Christ on earth**. If the devil can destroy the main principles of the church, the pure Word of God and His salvation, then he can destroy the church.

If we look around us, we will find that Satan is convincing people that the Bible is just another book and not divinely inspired. Many today do not believe in eternal judgement; they do not even believe in sin, or that **Jesus died on the cross for them**. The message that goes forth today from most pulpits is **a powerless message that cannot do what is needed in today's world**. Ministers, teachers, it is time to preach the word just like it is. Do not be afraid, for God has always provided for his people. The truth will set you free. You may need to get down on your knees and pray through and touch God first, but **do whatever it takes to build your courage and trust**. Then obey the gospel, tell the people thus sayeth the Lord and **do it with love, compassion and concern for the lost souls** on their way to a devil's hell. Preach and teach with **the authority and power of Jesus Christ behind you**, and souls can and will be saved. We are not called to tickle people's ears and tell little stories. We are called to **give out the words of life**; to tell those around us that there is a way for the soul of man to enter into the glories of heaven and **live there with God and Christ forever more**.

2 Peter 2:2

And many shall follow their pernicious ways; by reason of whom the way of truth shall be evil spoken of.

As Peter spoke of false teachers who pervert the Word of God and lead weak Christians away from God, he was sending a warning to beware, **to know those who labor among us, to be ever vigilant for Satan's lies**.

I Thessalonians 5:12

And we beseech you, brethren, to know them which labour among you, and are over you in the Lord, and admonish you;

What is a weak Christian? A weak Christian is one who neglects their spiritual life. They don't pray, they don't read and study God's word, and oh yes, they do not pray. We must have a spiritual relationship with the Lord on a daily basis or our spiritual lives fail. Here in this second verse Peter speaks of how people will follow these false leaders rather than the truth. To satisfy their own fleshly lust and desires, these people seek out those who will teach a compromised or perverted gospel, a gospel in which they can live the way they desire and still be told that they are good Christian folks. This lie, this pernicious way is being taught today the world around. Christians are falling for this doctrine because it allows them to live worldly life styles and still be told that they are right with God.

The John Phillips Commentary Series – Exploring the Epistles of Peter:

> Peter had no illusions as to the success of these false teachers. They would attract a considerable following. The expression "pernicious ways" points to "their lascivious ways." Peter has already warned his readers of this kind of thing (1 Peter 3).
>
> A lascivious person is one who has abandoned all restraint and revels in indecent behavior. Sodomy, bestiality, and pornography are the final expressions of such abandonment of all morals (1 Peter 3:7). Peter has in mind the shameless conduct of apostate teachers who, having abandoned the truth, soon endorse as normal the most foul and filthy lifestyles imaginable. As a result of such teaching and example, "the way of truth" is "evil spoken of." That is, it is blasphemed (as in 1 Peter 4:4).

The followers of Jesus separate themselves from these false

teachers lest they be led astray. One of Hitler's spokesmen said, "Tell a lie loud enough and long enough and it becomes the truth in people's minds." This is what the devil is doing today, in the here and now.

2 Peter 2:3

And through covetousness shall they with feigned words make merchandise of you: whose judgment now of a long time lingereth not, and their damnation slumbereth not.

This verse begins "*and through covetousness shall they with feigned words make merchandise of you.*" What this is saying is that through our own lust, our own desire to have more, be it money, fame, prestige, or whatever, **we are led astray of our own desires**. There have always been those who seek to use other people to achieve their goals. These false teachers, these destroyers, these tellers of lies, care not for the spiritual welfare of those around them. People are only a means to achieve their own goals. These purveyors of error and misguidedness **do not even care about the spiritual condition of their own souls**. Their goals are natural, worldly, to the building up of themselves, no matter how many they must destroy to get where they desire to be. But we may rest assured that **their day of judgement is coming**. The question is how many have they destroyed on their road to destruction? Too many, I am afraid. But judgement is coming.

Wiersbe's Bible Commentary NT states:

Peter saw no hope for these apostles; their doom was sealed. His attitude was different from that of "tolerant" religious people today who say, "Well, they may not agree with us, but there are many roads to heaven." Peter made it clear that these false teachers had "forsaken the right way" (2 Peter 2:15), which simply means they were going the wrong way! Their judgement was sure, even though it had not yet come. The trial was over, but the sentence had not yet been executed. It would not linger or slumber, Peter affirmed; it would come in due time.

I learned a long time ago that for **every action there is an equal reaction**. People think they are getting away with all kinds of things, but there is a day coming when we must answer for the things that we have done. Unforgiven sin leads to a devil's hell. Don't let people make merchandise of you. Peter could see what was to take place in the church after the disciples and the apostles all died and left the scene. The successors that would follow were men who did not walk with Jesus or sit at His feet as He taught them the words of life, hope, and health. The large number of them would be men who were **only concerned with what they could get for themselves**. These counterfeit teachers were ready to buy and sell their favors as the need arose. During the Dark Ages (or Middle Ages), the merchandising of religion was at a high point. The Roman Catholic Church held a stranglehold upon the people, selling its favors to the highest bidders, even charging large sums of money for priests to pray their dead loved ones out of purgatory. This is a place that does not, nor ever did exist. **The blessings of God are not for sale. They are freely given to those who are worthy.**

2 Peter 2:4

For if God spared not the angels that sinned, but cast them
down to hell, and delivered them into chains of darkness,
to be reserved unto judgment;

Verse four begins with a very sobering thought, that if God did not spare the angels that sinned, but brought them to judgement; then **why do people today think that God will excuse their sins?** One consensus is a generally held agreement among some that Jesus died for the sins of the whole world. So, no matter what we do or say, or how we might live, our sins are forgiven. Another group believes that since Jesus died to forgive the world of sin, each and every one of us are born saved. It seems the nearer we get to the rapture of the church, the wilder and more demented the church gets in its beliefs, drifting further from the truth of the Word. These theories, these false teachings absolve everyone from any aspect of personal responsibility, **which goes strictly against the Word of God**.

So, what is sin? **Sin is anything that comes between you and God.** God has laid down the ground rules. To disobey is sin, and sin pulls us away from God. The question is, where did sin come from? Note that sin did not originate in the garden with Adam and Eve. Neither did it originate on the earth. **Sin's origin occurred in heaven with the angel Lucifer.**

Lucifer, because of self-pride and self-importance, began to covet and desire power. He esteemed himself to be as great as God and began to devise a plan to overthrow God and to take God's place in heaven. Lucifer's failed plan to overthrow God caused Lucifer and one third of the angels of Heaven to be cast out of heaven and down to the earth.

I was once asked the question: Do angels have free will?

My reply was yes, they do. I was rebuked for my answer and told that I did not know what I was talking about. My answer was that if angels did not have free will, then how could they have come into league with Lucifer to overthrow God and become the leading force in heaven? **These fallen angels made a conscious free will decision to join with Lucifer and are now suffering the consequences of their decision.** Do angels obey God and serve God? Yes, they do. But they (the angels) are not mind-controlled slaves. **They serve God because they love God, and it's their desire to serve and please God.**

The John Phillips Commentary Series – Exploring the Epistles of Peter:

> By contrast, the entire company of rebellious angels acted of their own volition in planned, deliberate, and organized rebellion against both God and the background of full light and knowledge; hence, no salvation is provided for them.
>
> Peter's brief comment casts a flood of light upon the mysterious spirit world. Perhaps, in some of His private talks with the Twelve, the Lord Jesus told them of things that are not openly revealed in Scripture.
>
> The "angels that sinned" fall into two categories. When Satan fell, he seems to have dragged down a third of the heavenly host with him (Rev. 12:3-4; Luke 10:18). Their current sphere of activity is our planet and its environs in space. Large numbers of these fallen angels are still free and are actively engaged in holding our world in bondage. They

work ceaselessly to hinder God's redemptive purposes. They harbor special malice toward the Jewish people (Dan. 10:12-13, 20-21) and the church (Matt. 16:18). These mighty beings are organized and seem to have a hierarchical structure with Satan as their titular head. Paul tells us that we are obstructed by these beings when we pray and that we need "the whole armor of God" if we are to break through their ranks. They are organized as principalities and powers, as the rulers of this world's darkness, and as wicked spirits in high places (Eph. 6:10-18). They are of a different order than demons, which have a craving to possess human bodies. The inference is that demons, foul beings that they are, once had bodies but are now disembodied spirits of great malice and wickedness. Fallen angels, by contrast, are beings of enormous power and high rank that have supernatural gifts and abilities. They do not need to steal bodies; they can fashion them for themselves.

From the ranks of these "high ones that are on high" (Isa. 24:21) came a group of angels who had a further fall. Jude gives us information about them: "And the angels which kept not their first estate [i.e., their own principality], but left their own habitation [i.e., their own house], he hath reserved in everlasting chains under darkness unto the judgment of the great day" (Jude 6). Both Peter and Jude put this incident in the context of the sin of Sodom—going after strange flesh. This particular group of fallen angels lusted after human women. In pursuit of this alien desire, they violated the order of their being and, in consummating their craving, brought down upon their heads the wrath of God. Peter compares this incident to the days of Noah and to the judgment of the Flood. Evidently, the two events are closely connected.

These few paragraphs by John Phillip are very widely held to be truth. Whether you agree is up to you.

We need at this time to take a closer look at what the scriptures have to say, starting with Isaiah 14:12-15.

Isaiah 14:12-15

12 How art thou fallen from heaven, O Lucifer, son of the morning! how art thou cut down to the ground, which didst weaken the nations!
13 For thou hast said in thine heart, I will ascend into heaven, I will exalt my throne above the stars of God: I will sit also upon the mount of the congregation, in the sides of the north:
14 I will ascend above the heights of the clouds; I will be like the most High.
15 Yet thou shalt be brought down to hell, to the sides of the pit.

The scriptures, God's Holy Word, if we will study it, give us many answers to questions that we have often wondered about. Here in Isaiah we find part of the story of Satan's fall from heaven; of Satan's pride and his desire to be as God; and how that through his desire and rebellion, sin came into being. **By searching the**

Word, we can bring many hidden things into the light. This is why God tells us to study the Word.

Next, let us go to the book of Ezekiel.

Ezekiel 28:11-19

> *[11] Moreover the word of the LORD came unto me, saying,*
> *[12] Son of man, take up a lamentation upon the king of Tyrus, and say unto him, Thus saith the Lord GOD; Thou sealest up the sum, full of wisdom, and perfect in beauty.*
> *[13] Thou hast been in Eden the garden of God; every precious stone was thy covering, the sardius, topaz, and the diamond, the beryl, the onyx, and the jasper, the sapphire, the emerald, and the carbuncle, and gold: the workmanship of thy tabrets and of thy pipes was prepared in thee in the day that thou wast created.*
> *[14] Thou art the anointed cherub that covereth; and I have set thee so: thou wast upon the holy mountain of God; thou hast walked up and down in the midst of the stones of fire.*
> *[15] Thou wast perfect in thy ways from the day that thou wast created, till iniquity was found in thee.*
> *[16] By the multitude of thy merchandise they have filled the midst of thee with violence, and thou hast sinned: therefore I will cast thee as profane out of the mountain of God: and I will destroy thee, O covering cherub, from the midst of the stones of fire.*
> *[17] Thine heart was lifted up because of thy beauty, thou hast corrupted thy wisdom by reason of thy brightness: I will cast thee to the ground, I will lay thee before kings, that they may behold thee.*
> *[18] Thou hast defiled thy sanctuaries by the multitude of thine*

iniquities, by the iniquity of thy traffick; therefore will I bring forth a fire from the midst of thee, it shall devour thee, and I will bring thee to ashes upon the earth in the sight of all them that behold thee.

[19] All they that know thee among the people shall be astonished at thee: thou shalt be a terror, and never shalt thou be any more.

Here in these verses we learn that Satan is called a king in this world. Scripture goes on to tell us that Satan was in Eden, the garden of God, and how **he was beautiful in the day that he was created**. How that he (Satan) held a special place in heaven, that he was **perfect in his ways from the day he was created until iniquity was found in him**. Pride and self-importance caused envy to rise up in Lucifer, and this **turned to sin and caused him to be cast out of heaven**, along with a third of the angels, those that rebelled with him. They were cast out from the presence of God for ever.

The next group of scriptures we need to look at are found in Revelation.

Revelation 12:3-9

[3] And there appeared another wonder in heaven; and behold a great red dragon, having seven heads and ten horns, and seven crowns upon his heads.

[4] And his tail drew the third part of the stars of heaven, and did cast them to the earth: and the dragon stood before the woman which was ready to be delivered, for to devour her child as soon as it was born.

[5] And she brought forth a man child, who was to rule all

nations with a rod of iron: and her child was caught up unto
God, and to his throne.
⁶ And the woman fled into the wilderness, where she hath a
place prepared of God, that they should feed her there a
thousand two hundred and threescore days.
⁷ And there was war in heaven: Michael and his angels
fought against the dragon; and the dragon fought and his
angels,
⁸ And prevailed not; neither was their place found any more
in heaven.
⁹ And the great dragon was cast out, that old serpent, called
the Devil, and Satan, which deceiveth the whole world: he
was cast out into the earth, and his angels were cast out
with him.

These scriptures again tell us of the fall of Lucifer and that
he was cast out of heaven. As he was cast out, those angels that
followed him were cast out also, again about one third of the angels
of heaven. Where are these fallen angels today? Second Peter says
that they are **reserved in chains of darkness awaiting the
judgement**. The book of Jude agrees with Peter. Again, we look at
verse four where it says that **these fallen angels are reserved in
chains of darkness awaiting the coming judgement**, which they
will surely face.

Here in Revelation it states that **Satan was cast out into the
earth**. In the Interlinear Bible (Hebrew, Greek and English), the
Greek translation says that **Satan was cast out onto the earth**.
Here in comes the problem. **Were all the angels cast into the
chains of darkness or just part of them?** The Greek translations
say that **Satan and the angels were cast out onto the earth**. So,
is "cast into the earth" the same as "cast onto the earth"? I believe

it is. This would account for the angels being on the earth and taking wives of the daughters of men as in the book of Genesis before the flood. Bible scholars believe that the angels chained in darkness are the angels who committed sin with mankind. The sin of intermarrying with women on the earth, is it true? I cannot say, but I do believe that **the sons of God in Genesis are fallen angels, and they did take wives of the daughters of men to produce the race of giants** that were in the land before the flood, as told in Genesis 6:1-7.

Genesis 6:1-7

> [1] *And it came to pass, when men began to multiply on the face of the earth, and daughters were born unto them,*
> [2] *That the sons of God saw the daughters of men that they were fair; and they took them wives of all which they chose.*
> [3] *And the LORD said, My spirit shall not always strive with man, for that he also is flesh: yet his days shall be an hundred and twenty years.*
> [4] *There were giants in the earth in those days; and also after that, when the sons of God came in unto the daughters of men, and they bare children to them, the same became mighty men which were of old, men of renown.*
> [5] *And GOD saw that the wickedness of man was great in the earth, and that every imagination of the thoughts of his heart was only evil continually.*
> [6] *And it repented the LORD that he had made man on the earth, and it grieved him at his heart.*
> [7] *And the LORD said, I will destroy man whom I have*

created from the face of the earth; both man, and beast, and the creeping thing, and the fowls of the air; for it repenteth me that I have made them.

At this time, I would like to point out verse four, which tells us "there were giants in the earth in those days." This we all agree on, but the next part of the verse says, "and also after that." I contend or believe that **all flesh died in the flood except for Noah and his family**. But we know that again in the land, even before Moses, there was again a race of giants. I believe that after the flood, when men began to multiply and reclaim the land, we have the **same thing happening again but on a much smaller scale**. Fallen angels took wives of the daughters of men, and again there was a race of giants, Goliath being a good example. So, are the angels chained in darkness all of the angels, or just the ones who sinned once by following Satan and twice by marrying the daughters of men? I tend to believe they are **the angels who sinned by taking wives of mankind**. But you must search it out for yourselves and find out what God would have you to believe.

The one thing we must not lose sight of is Peter's point. **If God spared not the angels that sinned, then we can rest assured that God will not spare man because of his sin.** All through scripture God teaches that man is accountable for his wrongdoings, his sin.

In the *Biblical Illustrator* we find a quote from C.H. Spurgeon that speaks to the problem.

This warning, be it noted, applies itself to the very foulest of sin. The angels did not merely sin and lose heaven, but they passed beyond all other beings in sin, and made themselves fit denizens for hell. Oh my unrenewed hearer, I would not slander thee, but I must warn: there are all the makings of a hell within thy heart! It only needs that the restraining hand of God should be removed and thou wouldest come out in thy true colors, and those are the colors of iniquity.

If a person accepts the Lord Jesus as his personal savior, old things are passed away. **We become a new creature in Christ Jesus, and we are blessed beyond measure.** We have a personal relationship with our Lord, **a one-on-one relationship where we can talk to Him as a friend and He will talk to us**. Jesus is not a Lord far away, but He lives within our hearts. If at any time we allow sin to come into our hearts, our lives, then we lose that relationship with the Lord. Jesus and sin will not reside in the same temple. **You are either saved, or you are a sinner.** You cannot be both at the same time. A relationship with Jesus takes us to heaven. Sin takes us to hell.

2 Peter 2:5

And spared not the old world, but saved Noah the eighth person, a preacher of righteousness, bringing in the flood upon the world of the ungodly;

Peter once again is trying to prove to the people that **a just God cannot and will not continue to put up with man committing sin**. In this verse he gives the example of God destroying the old world with a flood.

Matthew 24:37-39

37 But as the days of Noe were, so shall also the coming of the Son of man be.
38 For as in the days that were before the flood they were eating and drinking, marrying and giving in marriage, until the day that Noe entered into the ark,
39 And knew not until the flood came, and took them all away; so shall also the coming of the Son of man be.

In these scriptures, Jesus is describing the conditions before the flood. Man had gotten so totally involved in himself and his base desires and fleshly lust that **he had lost all sight of God the creator**. The only ones serving God were the line of Seth (and not all of them). How do we know this? Because **only Noah and his family were saved alive**. The antediluvian age was, I believe, the worst time that has ever been on this earth. Judging by what is happening today, the lust of the people and their extraordinary wickedness had to have been great. Evil left unchecked grows in the heart of man. It turns man into a slave to sin. The more man sins, the more he desires to sin until he is totally consumed and ruled by sin. Every thought, the very intent of man's heart is to go deeper and deeper into the quagmire of sin until he reaches the place where there is no hope at all. Although he struggles, there is no hope to be found. **We in ourselves cannot overcome, but with Jesus there is victory.** Jesus is man's only hope; without Jesus we are lost, with no future to be seen. When we come to Jesus and repent, **He washes us clean**. We become white as snow, and the past is forgiven, **for there is hope for the future because of Jesus**. Jesus is our Savior, our Lord, and our King. Give Him praise and glory, for in Him we are more than conquerors. **The blood of the**

Lamb saves us.

Jesus is our savior. In the old world, Noah was the natural savior of the world. He preached for one hundred and twenty years. His only converts were his family. No one seemed to believe or care. Scripture tells us that **Noah was a preacher of righteousness**. Noah's great grandfather was Enoch, a prophet who prophesied of the judgement that was to come upon the earth.

Jude 14-15

14 And Enoch also, the seventh from Adam, prophesied of these, saying, Behold, the Lord cometh with ten thousands of his saints,
15 To execute judgment upon all, and to convince all that are ungodly among them of all their ungodly deeds which they have ungodly committed, and of all their hard speeches which ungodly sinners have spoken against him.

Enoch was also spoken evil of and not believed. Enoch went so far as to name his son Methuselah, which was a prophecy in itself. The name Methuselah means that **when he dies, it shall come**. Methuselah died in the year of the flood, and just as Enoch had prophesied, at Methuselah's death, **the flood came to destroy man from the face of the earth**. Man was warned and did not heed the call of God. Today, just as then, the world is being warned, and **most of the world pays no heed to the warnings from God.**

2 Peter 2:6-9

6 And turning the cities of Sodom and Gomorrha into ashes condemned them with an overthrow, making them

an ensample unto those that after should live ungodly;
⁷ And delivered just Lot, vexed with the filthy conversation
of the wicked:
⁸ (For that righteous man dwelling among them, in seeing
and hearing, vexed his righteous soul from day to day with
their unlawful deeds;)
⁹ The Lord knoweth how to deliver the godly out of
temptations, and to reserve the unjust unto the day of
judgment to be punished:

The third example Peter gives us is about how God dealt with the cities of Sodom and Gomorrah. The cities of the plain were exceedingly wicked, and their wickedness came up before God. **The things we do not only affect us but also those around us.** The wickedness man does has a way of spilling over on others. Which of these cities was the most wicked? We do not know. But Lot lived in Sodom. We often speak of Sodom and Gomorrah, but did you know that Sodom and Gomorrah were not the only cities to be destroyed by God? The scriptures tell us of **three other cities on the plain that were destroyed,** for all the plain was destroyed. These cities were Admah, Zeboim, and Lasha. You can find them mentioned in Genesis 10:19 (and Admah and Zeboim in Genesis 14:2) if you care to look them up.

James 4:4

Ye adulterers and adulteresses, know ye not that the friendship of the world is enmity with God? whosoever therefore will be a friend of the world is the enemy of God.)

God hates sin, and the Word tells us the **friendship of the**

world is enmity with God. Why? Because the world is evil.

I John 2:15-17

> [15] *Love not the world, neither the things that are in the world. If any man love the world, the love of the Father is not in him.*
> [16] *For all that is in the world, the lust of the flesh, and the lust of the eyes, and the pride of life, is not of the Father, but is of the world.*
> [17] *And the world passeth away, and the lust thereof: but he that doeth the will of God abideth for ever.*

Here God tells us **not to love the world or the things that are in the world**. Therefore, we can see that the scripture as written by John sums up the world as the lust of the flesh, lust of the eye, and wanton foolish pride. None of this is of God. The cities of the plain were guilty of these three conditions compounded. They were obsessed with fleshly desires in the extreme, just as we see happening today. **Just because we are not living under the law but under grace does not mean that God has changed his mind about what is sin.** Sin is still sin, and what brought judgement in the Old Testament will also bring judgement today. People try to fool themselves, to justify themselves, but **sin will still take a soul to hell**. Sodom and Gomorrah are examples to us of what will happen to us if we live a life to ourselves without God.

In *Wiersbe Bible Commentary NT* we read the following:

> The men of Sodom practiced filthy behavior and unlawful deeds (2 Peter 2:7-8). Since the law of

Moses had not yet been given, the word unlawful cannot refer to some Jewish law. In what sense were their filthy deeds "unlawful"? They were contrary to nature (see Romans 1:24-27). The flagrant sin of Sodom and the other cities was unnatural sex, sodomy, or homosexual behavior, a sin that is clearly condemned in Scripture (Leviticus 18:22; Romans 1:24-27; I Corinthians 6:9).

Yes, Lot was spared, but not because of anything Lot was doing. He was spared because of **his uncle Abraham who prayed for him**, an uncle who had a personal relationship with God. Therein lies the victory, **a personal relationship with God**. We can have that same relationship with God, if we are willing to pay the price. In this world a person can have most anything if they can pay the price. Homes, cars, riches, all can be had for a price. **In God, we can have the victory, contentment in the storm, a peace that passes all understanding**; it can all be ours if we are willing to pay the price. What price? **Giving ourselves over totally to God, accepting His plan for our lives and living as He would have us to live.** As we read and study the Bible, what is the one thing God wants us to learn? It is to learn from the experiences of others and not to walk in their ungodly ways. Learn from those who won the victory; learn that by obeying God's Word and living godly **we shall be overcomers and dwell with God forever**.

There is an old saying that says if you do not learn the lesson the first time, you are doomed to repeat it over and over again until you learn that lesson. **Well, the world has not learned its lesson.** Sin and exceeding wickedness destroyed the old world. God started over with Noah and his family, all told, eight souls. Man has multiplied on the face of this world to repeat the same mistakes; a perfect example is the cities of the plain. **Because of exceeding evil and wickedness, God destroyed them and still man has not learned.**

Now in this present age man once again is repeating the same sins over again. Man is going after strange flesh; homosexuality is no longer a hidden life style. They plan their sinfulness and demand that the world accept it as normal. We are back to the days of Noah and the days of Sodom and Gomorrah. And one more time **God is going to rain judgement upon this world.** Lift up your head, Child of God, for our redemption draws nigh. For just as in verse nine, **the Lord knows how to deliver the just and to reserve the unjust for judgement**.

2 Peter 2:10-13

10 But chiefly them that walk after the flesh in the lust of uncleanness, and despise government. Presumptuous are they, selfwilled, they are not afraid to speak evil of dignities.
11 Whereas angels, which are greater in power and might, bring not railing accusation against them before the Lord.
12 But these, as natural brute beasts, made to be taken and destroyed, speak evil of the things that they understand not; and shall utterly perish in their own corruption;
13 And shall receive the reward of unrighteousness, as they that count it pleasure to riot in the day time. Spots they are and blemishes, sporting themselves with their own deceivings while they feast with you;

These four verses combine to make up one main thought, but at the same time as they make up one thought, we want to look at them individually, also. **Peter was a man who was deeply troubled by what was happening in the church.** The church was in its infancy, some thirty years old, and already the devil was trying to tear it down by bringing in false teachers. Peter knew these false teachings were subtle, but what they espoused was fatal to the soul. It was his aim to **warn the churches about this trick of the devil.** These false teachers were trying to build themselves up in the eyes of everybody, while at the same time tearing down what everyone else believed.

There are certain rules of authority in this world, and **we as the children of God are to obey them and respect them.**

1. Parents are to **have rule or authority over their children.**

Ephesians 6:1-4

> *¹ Children, obey your parents in the Lord: for this is right.*
> *² Honour thy father and mother; (which is the first commandment with promise;)*
> *³ That it may be well with thee, and thou mayest live long on the earth.*
> *⁴ And, ye fathers, provoke not your children to wrath: but bring them up in the nurture and admonition of the Lord.*

2. Employers are to **have authority over their workers.**

Ephesians 6:5-8

> *⁵ Servants, be obedient to them that are your masters according to the flesh, with fear and trembling, in singleness of your heart, as unto Christ;*

[6] Not with eyeservice, as menpleasers; but as the servants of Christ, doing the will of God from the heart;
[7] With good will doing service, as to the Lord, and not to men:
[8] Knowing that whatsoever good thing any man doeth, the same shall he receive of the Lord, whether he be bond or free.

3. We as Christians are to **respect and honor those who have authority over us in the Lord**.

Hebrews 13:7

Remember them which have the rule over you, who have spoken unto you the word of God: whose faith follow, considering the end of their conversation.

I Peter 5:1-5

[1] The elders which are among you I exhort, who am also an elder, and a witness of the sufferings of Christ, and also a partaker of the glory that shall be revealed:
[2] Feed the flock of God which is among you, taking the oversight thereof, not by constraint, but willingly; not for filthy lucre, but of a ready mind;
[3] Neither as being lords over God's heritage, but being ensamples to the flock.
[4] And when the chief Shepherd shall appear, ye shall receive a crown of glory that fadeth not away.
[5] Likewise, ye younger, submit yourselves unto the elder. Yea, all of you be subject one to another, and be clothed

with humility: for God resisteth the proud, and giveth grace to the humble.

4. Elders, you are not to be **a dictator over God's flock, for in this God is not pleased**.

Hebrews 6:1-6

1 Therefore leaving the principles of the doctrine of Christ, let us go on unto perfection; not laying again the foundation of repentance from dead works, and of faith toward God,
2 Of the doctrine of baptisms, and of laying on of hands, and of resurrection of the dead, and of eternal judgment.
3 And this will we do, if God permit.
4 For it is impossible for those who were once enlightened, and have tasted of the heavenly gift, and were made partakers of the Holy Ghost,
5 And have tasted the good word of God, and the powers of the world to come,
6 If they shall fall away, to renew them again unto repentance; seeing they crucify to themselves the Son of God afresh, and put him to an open shame.

5. Saints of God, we as true Christians are to **pray for those who are in authority**.

I Timothy 2:1-4

1 I exhort therefore, that, first of all, supplications, prayers, intercessions, and giving of thanks, be made for all men;
2 For kings, and for all that are in authority; that we may

lead a quiet and peaceable life in all godliness and honesty.
³ For this is good and acceptable in the sight of God our Saviour;
⁴ Who will have all men to be saved, and to come unto the knowledge of the truth.

6. We are to pray for our government and those in authority that they will **listen to the voice of God and make the right decisions so that the church of God may grow and prosper**.

I Timothy 2:1-8

¹ I exhort therefore, that, first of all, supplications, prayers, intercessions, and giving of thanks, be made for all men;
² For kings, and for all that are in authority; that we may lead a quiet and peaceable life in all godliness and honesty.
³ For this is good and acceptable in the sight of God our Saviour;
⁴ Who will have all men to be saved, and to come unto the knowledge of the truth.
⁵ For there is one God, and one mediator between God and men, the man Christ Jesus;
⁶ Who gave himself a ransom for all, to be testified in due time.
⁷ Whereunto I am ordained a preacher, and an apostle, (I speak the truth in Christ, and lie not;) a teacher of the Gentiles in faith and verity.
⁸ I will therefore that men pray every where, lifting up holy hands, without wrath and doubting.)

Peter, in verse 10, begins to point out that **flesh is**

288

responsible for all the trouble that occurs in the world. Scripture teaches us that we must crucify this flesh, for the desires of the flesh are the cause of evil, hatred, lust, pride, murder and so on. **The world walks after the fleshly lust of uncleanness.** This lust pushes man to do whatever he perceives is necessary to obtain his goals in life. The golden rule is no more. Today's rule is **to do unto others before they can do it to you**. Our children are taught by their parents to achieve their goal no matter who they have to use or step on or lie about. The only thing that is important is to get what you want in life. We live in a world that has learned from the devil that **winning is the only important thing in this life**. Man is so arrogant that he is not even afraid to defy God.

As we watch the television and listen to the radio, we hear preachers who pervert the word of God, openly stating that they do not believe all the Bible. They **openly criticize the scriptures as wrong**, that they were written by men who should be openly rebuked because of what they wrote, because it hurts people's feelings and makes them feel bad. These preachers and teachers should realize **there is a judgement day coming, and at that day they will have to give an account before God**. They may have taken everything they don't like out of their Bibles, but God is not going to judge them by their Bibles and what they believe to be right. God is going to judge **according to His Word and what He knows to be right**. All that I can say is what Hebrews 10:31 says: "It is a fearful thing to fall into the hands of the living God." **May God have mercy upon their souls.**

In this eleventh verse, Peter is trying to teach a very important lesson that all Christians need to learn, **how to control our mouth and tongue**. To think before we speak. In the church of Peter's day, false teachers were already at work condemning various teachings of God's Word. Not much has changed in all these years. **The church still has those who would and do pervert the gospel of Jesus Christ.** They bring railing accusations against everyone who does not agree with them. **They are condemning themselves in the face of God and will soon face their punishment.** Peter gives an example of the angels who do God's bidding. They're wise enough to hold themselves in check or face punishment. How then should we act?

As we look at this twelfth verse, Peter brings strong accusations against these false teachers, those who destroy the power and authority of God's Word. Peter likens them to brute beasts. These men and women **live only in the natural**. Sadly, a large majority of these people have at one time known the truth. But today, because of something that has happened to them in their past, **they have turned from the truth**. They endeavor to put forth the appearance of being a Christian founded upon the Word of God, but this is not so. They try to destroy everything that points to their true self and where they stand with God. They speak evil of the things of God that they do not understand, or do not want to understand. **They want to live their lives the way they desire.** They want no rules applied to them. Instead, they **make their own rules**.

The Word tells us these individuals will **perish in their own corruption**. The question is how many they will pull down with them, those who choose to trust in their false doctrine and those who try to pattern themselves or conform to what their false teachers are teaching. They not only destroy themselves but **the multitudes that follow them**. They have left the divine anointing of God's spirit and have taken the worldly path of human reasoning and stupidity. Their stupidity is very apparent, because they **criticize and denounce the things of God which they know nothing about** or have walked away from.

Going on to verse 13, there have always been those who refuse to believe.

The John Phillips Commentary Series – Exploring the Epistles of Peter:

> George Bernard Shaw was an avowed atheist. He, too, was not afraid to speak evil of dignities, even the Highest. "It is high time," he said, "that we got rid of Jehovah." He openly advocated government persecution of the church. He said, "As to the belief that Jesus was the Christ who would rise from the dead and return in glory to judge the world, and all the rest of it, we must believe exactly what we should believe of any other man who fell into a similar delusion: that he went mad, just as Swift and Ruskin did, both of them being driven out of their minds by the wickedness of the human species."

There are many more that have spent their lives **bashing the church and the things of God**. Do they think that in their rantings they can do away with the Creator of the universe, the Creator of man? **It is unbelievable that men think that in the eons of the past somewhere, the ancestors of man crawled out of the primordial ooze.** It seems the wiser man becomes, the more ignorant he becomes. He can believe he is a product of evolution, but **he cannot believe in the divine creation**. These men and women who choose to turn their backs on God will reap the rewards of their decision. They will stand before the righteous judge, God, and be **judged by the very God they refused to believe in or**

accept.

Peter calls this type of people spots and blemishes, a **disgrace to the church**, because many of them try to put forth a Christian-like appearance **but are far from being Christians**. Some of these men and women even try to invade the ministry, and some succeed. You hear them on television and radio begging for money, not for the work of God, but **for their own selfish lusts and desires**. They think they are fooling everybody, but **they cannot fool God**. If we watch them from afar, sooner or later we will see or hear of things they have been caught doing, and **it always brings shame and reproach upon the church**. I realize that ministers, teachers, and Christians get tempted and fall. We all from time to time will fail God in one way or another. We are human, but **scripture teaches that we must strive for perfection**.

Do not put all your trust in any one person no matter how much we look up to them. They are subject to temptations and can fail. **All our trust must be anchored in the one who can never fail, Jesus Christ our Lord.** We see on every hand those of the world who would cause us to fall, but be not dismayed, for **Jesus is your strength, your redeemer**.

2 Peter 2:14

Having eyes full of adultery, and that cannot cease from sin; beguiling unstable souls: an heart they have exercised with covetous practices; cursed children:

Here Peter gives us a description of individuals and denounces their ungodly conduct. Peter begins with, "Having eyes full of adultery, and that cannot cease from sin." A life that is turned over to the devil is **a life out of control**. The sinner is bound by sin.

292

They may have set boundaries they do not want to cross such as murder but make no mistake, **they are controlled by the devil.** Peter makes it plain that these people cannot stop committing sin. The only way a person can stop sinning is to **repent of their sins and accept Jesus Christ as their personal savior.** Jesus is the only one who can break the stranglehold of sin. Every one of us is tempted to sin. The devil tempts us **where we are the weakest.** Sexual attraction is normal. It is given to us by God for finding a mate, a partner for life. The devil takes this God-given part of our lives and **blows it all out of proportion.** He uses this to tempt men and women to sin. He also **compounds the situation by going after Christians.** He wants to focus people's attention **on the church and its failures.**

The John Phillips Commentary Series – Exploring the Epistles of Peter:

> There has been a veritable epidemic in recent years of pastors, youth leaders, ministers of music, and other church leaders who have been forced from the ministry by their unrestrained lusts. Worse still are the cases of numerous others who remain in the ministry, tolerated or even supported by a spineless or hoodwinked congregation, even though they have been guilty of flagrant misconduct. It is part of the general growth of end-times Laodicean apostasy in the church that moral collapses are now so frequent and viewed in so many cases with general apathy. Apathy and apostasy are fellow travelers.

Next Peter talks about "beguiling unstable souls." An

unstable soul is one who is **not rooted and grounded in the Word of God**. Where the true gospel is not being preached, there you will find unstable souls. **It is the true, pure Word of God that causes souls to be established on the solid rock, God's Word.** Where a perverted gospel is being preached, there you will find the devil **hard at work leading souls astray**. I remember back in the early 50s, 60s, and 70s, there was a movement that hit the Pentecostals very hard. This movement promised liberty to people, calling, "Come out of your churches and join us. You do not have to live by the rules that your churches preach and teach. Come and join us and be free from the dos and don'ts. We will give you liberty." However, their liberty turned into **bondage and slavery, entrapped in the devil's snare.** Do not let the devil beguile you with promises. **He promised Eve and Adam they would become like God, and you see where that has gotten us.**

Many people I could name today are following the same road as Bishop John Shelby Spong of the American Episcopal Church. **Spong has no use for fundamental Christians that take the word of God literally.** Bishop Spong wrote several books condemning the fundamental beliefs and espousing the view much of the world holds today. One book he co-wrote, *Sexuality: A Divine Gift*, went against everything the Bible teaches about sex and sexual conduct. Bishop Spong claims that Paul was ignorant in the first chapter of Romans. Bishop Spong declares that the church **should repent of its past ignorance and prejudices concerning sexual conduct, that all sexual acts are permissible between individuals, men with women, male with male, and female with female.** He concludes that nothing is wrong. If you want to do it, do it. Bishop Spong goes so far as to portray Jesus as narrow-minded and vindictive. **He denies that Jesus rose from the dead.** He denies the virgin birth and denies a Godhead or trinity. He rejects the scriptures that Jesus came into this world to save sinners. He also states that **the God of the Old Testament is a sadistic God** and He imposed a vicious code of conduct on mankind which went against their rights of free will. Is it any wonder that the church world is in the shape it is in, with men like this in leadership? **The very fabric of social life and law and order are rooted in the Ten Commandments given by God.** We are living in very perilous times. In the *Wiersbe Bible Commentary*, Wiersbe speaks of these ministers and how that they have perfected their skills in getting what they desire.

Wiersbe Bible Commentary NT:

> "They are experts in greed" says the New International Version, and the Philips translation is even more graphic: "Their technique of getting what they want is, through long practice, highly developed." They know exactly how to motivate people to give. While the true servant of God trusts the Father to meet his needs and seeks to help people grow through their giving, the apostle trusts his "fundraising skills" and leaves people in worse shape than he found them. He knows how to exploit the unstable and the innocent.

Peter goes on to describe these people as "cursed children." As cursed, they cannot enter into the blessings of the Lord.

Matthew 25:41

> *Then shall he say also unto them on the left hand, Depart from me, ye cursed, into everlasting fire, prepared for the*

devil and his angels:

Matthew 16:26-27

^{26} For what is a man profited, if he shall gain the whole world, and lose his own soul? or what shall a man give in exchange for his soul?
^{27} For the Son of man shall come in the glory of his Father with his angels; and then he shall reward every man according to his works.

But to the righteous the Lord shall say:

Matthew 25:33-34

^{33} And he shall set the sheep on his right hand, but the goats on the left.
^{34}Then shall the King say unto them on his right hand, Come, ye blessed of my Father, inherit the kingdom prepared for you from the foundation of the world:

2 Peter 2:15-16

^{15} Which have forsaken the right way, and are gone astray, following the way of Balaam the son of Bosor, who loved the wages of unrighteousness;
^{16} But was rebuked for his iniquity: the dumb ass speaking with man's voice forbad the madness of the prophet.

Peter begins these two scriptures speaking about how **most people have forsaken the right way**. The world and a goodly part of the church are following in the footsteps of the prophet Balaam who, like many, loved the wages of sin. The story of Balaam is found in Numbers, chapters 22-24. Balaam was gentile; he was not Jewish, but somehow **he had knowledge of God and talked with God**. Balaam had the same problem that many preachers and false leaders have today. They are **overcome with the spirit of covetousness**.

Covetousness is an overcoming desire for more of everything. They are **never satisfied with what they have**. They always want more. They want more money. They want more power and prominence than anyone else. Everything has to be about them. **Cursed is the man or woman who makes merchandise of God's children.** These are the words of Peter. Balaam received his reward in Numbers 31:8. He was slain with a sword; **God always has the last word and punishes the wicked**.

If we are not careful in our service of and for God, **we sometimes get sidetracked**. In those times God will get our attention, just as **He got Balaam's attention by opening the mouth of the ass**. The ass speaking with man's voice forbad the madness of the prophet. In these last few years I have seen and heard things said and preached that I would never have dreamed of even ten years ago. People have **no respect for God or the things of God**. Preachers, pastors, teachers, and church leaders **discount much of what the Bible says**. They pick and choose what they want to believe **and throw the rest aside**. I ask myself what has happened, what is going on in the minds of the world and the church? Then God brings me back to scripture and what the scripture says in Revelations. We are surely **living in the last days**. We are living in the Laodicean church age. **Jesus is soon to come, and we are going home.** Praise God, we are going home.

2 Peter 2:17-19

[17] These are wells without water, clouds that are carried with a tempest; to whom the mist of darkness is reserved for ever.
[18] For when they speak great swelling words of vanity, they allure through the lusts of the flesh, through much wantonness, those that were clean escaped from them who live in error.
[19] While they promise them liberty, they themselves are the servants of corruption: for of whom a man is overcome, of the same is he brought in bondage.

Peter changes his examples in verse seventeen **from scriptural examples to everyday examples**. Examples that even the sinner can understand. Peter uses the **natural things to bring home his point**. First, he speaks of wells without water.

Barnes Notes, page 248, states:

> Nothing to an oriental mind would be more expressive than to say of professed religious teachers, that they were "wells without water". It was always a sad disappointment to a traveler in the hot sands of the desert to come to a well were it was expected that water might be found, and to find it dry. It only aggravated the trials of the thirsty and weary traveler. Such were these religious teachers. In a world, not unaptly compared in regard to its real comforts, to the wastes and sands of the desert, they would only grievously disappoint the expectations

of all those who were seeking for the refreshing influences of the truths of the gospel. There are many such teachers in the world.

As we draw closer to the Lord's return, we see more and more **the hand of Satan working in the churches and around the world**. Where the churches at one time preached the true and pure word of God; today **they bow before the desires of the ungodly in high places and before the unholy masses**. The church that lived upright before the world and kept the faith now is only a shadow of what it used to be. **It no longer draws water out of the wells of salvation.**

Isaiah 12:2-3

> *[2] Behold, God is my salvation; I will trust, and not be afraid: for the LORD JEHOVAH is my strength and my song; he also is become my salvation.*
> *[3] Therefore with joy shall ye draw water out of the wells of salvation.)*

A well without water is of no use to anyone, **it is simply an empty hole**. Jesus told the woman at the well that he would give people water whereby **they would never thirst again**, a living water to satisfy the longing of the thirsty soul. Satan's aim is to **draw people's attention to natural things**. His plan is to blind their eyes and **make them think natural possessions** will satisfy their inner longing. But **there is no freedom in possessions**. There is no freedom **in the world and what it can offer**. Freedom comes through Jesus Christ. **Jesus is the only one who can set the soul free.** The cults of this world promise their followers freedom, and today many who used to be in the church are caught up in the occult. They say that they feel free, free from religion, free from rules that govern their lives.

However, if you look at freedom, being free, you will find that **freedom is a concept**. It is a concept that, in today's world, holds many connotations. We find in talking to many people, **everybody has their own ideal of what true freedom really is**. The apostates offer freedom if you will come and follow them, but **it is a misguided freedom that is not freedom at all**. These people who follow these apostate teachers are more often than not brainwashed to the point that they have **no independent thoughts of their own**. This is the only way these groups can hold their followers.

Jesus is the only one who offers true freedom. In Christ there is **liberty, there is true peace**. There are some that ask, "How can you say that you are free when there are things you cannot do and places where you are not supposed to go? Where is your freedom?" Our freedom comes because we are **no longer bound by sin to spend eternity in a devil's hell**. We are free moral agents to do as we please; we are not forced to do anything. We are not forced to serve God or to learn His word. **We do so because we desire to.**

There is within every person a place that is empty, and from this inner place, there is a **longing that cries out to be filled**. Souls try everything to fill that longing, but no matter what they try, it **just cannot be satisfied**. Oh, sometimes for a short while it seems the longing is filled, but **it keeps coming back**. Why? Because we were created by God, and **that place, that longing, cannot be filled except with God's spirit**. We were made to have fellowship with God, to be His friends, His servants, and His companions, and **only God can make us fully whole, fully complete**.

As Peter writes, *"wells without water."* How dreadful! Next, he speaks of *"clouds without water carried about of winds."* This verse gives us **a perfect picture of many in the churches today**. They look good, they talk good, but **they do not possess what they profess to have**. They are unstable in the Word and their faith. Peter goes on to say that **such souls have a place reserved for them in the mist of darkness forever**. Soul astray, there is completeness, but it can **only be found in God through His beloved son Jesus Christ**.

Everyone wants to be accepted, to be a part of something, to be loved. The apostate plays on our need to belong and our willingness to accept what people say. If God teaches us anything, it is **to be wary of people and what they say**. Therein is part of the problem: We like to hear our own voices. When we ought to be listening, too many times we are talking, and it is a fact that **when you are speaking, you are not listening**.

Church, let me say one more time, **we are living in the last days before Jesus comes**. We must reach the lost as quickly as possible. The devil's crowd is hard at work, making all kinds of promises they cannot keep. But they can **lead those astray who are seeking something to satisfy their souls**.

Verse eighteen gives us a better picture of how the apostate work. Peter says that **they speak with "great swelling words of vanity, they allure through the lust of the flesh, through much wantonness."** These false teachers allure by **telling people what they want to hear**. Everybody likes to be told that they are right. I do not know of anyone who likes being told that they are wrong; some will accept that they are wrong if you can prove it to them. But to admit that you are wrong **goes against the fleshly grain**. These false preachers and teachers are **masters at misleading people**.

How are they so adept at what they do? It is easy, just twist the Word of God, **take it out of context**, and you can prove nearly anything that you want to say. Satan is very good at **telling half-truths to prove his lies**. Look at Eve in the garden. Satan told Eve that if she ate of the tree, she would not die. Satan was talking of the natural body, and after she ate, she did not die in the natural. **But she did die in the spiritual.** It is human to look at things in a natural way. God however wants us **to see things in a spiritual way**. This natural body, this natural world will pass away, but the **spiritual body will live on in eternity and never die**. For those of us who believe and are saved through the blood of Jesus Christ, God has **prepared for us an everlasting home with them in what we call heaven**. For the sinners, there is also an everlasting home, and that is **in hell with the devil and his angels**.

I remember when it was a **common thing for preachers to preach on hell** and sinners going there because of their ungodly lifestyles. Today it is **rare to hear hell preached about**. I have heard preachers say that **if you preach on hell and what it is going to be like, you will scare people and they will not come back to church**. Preaching on hell is what caused me to realize that I was lost and on my way there. This reality of hell and who is going there is what **brings conviction upon hearts to seek Jesus for salvation**. The scripture states:

Psalms 111:10

> *The fear of the LORD is the beginning of wisdom: a good understanding have all they that do his commandments: his praise endureth for ever.*

Proverbs 1:7

The fear of the LORD is the beginning of knowledge: but *fools despise wisdom and instruction.*

Proverbs 9:10

The fear of the LORD is the beginning of wisdom: and the knowledge of the holy is understanding.

The fear of the Lord is **the beginning of knowledge**. If there is no fear of God and His judgements, then there is no reason to seek Him for forgiveness. This is the main goal of these false teachers, **to get people into the mindset that there is nothing to fear from God**, that God is only love, and that He will not let anyone go to hell; that He is merciful and is not to be feared. **Live the way that you want; nothing is wrong, so do as you please and God will take you to heaven when you die.** Wrong, wrong, wrong. These false teachers promise a liberty, a freedom from all the dos and don'ts the church teaches, and that **you can go to heaven through their wrong teachings**. God has set His law in the Holy Scriptures and to live otherwise is foolishness. We either **live by God's Word or we perish by God's Word**. The last part of this verse says, "for of whom a man is overcome, of the same is he brought in bondage." **Who do you serve, for you cannot serve two masters.**

Matthew 6:24

No man can serve two masters: for either he will hate the one, and love the other; or else he will hold to the one, and despise the other. Ye cannot serve God and mammon.

2 Peter 2:20-21

²⁰ For if after they have escaped the pollutions of the world
through the knowledge of the Lord and Saviour Jesus
Christ, they are again entangled therein, and overcome,
the latter end is worse with them than the beginning.
²¹ For it had been better for them not to have known the
way of righteousness, than, after they have known it, to
turn from the holy commandment delivered unto them.

These two verses teach a scriptural doctrine that most denominational groups refuse to accept. They hold to the doctrine that **once you are saved you are forever saved**. They teach that a man can and does from time to time backslide, but **even if he dies in a backslidden condition that his soul will still go to heaven**. Here I must say I believe they are very, very wrong in their belief, and I am going to present scripture to back up my position. I believe that **people who trust in eternal salvation do so to cover up the lives they live**. I personally know of people who sin, do much evil, and say **they are all right because they are saved**.

The church of today and even in the past goes by a double standard. An example is this: The Bible, God's Word, says **all liars are going to hell.** The church preaches that **lying is a sin**. Yet **when professing Christians lie, it seems to be ok**. If the Word says all liars, then what is the **difference between sinners who are liars and Christians who are liars**? Again, we look at drunkards. The scripture says that **drunkards are going to hell**. The church teaches that **sinners who are drunkards are going to hell**, but the **Christians who are drunkards will go to heaven**. This makes no sense. Sin is sin, regardless of who commits it. Does not the scripture say that **God is no respecter of persons**? Let us look at

304

what the scripture says about sin and those who commit it. First, let us look at what Ezekiel has to say.

Ezekiel 18:24-32

> *24 But when the righteous turneth away from his righteousness, and committeth iniquity, and doeth according to all the abominations that the wicked man doeth, shall he live? All his righteousness that he hath done shall not be mentioned: in his trespass that he hath trespassed, and in his sin that he hath sinned, in them shall he die.*
> *25 Yet ye say, The way of the Lord is not equal. Hear now, O house of Israel; Is not my way equal? are not your ways unequal?*
> *26 When a righteous man turneth away from his righteousness, and committeth iniquity, and dieth in them; for his iniquity that he hath done shall he die.*
> *27 Again, when the wicked man turneth away from his wickedness that he hath committed, and doeth that which is lawful and right, he shall save his soul alive.*
> *28 Because he considereth, and turneth away from all his transgressions that he hath committed, he shall surely live, he shall not die.*
> *29 Yet saith the house of Israel, The way of the Lord is not equal. O house of Israel, are not my ways equal? are not your ways unequal?*
> *30 Therefore I will judge you, O house of Israel, every one according to his ways, saith the Lord GOD. Repent, and turn yourselves from all your transgressions; so iniquity shall not be your ruin.*

31 Cast away from you all your transgressions, whereby ye have transgressed; and make you a new heart and a new spirit: for why will ye die, O house of Israel?
32 For I have no pleasure in the death of him that dieth, saith the Lord GOD: wherefore turn yourselves, and live ye.

Now comes the pat answer: "That was **in the Old Testament**. We are living under the New Testament. We are living **under grace, now, not the law**." I contend that the same principles in the Old Testament are **carried over into the New Testament**. We are not living under the Law of Moses. These scriptures in Ezekiel are not part of the Law of Moses. They are part of **God's law on how people are to serve Him and live for Him**. But let us look at what the New Testament has to say on the subject.

Matthew 7:21-22

21 Not every one that saith unto me, Lord, Lord, shall enter into the kingdom of heaven; but he that doeth the will of my Father which is in heaven.
22 Many will say to me in that day, Lord, Lord, have we not prophesied in thy name? and in thy name have cast out devils? and in thy name done many wonderful works?,

Matthew 24:11-22

11 And many false prophets shall rise, and shall deceive many.
12 And because iniquity shall abound, the love of many shall wax cold.
13 But he that shall endure unto the end, the same shall be

saved.

14 And this gospel of the kingdom shall be preached in all the world for a witness unto all nations; and then shall the end come.

15 When ye therefore shall see the abomination of desolation, spoken of by Daniel the prophet, stand in the holy place, (whoso readeth, let him understand:)

16 Then let them which be in Judaea flee into the mountains:

17 Let him which is on the housetop not come down to take any thing out of his house:

18 Neither let him which is in the field return back to take his clothes.

19 And woe unto them that are with child, and to them that give suck in those days!

20 But pray ye that your flight be not in the winter, neither on the sabbath day:

21 For then shall be great tribulation, such as was not since the beginning of the world to this time, no, nor ever shall be.

22 And except those days should be shortened, there should no flesh be saved: but for the elect's sake those days shall be shortened.

Matthew 25:1-12

1 Then shall the kingdom of heaven be likened unto ten virgins, which took their lamps, and went forth to meet the bridegroom.

2 And five of them were wise, and five were foolish.

3 They that were foolish took their lamps, and took no oil with them:

4 But the wise took oil in their vessels with their lamps.

5 While the bridegroom tarried, they all slumbered and slept.

6 And at midnight there was a cry made, Behold, the bridegroom cometh; go ye out to meet him.

7 Then all those virgins arose, and trimmed their lamps.

8 And the foolish said unto the wise, Give us of your oil; for our lamps are gone out.

9 But the wise answered, saying, Not so; lest there be not enough for us and you: but go ye rather to them that sell, and buy for yourselves.

10 And while they went to buy, the bridegroom came; and they that were ready went in with him to the marriage: and the door was shut.

11 Afterward came also the other virgins, saying, Lord, Lord, open to us.

12 But he answered and said, Verily I say unto you, I know you not.

Here in Matthew, we find **three examples of how a person can be saved, backslide, and lose their salvation**. The story of the ten virgins is a type of the church at the time of the rapture. It is important to notice the following:

(1) They were **all virgins or born-again Christians**.
(2) Not all Christians are the same. Of these ten, five were wise in the Lord and His Word. The other five were like a lot of Christians today, **saved but not rooted and established or grounded in the Lord** like they truly need to be. They are saved, but they like the Hebrews of Moses' day; they still remember the leeks and onions of

Egypt.

(3) These virgins went forth to meet the bridegroom. They all had their lamps, and all their lamps were burning. The difference was the **wise carried extra oil for their lamps**.

There are many in the church today **who live for the now**. Their minds are on today. They are **not preparing for the future**. When the time came, and the cry went out, the foolish virgins found they had **not taken the necessary steps to be fully ready and thus were locked outside**. Then those final words were spoken by the Master, "Verily I say unto you, I know you not." He did not say I never knew you. He said **I know you not**. As we look at these ten, they were all the same, virgins. They were all pure; they were **all saved, born again**. They all had their lamps burning, which tells us that **the light, the spirit of God burned in them all**.

The difference showed itself as they all waited for the bridegroom. **Five of them let their lives grow cold and indifferent.** They lost that burning light of God's spirit, and their spiritual lights went out. Serving God is a **day-to-day walk with Him**. What we did yesterday, what we were yesterday is gone. Only **what we are today counts**. We cannot live on yesterday's blessings, on yesterday's salvation; the question is where we are with God today. God does not judge us on where we stood yesterday and the days before. What He judges us on is **where we stand now, today**. We cannot stand on the past, because it is gone.

Next let us look to the book of Luke and read what the scriptures say there.

Luke 8:11-14

[11] Now the parable is this: The seed is the word of God.

12 Those by the way side are they that hear; then cometh the devil, and taketh away the word out of their hearts, lest they should believe and be saved.

13 They on the rock are they, which, when they hear, receive the word with joy; and these have no root, which for a while believe, and in time of temptation fall away.

14 And that which fell among thorns are they, which, when they have heard, go forth, and are choked with cares and riches and pleasures of this life, and bring no fruit to perfection.

Luke 9:62

And Jesus said unto him, No man, having put his hand to the plough, and looking back, is fit for the kingdom of God.

Luke 11:24-26

24 When the unclean spirit is gone out of a man, he walketh through dry places, seeking rest; and finding none, he saith, I will return unto my house whence I came out.

25 And when he cometh, he findeth it swept and garnished.

26 Then goeth he, and taketh to him seven other spirits more wicked than himself; and they enter in, and dwell there: and the last state of that man is worse than the first.

As we look at what these scriptures say, we must realize that **salvation is given to whosoever will accept it**. Then after we are saved, **it is up to us, you and I, to nurture what God has given**. If we do not nurture this salvation, then it will slip away, and we will lose what God has given. This idea that at salvation our souls are set aside, and regardless of how we live or what we do, our soul is forever saved, is **misguided and wrong**. If sin condemns our soul before we are saved, then **it will also condemn our souls** after we are saved.

There are many today who are backslidden and away from God, living ungodly lives. Yet because of what they have been taught about eternal salvation, **they firmly believe they will still go to heaven**. One woman made the statement that she could be in bed committing adultery, and if Jesus came, she would still go to heaven, because **she had been saved years before**. What is the difference between a sinner committing adultery and a person who claims to be saved committing adultery? **The answer is none.** Sin is still sin, and **whoever is committing it will go to hell unless they repent** and ask for forgiveness. This teaching of eternal security gives many the false illusion that they can sin without any condemnation being laid upon them. Jesus, Himself, said, **"No man, having put his hand to the plough, and looking back is fit for the kingdom of God."** People, we are responsible for our actions, and when we are wrong, we will pay the price.

Galatians 1:6

I marvel that ye are so soon removed from him that called you into the grace of Christ unto another gospel:

Galatians 4:9

But now, after that ye have known God, or rather are known of God, how turn ye again to the weak and beggarly elements, whereunto ye desire again to be in bondage?

I Timothy 4:1-2

> *¹ Now the Spirit speaketh expressly, that in the latter times some shall depart from the faith, giving heed to seducing spirits, and doctrines of devils;*
> *² Speaking lies in hypocrisy; having their conscience seared with a hot iron;*

Over and over we find scriptures that speak of individuals departing from the faith. The mainstream denominational churches **try to tell you they were never really saved**. This is a cheap copout or reason to explain their doctrinal beliefs. But the **truth of God's Word is still there**. One preacher I heard said that at salvation, Christ's blood covers the sins of the past, the present, and the future, and **we do not have to do anything else**. I agree, in part, that at salvation, **Jesus' blood covers all the sins we have committed**.

I have heard people say over and over that I am just a sinner saved by grace, and this statement makes me realize **they do not understand God's Word**. Our testimony should be, "I used to be a sinner, but today I am saved by grace." The scripture teaches us that **we can be perfect because our Savior and King is perfect as God is perfect**. Matthew 5:48 gives us the words of Jesus: *"Be ye therefore perfect, even as your Father which is in heaven is perfect."* In John 17:20-26, we read the words of Jesus telling that He, Jesus, dwells **in the hearts and souls of believers**. Verse 23 tells us in Jesus' words that He becomes part of us by **making us perfect through Him**.

John 17:23

I in them, and thou in me, that they may be made perfect in one; and that the world may know that thou hast sent me, and hast loved them, as thou hast loved me.

We will never be perfect in the eyes of man, for man always looks for fault, but these scriptures tell us that **we can be perfect in and through Jesus Christ** and our Father, God. In I John 2:1, we read these words:

I John 2:1

My little children, these things write I unto you, that ye sin not. And if any man sin, we have an advocate with the Father, Jesus Christ the righteous:

Here, John tells us not to sin but if, and if is a small word with a huge meaning, we do sin, we can **go back to Jesus and ask Him to forgive us of the sin that we have committed**, whereby we can stay in the grace and presence of God.

2 Corinthians 13:11

Finally, brethren, farewell. Be perfect, be of good comfort, be of one mind, live in peace; and the God of love and peace shall be with you.

Here in 2 Corinthians, we see where **the Bible tells us to be perfect**.

Ephesians 4:11-13

[11] *And he gave some, apostles; and some, prophets; and*

some, evangelists; and some, pastors and teachers;
¹² For the perfecting of the saints, for the work of the ministry, for the edifying of the body of Christ:
¹³ Till we all come in the unity of the faith, and of the knowledge of the Son of God, unto a perfect man, unto the measure of the stature of the fullness of Christ:

Ephesians tells us that we are given pastors, teachers, and evangelists **for the perfecting of the saints that we may be perfect**. In two places in the book of Colossians, it also speaks of how the saints **are to be perfect before God**.

Colossians 1:28

Whom we preach, warning every man, and teaching every man in all wisdom; that we may present every man perfect in Christ Jesus:

Colossians 4:12

Epaphras, who is one of you, a servant of Christ, saluteth you, always laboring fervently for you in prayers, that ye may stand perfect and complete in all the will of God.

2 Timothy 3:16-17

¹⁶ All scripture is given by inspiration of God, and is profitable for doctrine, for reproof, for correction, for instruction in righteousness:
¹⁷ That the man of God may be perfect, thoroughly furnished unto all good works.

314

To the child of God, the believer, these scriptures should not be overlooked; we **do not have to sin every day**; that is a lie of the devil.

Ezekiel 18:24

> *But when the righteous turneth away from his righteousness, and committeth iniquity, and doeth according to all the abominations that the wicked man doeth, shall he live? All his righteousness that he hath done shall not be mentioned: in his trespass that he hath trespassed, and in his sin that he hath sinned, in them shall he die.*

Going back to un-repented sin will condemn souls to hell. The power of God through Jesus that saved us from sin, if we fall, **can restore us if we ask for forgiveness**. In I John 2:1, *"we have an advocate with the Father, Jesus Christ the righteous."* In these Bible studies, you will find that I repeat myself over and over. Why? Because I want you to know that **to serve God, we must daily take care of our salvation if we are to make heaven our home**. I was asked, "But what if you're wrong?" If I am wrong, I have not lost anything. I am still on my way to heaven. But my question to you is **what if I am right and you are wrong**? Then you have missed heaven.

I Timothy 4:1-2

> *[1] Now the Spirit speaketh expressly, that in the latter times some shall depart from the faith, giving heed to seducing spirits, and doctrines of devils;*
> *[2] Speaking lies in hypocrisy; having their conscience seared*

with a hot iron;)

We find that in later times, some will depart from the faith, backslide, or **go back into the world of sin**. Are these still saved? The answer is no, not unless they **return to Jesus and ask for forgiveness**. When a person walks away from God, **they leave God's grace and protection, and they are on their own**. If they never come back to God, then they have lost everything, **including their soul to the devil**. It is time for the church world to wake up, to realize the times we are living in, to preach that **we must live for God now, that yesterday is gone, and that what we had yesterday is gone**. The only time God looks at yesterday is when a saint dies and goes home. Then what he or she did yesterday helps determine their reward.

Hebrews 10:38-39

> [38] *Now the just shall live by faith: but if any man draw back, my soul shall have no pleasure in him.*
> [39] *But we are not of them who draw back unto perdition; but of them that believe to the saving of the soul.*

Here the writer tells us **the just shall live by faith**, but there will be those who will **draw back or backslide**. The scripture says, "back unto perdition or sin," and we know that the devil is called the son of perdition. **Sin condemns, grace sets free.** We cannot be both; **we are either saved or lost**. We cannot be both saved and backslidden at the same time.

Revelation 2:4-5

> [4] *Nevertheless I have somewhat against thee, because thou*

hast left thy first love.
⁵ Remember therefore from whence thou art fallen, and repent, and do the first works; or else I will come unto thee quickly, and will remove thy candlestick out of his place, except thou repent.

In verse four, Jesus was speaking to the church of Ephesus. But what is the church made up of? People, individuals, they are the church. So, we see here that **Jesus is talking to people**. Here Jesus is talking to the people **still going to church**. What does this have to do with backsliders and those who have left the church? It shows that **it is possible to be backslidden and still be sitting on the pew**. We are talking about losing your salvation, and here, Jesus **condemns those who have left their first love**. That love is the love we find when we first get saved. Jesus tells the people to remember where they have fallen from and **to repent or be removed forever from the presence of God**. People, this is extremely serious, and there are multitudes of souls at stake. We must pray as never before that **God will open blinded eyes to the truth before it is too late**. The eternal judgement will be worse for a soul that once knew the saving power of Jesus Christ and then turned away.

Revelations 3:5

He that overcometh, the same shall be clothed in white raiment; and I will not blot out his name out of the book of life, but I will confess his name before my Father, and before his angels.

In this verse, we see a basic simple truth: *"he that overcometh, the same shall be clothed in white raiment."* This is

317

the promise of God. Yet there is **another promise right under that**, and that promise is overlooked by almost everyone. What does this mean? It is very simple. When we get saved, our name is recorded in that great book of life. However, when we walk away from God and go our own way, **our names are blotted out of that book, the book of life.**

Revelations 3:15-16

15 I know thy works, that thou art neither cold nor hot: I would thou wert cold or hot
16 So then because thou art lukewarm, and neither cold nor hot, I will spue thee out of my mouth.

The question is this: Are you hot, are you passionate about God, or **are you lukewarm, to be cast away or spued away from God's presence**? Judge yourselves before you stand before God.

2 Peter 2:21

For it had been better for them not to have known the way of righteousness, than, after they have known it, to turn from the holy commandment delivered unto them.

This verse sums up everything. It is far better for a person to have **never known the truths of God's Word, to have never known the divine presence and touch of the Lord in our souls.** Because once we have felt that presence and power of God, our lives will **never be the same.** Then for a person to leave the divine and be drawn back into those weak, beggarly elements of worldly lust and pleasures is a travesty before God, for which **that soul will pay dearly**.

2 Peter 2:22

But it is happened unto them according to the true proverb, The dog is turned to his own vomit again; and the sow that was washed to her wallowing in the mire.

This verse paints a picture of **how bad it is for a person to walk away from God**. There is a song which I have not heard sung in over thirty years called *Standing Outside*. Where are you standing?

Songs We Sing Complete:

> 1. Judgement is surly coming.
> Coming to you and me,
> We will be judged that morning
> For all eternity;
> Some will go into Heaven,
> Others will be denied:
> Will you be in that number
> Standing outside?
>
> Chorus: Standing outside the portals,
> Standing outside denied,
> Knowing that with the demons
> Ever you shall abide;
> Never to share the beauties,
> Waiting the sanctified,
> O what an awful picture,

Standing outside.

2. Standing outside while loved ones,
Enter the pearly gate,
Knowing that there forever,
You will then separate;
To be away from loved ones
And by God denied:
O what an awful picture,
Standing outside.

3. Can you not see the picture
Of those who're lost in sin,
Standing outside the portals,
Without a hope to win?
Souls crushed with deepest sorrow,
Without a friend to guide?
O what an awful picture
Standing outside.

Chapter 2 Review Questions

1. For everything that God has the devil has a _____

_____?

2. Peter, in verse one, warns that there would be what among the

people? _____

_____

3. The Mormons believe the same lie that Satan used with Eve

and Adam in the garden, and that lie is? _____

_____

4. The Catholic Church worships Mary and puts her on an equal

_____

5. What is Polytheism? _____

_____

6. One of Hitler's spokesman made what statement about truth?

_____

_____

7. What is sin? _____

_____

8. Where did sin originate? _____

_____

9. How many of the angels were cast out of heaven with Lucifer?

_____

10. What other cities besides Sodom and Gomorrah were

destroyed on the plain? _____

_____

11. In verse eleven what important lesson is Peter trying to teach

us? _____

_____

12. In this fourteenth verse, how does Peter describe these

apostates? _____

_____

13. What is the only way that a person can cease from sin?

_____

14. Of the seven church ages, which ones are we living in today?

_____

_____

15. The church today is only a _____ of what it

    used to be.

16. What is one of the hardest things for a person to admit?

    _____

17. The scripture tells us the fear of the Lord is the beginning of

    _____.

18. No man can serve two _____.

19. In verses 20-21, we find a scriptural doctrine which goes

    against what most denominations teach their people. What is

    this false Doctrine? _____

    _____

20. What does Ezekiel 18:24 say happens when a righteous man

    turns away from his righteousness and commits sin?

    _____

    _____

21. Does what we did and were before we gave our lives to God,

    make a difference when God judges a backslider?

    _____

22. In I Timothy 1-2, the scripture tells us that in later times some shall depart from the faith. Do you believe that we are living in those later times? _____

23. In the book of Revelation, Jesus speaks of a first love explain what is he talking about? _____

_____

24. Do you believe after reading these past scriptures, and what I have said, that a person's name can be blotted out of the book of life? _____

25. When a Christian becomes lukewarm in their salvation, what happens to them? _____

_____

26. Do you believe in the doctrine, once you are saved you are forever saved? Explain. _____

_____

Chapter 3

¹ This second epistle, beloved, I now write unto you; in
both *which I stir up your pure minds by way of*
remembrance:
² That ye may be mindful of the words which were spoken
before by the holy prophets, and of the commandment of
us the apostles of the Lord and Saviour:
³ Knowing this first, that there shall come in the last days
scoffers, walking after their own lusts,
⁴ And saying, Where is the promise of his coming? for
since the fathers fell asleep, all things continue as they
were *from the beginning of the creation.*

Peter in the first verse tells us why he has written this second epistle. For, you see, it is needful for us from time to time to be **put in remembrance of things that are important to us**. What can be of more importance than the gospel of our Lord Jesus Christ? This is why the scriptures teach us **not to forsake the assembling of ourselves together**. This is why going to church is so vital to the child of God. Sunday school teaches us the Word of God, and the song service is a time of praise and worship of our Lord. The preaching of the Word is to **bring to our remembrance the things we have learned,** to instruct and remind us on how we are to live **an upright life before God and how we should present ourselves before the world** in a way that promotes the love and joy Christians should possess.

The world has fallen for the devil's trickery. The world thinks Christians **never have any fun or pleasure, that we are mind-robbed or mindless robots.** This could not be further from the truth. Yes, we teach that sex is reserved for the marriage bed and that getting drunk is a moral sin. In all my years, I do not know of any person who got drunk, that the next day they **did not regret doing so.** In fact, I worked with a man who told me time and time again that he hated to see the weekend come because **he knew he was going to get drunk.** I told him he could stop, but **he had to want to.** If we want something from the Lord, we must **ask and show God that we are serious.** The way we do this is to **learn God's Word, pray and seek his face.** As we commit God's Word into our memory, as David said, it **becomes a light unto our path.**

Psalm 119:105

Thy word is a lamp unto my feet, and a light unto my path.

Yet still from time to time, we must have our pure minds stirred **lest we forget and fall back into slackness.** Verse two states, "That ye may be mindful of the words which were spoken by the holy prophets." Why? Because we, as mortal humans, if we are not careful, **begin to take things for granted.** As Americans, we take for granted our freedom of religion and our freedom of speech, not realizing that **our freedoms are being taken away**

every day. It is sad to think of what is happening in America today, and **not just here, but all around the world**.

The freedom to worship is slipping away. As the scripture tells us, there are many today **saying we have heard all of this and it has not happened yet**. However, I say unto you that it is going to happen, and **it will not be long**. Jesus is coming back, and the church needs to get ready, because **the church as a whole is not ready for Christ to return**. The commandment of the apostles was this: Jesus is the Son of God, the sacrifice for sin. Seek His face, and repent of your sin, because **He is coming back to catch the believers away and take them to heaven to live with Him forever**.

In verses three and four, God's Word tells us that the way we will know when Jesus' coming is nigh **is to look at what is going on around us**.

Verse three tells us that "in the last days scoffers" shall come "walking after their own lusts." We have never seen, nor has there ever been a time like today. Preachers **ridicule the Word of God**. They say **the apostles should be publicly shamed for what they wrote in the Bible**. Preachers in public say that **they do not believe the whole Bible**.

Now preachers are calling for the Bible to be re-written, to **do away with everything in the Bible that names sin and talks about hell being a real place**. They want a Bible where nothing is sin, and if you want to do it, do it. Nothing is wrong. What they truly want **is a state of anarchy like it was before the flood, before the law of God was given**. If Satan could achieve this, he could condemn the total of humanity, but Satan forgets that **God will always have a remnant that will serve Him**.

Already much of the church is asking where the promise of His coming is. We have heard of it for years, and the church has preached it for hundreds of years. Surely, it must be a fable, just a lie preached and taught for so long that people accept it as truth.

Saints, do not give up hope and belief, because **we are near to the coming of the Lord**. Ask yourself this question, why would people be turning away from God and His Word? Could it be because **they want to live a sinful life**? If they can do away with God's Word, they think **they can escape God's condemnation of their sins**.

Peter makes it very plain in the Word that times like these will come but **be not dismayed. God is still on the throne.** For some reason, **people, preachers, teachers and church leaders have decided that if your lifestyle goes against God's Holy Word and the scriptures, then the only thing left to do is to change the Word of God**. They forget what Revelation says in chapter 22.

Revelation 22:18-19

> [18] *For I testify unto every man that heareth the words of the prophecy of this book, If any man shall add unto these things, God shall add unto him the plagues that are written in this book:*
> [19] *And if any man shall take away from the words of the book of this prophecy, God shall take away his part out of the book of life, and out of the holy city, and from the things which are written in this book.*

As we read these words, it should be plain that **God demands that His Word not be changed**. We are not to add anything, nor are we to take anything away from God's divinely inspired Word. To do so is to bring damnation to one's soul. When

328

we look around us, we see God's Word being changed every day. There are now nearly two hundred different versions of the Bible, and I can tell you that **they all read differently, meaning something was changed**. The answer I get is, well, we are making it easier to understand. The meaning is still the same; we have just changed the words. However, **change is still change, and change is forbidden**. There will be a lot of people who stand guilty on judgement day. People desire to follow the fleshly lust of this world and **still be told they are all right with God**. The number is getting greater every day. Men have become scoffers.

The John Phillips Commentary Series – Exploring the Epistles of Peter:

> Those scoffers have arrived. In 1982, the June issue of *Atlantic Monthly* devoted its cover and its leading article to ridiculing those who believe in the second coming of Christ. The article was by William Martin and was titled, "Waiting for the End." The cover depicted a fussy little man dressed in a poorly tailored blue suit, with a Bible tucked under his arm, impatiently pointing to his watch. Coming toward him was an army of giant locusts.

It is now over thirty years since this article, and the scoffers have multiplied many times over. However, it does not change a thing, because **Jesus is still going to come**.

2 Peter 3:5-7

⁵ For this they willingly are ignorant of, that by the word

of God the heavens were of old, and the earth standing out
of the water and in the water:
⁶ Whereby the world that then was, being overflowed with
water, perished:
⁷ But the heavens and the earth, which are now, by the
same word are kept in store, reserved unto fire against the
day of judgment and perdition of ungodly men.

Peter begins in verse five by speaking about **people being willingly ignorant**.

The Wiersbe Bible Commentary (NT):

> "Everybody is ignorant," said Will Rogers, "only on different subjects."
>
> How true, and yet that is not the whole story because there is more than one kind of ignorance. Some people are ignorant because of lack of opportunity to learn, or perhaps lack of ability to learn; others are (to use Peter's phrase in 2 Peter 3:5) "willingly ... ignorant." "Not ignorance, but ignorance of ignorance, is the death of knowledge," said a famous philosopher, and he is right.

There are two opinions on these three scriptures as to what is being referred to. The first opinion we will look at is the one most generally accepted. This opinion **says these three scriptures refer to the creation of the world in Genesis**. We know the account of creation in Genesis chapter one **is true just as recorded**. In the beginning, the earth was without form and void, and darkness was upon the face of the deep. Then God made the land to appear, and then the plants appeared. Then God made the animals, birds, and fish. Then he made man. He took the dust of the ground and formed man.

Here is where the creation of man differs from all the rest. For God **breathed into his nostrils the breath of life**, and man became a living soul. We know that mankind as a whole turned their backs upon God. However, **God has always and will always have a people that will serve Him**. Sometimes they may become few as in the days of Noah, but **God will have a people**.

Scripture tells us that God spoke to Noah to build an ark because **He was going to destroy man**. It took Noah one hundred and twenty years of preaching and working on the ark. Just think, this man **preached every chance he could while building the ark**, and for one hundred and twenty years **he had no converts**. The one thing that he truly had was **faith, a deep-down conviction that God was going to do exactly what He said he would**. Scripture says that Noah preached until time to enter the ark. As Noah and his family entered the ark after the animals, scripture states that **God shut them in**.

Genesis 7:13-16

> *13 In the selfsame day entered Noah, and Shem, and Ham, and Japheth, the sons of Noah, and Noah's wife, and the three wives of his sons with them, into the ark;*
> *14 They, and every beast after his kind, and all the cattle after their kind, and every creeping thing that creepeth upon the earth after his kind, and every fowl after his kind, every bird of every sort.*
> *15 And they went in unto Noah into the ark, two and two of all flesh, wherein is the breath of life.*

[16]And they that went in, went in male and female of all flesh, as God had commanded him: and the LORD shut him in.

All these scriptures, I believe with all my heart, **are true, just as everything the Bible says is true**. I also believe that the next time this world is to be destroyed, it will be **destroyed by fire just as God's Word records**.

However, there are questions the Bible alludes to but does not answer. The question that I would like to put before you is this: **Is there any basis for the belief that there was a Pre-Adamite world which was destroyed by water?**

When we look at these three scriptures, is there a double meaning in them, just as there are in other scriptures? Some Bible scholars believe there is, and if so, **it would explain a multitude of questions**. Questions about the fossil records that are being found on a daily basis. About innocent people from thousands of years ago. The Bible's recorded history is only some seven thousand years. **What of fossil records tens of thousands of years old, or fossil records of millions of years ago.** Are all these fake?

This belief that the world was made and destroyed before the creation in Genesis holds some merit. This would also answer many of today questions by science. **Science tells us that the world is millions of years old.** The church says that the world is something over **seven thousand years old**. How long Adam and Eve were in the garden **we have no way of knowing**. We know that Adam was about nine hundred and fifty years old when he died. The question is this, **was his age recorded from the time that he was created, or did it begin the day that they were expelled from the garden?** Some say it was from the day that he was created, some from the time that he was cast out of the garden. Remember, too, that **God does not count time as we do**. For with

332

the Lord a day could be a thousand years and a thousand years could be as a day. We have no way of knowing for sure the answers to these questions. So, mine or your opinion is as good as anyone else's.

Now back to the question, was there a pre-Adamite world that was destroyed by water before Genesis? **There is some basis for this belief.** We will never know the answer until we get to heaven, and then it will not matter, anyway. However, as we look at these three verses, does it refer to a world that existed before the Genesis creation? In the King James Version, Genesis 1:28, God tells Adam and Eve to **multiply and replenish the earth**. Now the question is how you can replenish the earth if it was not first plenished, or had people there at some time before.

My Hebrew translation says to fill the earth, but I also know that **not all Hebrew translations read the same**. It depends on who does the translation. Whether you believe in a pre-Adamite world or not; it **does not change the Word of God**. From Genesis to Revelation, God's Word is true. The reason I am including this point of view is to try to **give you a well-rounded look at the Word and what some people believe**.

I will be using mostly the *Dake Bible* because it is the most informational source I have at this time. There are articles on the web you can pull up on your computer but be very careful. Some of these articles go **into the realm of science fiction, without any biblical basis**. Therefore, let us look at *Dake's Annotated Reference Bible*.

The Dake Annotated Reference Bible KJV:

1. Two social systems are mentioned here by Peter: one was <u>before</u>, the one <u>which is now</u>, and the other, <u>after</u> the one <u>that then was</u> (v 6-7).

2. The former social system was created "In the beginning" and was destroyed by the flood of Genesis 1:1-2. The present social system was created in 6 days since the flood of Geneses 1:2 (Gen. 1:3-2:25).

The belief here is that **the world was not totally destroyed by the flood of Noah's day**, because Noah and his family were saved by the ark; also the animals were not destroyed, because like Noah, they were safe in the Ark. **If there was a pre-Adamite world that God destroyed, then everything was destroyed.** There was nothing left, not one surviving thing. We have looked at 2 Peter 3: 5-7, and now we will look at Jeremiah 4:23-26.

Jeremiah 4:23-26

> [23] *I beheld the earth, and, lo, it was without form, and void; and the heavens, and they had no light.*
> [24] *I beheld the mountains, and, lo, they trembled, and all the hills moved lightly.*
> [25] *I beheld, and, lo, there was no man, and all the birds of the heavens were fled.*
> [26] *I beheld, and, lo, the fruitful place was a wilderness, and all the cities thereof were broken down at the presence of the LORD, and by his fierce anger.*

As we look at these scriptures, **there is no reference to any change made in the heavens in the flood of Noah's day**. *Dakes* and others say that:

The Dake Annotated Reference Bible KJV:

This proves that the world that then was had to

334

be before Adams' day because the heavens and the earth, <u>which are now</u> come into existence at that time and not at the time of Noah.

As we read in Genesis chapter one, that **dry land did not appear until verse nine**. If we look at Jeremiah 4:23-26, we see in verse twenty-three that the earth *"was without form, and void; and the heavens, and they had no light."* In verse twenty-four, **the mountains trembled and the hills moved lightly**. Verse twenty-five, *"I beheld, and, lo, there was no man, and all the birds"* had all fled or gone. Verse twenty-six, *"the fruitful place was a wilderness, and all of the cities were broken down"* or **destroyed by the fierce anger of the Lord**.

As we look at what is said, we must conclude that **the only time that the earth was without form and void was before the Genesis creation**. Theory is that at the fall of Lucifer the world was thrown into chaos. Sin and evil prevailed, and at this point, **God utterly destroyed the earth and everything concerned with the world**. The world was left in darkness without any light.

We know the flood of Noah's day did not destroy everything. Yes, sinful mankind was destroyed, but **not all of mankind, because of Noah and his family**. Some of the animals were not destroyed, because **God made provision for them in the ark**.

The sun and moon also were not destroyed. So, were Peter and Jeremiah speaking of a pre-Adamite world that once existed and was then destroyed by God before the Genesis creation? I will leave you to pray about it and see what God leads you to believe.

In the scope of the Bible, every verse, chapter, and book are one hundred percent true. It holds no mistakes. Then why bring in the possibly of a pre-Adamite world? Because I **do not want you**

to be taken unaware. If there was or wasn't a pre-Adamite world, it doesn't change one thing about God's Word or our salvation. However, I desire to **give you as full a picture of scripture as I can**.

Be led by the spirit of God, for God will lead you into all truths. If you keep your mind on God, it will surprise you what God will reveal. Do not allow yourselves to be led off track by the enemy, because he will if he can. **Pray and study, seek God's will for your lives, and hold to God's unchanging hand.**

2 Peter 3:7

But the heavens and the earth, which are now, by the same word are kept in store, reserved unto fire against the day of judgment and perdition of ungodly men.

I would like to point out this verse because it carries a **dire warning to men and women today, more than ever before**. Because the Lord's return is closer than ever before, Peter speaks of the heavens and the earth, which is now, that will **one day be destroyed**. Scripture states that **this world is kept in store, or it is reserved unto fire for a coming day of judgement**, a judgement of all the sinful men that have ever lived from the beginning of creation.

Will this world be destroyed by nuclear power? No. There may be a nuclear war, but it **will not destroy the world**. What does God have in store for man in the future? We have a rapture to take place. The world faces a tribulation period. Then the triumphant return of Jesus Christ to **rule the world through a thousand years of peace**. After this comes a war with evil one last time. Then comes the final judgement and **the world being destroyed by fire.**

We can truly say that **sin has left its permanent mark upon this world as well as in heaven**. You may ask why in heaven. Yes, even in heaven. Contrary to what many may believe, sin did not originate with Adam and Eve in the garden. It originated **in heaven with Lucifer when he rebelled against God and sought to replace God with himself.**

The John Phillips Commentary Series – Exploring the Epistles of Peter:

> The "Day of Judgment," which will be ushered in by the dissolution of the universe, has already been noted on God's calendar (Rev. 20:11). The day will coincide with the setting up of the Great White Throne, before which "ungodly men" will be arraigned on their way to perdition.
>
> The word for "perdition" (*apōleia*) can be rendered "destruction." The word is used of the doom of the sinner and is one of the strongest words in the Greek language to express the final and irreversible doom of the lost.

During this time, the world as we know it will be **destroyed by fire**, and in its place, **there will be a new heaven and a new earth**.

2 Peter 3:8-9

[8] But, beloved, be not ignorant of this one thing, that one day is with the Lord as a thousand years, and a thousand years as one day.

⁹ The Lord is not slack concerning his promise, as some men count slackness; but is longsuffering to us-ward, not willing that any should perish, but that all should come to repentance.

As we look at verse eight, it tells us one very important thing we need to remember. **God does not count time as we do.** The scripture says that to the Lord one day **could be as a thousand years or a thousand years could be counted as a single day.** On this scale of counting time, Jesus has only been gone away for two days since He returned to Heaven, but it is not important because **everything happens in God's time.** The one thing we must remember is that **God is not slack concerning his promise.** What God says, He will do. Rest assured He will do it.

One thing we need to be thankful for is that **God is longsuffering to us.** His mercy is from everlasting to everlasting. God's will is that **all men should come to repentance and be saved.** In God's mercy, God has given all men the opportunity to be saved but **He will not force men to accept Jesus as their savior.** The Word says all men <u>might</u> be saved, but **we must make that decision.**

2 Peter 3:10-13

¹⁰ But the day of the Lord will come as a thief in the night; in the which the heavens shall pass away with a great noise, and the elements shall melt with fervent heat, the earth also and the works that are therein shall be burned up.
¹¹ Seeing then that all these things shall be dissolved, what manner of persons ought ye to be in all holy conversation

and godliness,
¹² Looking for and hasting unto the coming of the day of
God, wherein the heavens being on fire shall be dissolved,
and the elements shall melt with fervent heat?
¹³ Nevertheless we, according to his promise, look for new
heavens and a new earth, wherein dwelleth righteousness.

Many preachers have used these scriptures thousands of times. Peter warns that Jesus is going to return **when we least expect Him**. We must be careful. We must be **vigilant always looking and waiting for the Lord's return**. This tenth verse speaks of the rapture of the church, when **Jesus shall come and catch away His waiting bride**. Then the verse next speaks of the end of time, a time when this world will come to an end. As scripture states, "the heavens shall pass away with a great noise, and the elements shall melt with fervent heat, the earth also and the works that are therein shall be burned up." The heavens shall come to an end, the skies, the heavens shall be destroyed, and then the earth. **All that God has created will be no more, gone forever.**

Some people believe this world will be destroyed by nuclear weapons, and I do not know why. **God needs no help from man.** All of this will take place after the thousand-year reign. God is well able to **destroy the world without man's help**. Just look at Sodom and Gomorrah and the cities of the plain. They were destroyed as fire fell from heaven. Even today, many scientists say it appears that they were destroyed by nuclear weapons. **God needs no help from man.** Besides, there will **be no people on earth at this time**. The saints will be in heaven with Jesus Christ. The sinners will be at the Great White Throne Judgment standing before God and giving an accounting of their lives and actions.

People, make no mistake. **God is no respecter of persons.**

Every person will be judged **according to their deeds**. In verse eleven, we read where Peter is trying to make people think about God and His judgments. Peter is saying to think, for heaven's sake, think, **if God is going to destroy this world because of sin and man's ungodly deeds, then what kind of a person should you be**? What manner or what kind of person will you be when the Lord returns? What manner of conversation do you use? Do you magnify and praise God with your speech? Do you show forth godliness? **Do you put forth a Christ-like example before this lost and dying world?** If God judged you today, what would He say? Let us examine ourselves now, so that when the day of Jesus' return comes, **there will be no guilt found in us**.

1 Corinthians 11:28

> But let a man examine himself, and so let him eat of that bread, and drink of that cup.

Let us look with anticipation for our Lord to come again and take us home to heaven. You see, to the child of God **there is given a promise**. That promise tells us that **we will inherit a home and that home will be upon a new earth which is overshadowed by a new heaven**. There will come down out of this new heaven a new city called the New Jerusalem. There will be **no more sadness, no pain, no sickness, for righteousness will reign there forever**. Child of God, look at what the world offers and then look at what God offers. Does it not make sense **to prepare for eternity, a time where the soul that now dwells in this mortal body will live on throughout the ceaseless ages of eternity**? Everyone is going to live forever. The only question is **where you are going to live**.

2 Peter 3:14

Wherefore, beloved, seeing that ye look for such things, be diligent that ye may be found of him in peace, without spot, and blameless.

Now Peter begins to make some final remarks that are of a more practical nature. If we will heed what he is saying, it will be to our benefit. **We cannot afford at this late date in time to play with the world and all the things the world has to offer.** The child of God lives in this world, but we **cannot be part of this world**. As the children of God, we must **ever be diligent looking for our savior to return**. It seems that the church, the believers, **ought to be doing everything in their power to make their calling and election sure.**

However, this is not the case. **The church should be expecting Jesus to return.** They are doing just the opposite. The church world as a whole is beginning to **turn its back upon the gospel**. The church is beginning to **change its doctrine from the truth of God's Word**. It is taking what scripture tells us is sin and removing those parts from their doctrine. Homosexuality, immoral sex (such as adultery), stealing, cursing, taking the Lord's name in vain, any kind of preaching that tells the truth of God's Word. **Anything that might offend or hurt someone's feelings is forbidden.**

They care more about public opinion than they do about the souls of the lost and dying. **The truth of God's Word will keep you in peace, without spot, and blameless.** In these last days, the Word tells us that **there will be a great falling away**. This falling away is not that everyone will stop going to church. It is the fact that men and women will **turn their backs upon the truth of the**

341

gospel. They will not stop going to church; they just **stop believing the Word**. They heap to themselves preachers and teachers to tell them what they want to hear. As the Gospel says, **they will be turned unto fables.**

2 Thessalonians 2:11-12

> [11] *And for this cause God shall send them strong delusion, that they should believe a lie:*
> [12] *That they all might be damned who believed not the truth, but had pleasure in unrighteousness.*

More scriptures of how people will turn from God:

2 Timothy 4:3-5

> [3] *For the time will come when they will not endure sound doctrine; but after their own lusts shall they heap to themselves teachers, having itching ears;*
> [4] *And they shall turn away their ears from the truth, and shall be turned unto fables.*
> [5] *But watch thou in all things, endure afflictions, do the work of an evangelist, make full proof of thy ministry.*

Keep your mind upon the Lord, watch for His returning, because **He is surely coming back.**

2 Peter 3:15

> *And account that the longsuffering of our Lord is salvation; even as our beloved brother Paul also*

according to the wisdom given unto him hath written unto you;

Peter stresses in this verse that the longsuffering of God is counted for salvation. Scripture tells the child of God that **we must learn patience. We must learn to wait upon the Lord.**

In *The John Phillips Commentary*, we find a quote from George Muller.

The John Phillips Commentary Series – Exploring the Epistles of Peter:

> I myself have for twenty-nine years been waiting for an answer to prayer concerning a certain spiritual blessing. Day by day have I been enabled to continue in prayer for this blessing. At home and abroad, in this country and in foreign lands, in health and in sickness, however much occupied, I have been enabled, day by day, by God's help, to bring this matter before Him; and still I have not the full answer yet. Nevertheless, I look for it. I expect it confidently. The very fact that day after day, and year after year, for twenty-nine years, the Lord has enabled me to continue, patiently, believingly, to wait on Him for the blessing, still further encourages me to wait on; and as fully am I assured that God hears me about this matter, that I have often been enabled to praise Him beforehand for the full answer, which I shall ultimately receive to my prayers on this subject. Thus, you see, dear reader,

that while I have hundreds, yea, thousands of answers, year by year, I have also, like yourself and other believers, the trial of faith concerning certain matters.

Why has God waited for so long to return? Maybe it is to give more souls the opportunity to find Him as their personal savior. I know there are **countless numbers of people who are praying for lost loved ones**; asking God to wait upon His coming so their loved ones might be saved. Truthfully, **the longer the Lord waits, the more can be saved**. Yet the longer the Lord waits, the more will backslide. Therefore, **we must trust God in all His wisdom to do what He considers to be right**.

In the last part of this verse, Peter refers to the writing or sayings of Paul. Paul, like Peter, was a preacher of the gospel. In fact, Paul wrote many of the books of the New Testament, with 13 attributed to him. **Paul was led by God to be the apostle to the Gentiles, to carry the message of the gospel.** We know the other apostles also went and preached to the Gentiles but very little is known of their work.

Paul, like Peter, preached the Lord's return. He preached that Christians must learn to be patient before the Lord, because **God moves in His own good time**. The one thing that is important to know is that **God is never early, but He also is never late**. He answers just in time. Read the Word and study the scriptures, for in them we find life everlasting through Jesus Christ our Lord. **Be patient, trust, believe, and see the hand of the Lord work.** Like Paul, Peter, James, John, and the others, believe, for as the Word says, all things are possible if we only believe.

2 Peter 3:16

As also in all his epistles, speaking in them of these things;
in which are some things hard to be understood, which
they that are unlearned and unstable wrest, as they do
also the other scriptures, unto their own destruction.

In this sixteenth verse, Peter is trying to address a problem that still exists even today. That problem is twofold. Looking at the first part of the problem, we see **false preachers and teachers who twist God's Word to make it say what they want it to say.** This has been going on since the time of the apostles. It started just after their epistles (letters) were written and then sent out to the churches.

Our enemy the devil is quick to twist and change the Word that we hear and read. This is why it is so important to study the Word, to know the Word. The psalmist David said in Psalms 119:11, *"Thy word have I hid in mine heart, that I might not sin against thee."* **If we are ignorant of God's Word, we will fall prey to the devil.** The occult looks for people who are not established in the Word of God because **it is easy to lead them astray.**

Then we have within the church liberal Bible scholars who try to say that there was much disagreement between the apostles. This is not true. **Peter and Paul believed the same thing, as did the other apostles.** They all believed the teachings of Jesus Christ our savior. The reason for these liberal scholars to say that Jesus and the apostles did not believe the same thing is so that they can denounce what the apostles wrote. **If they can make people believe this lie of the devil, they can take away what sin is and take away the teaching that sin demands punishment.**

If all you preach and teach is love, that there is no sin that should be punished, then **you destroy the fear of God.** If there is no fear of God, then **every man does what is right in his own sight**. But – and it is a big but – does not the scripture say that the fear of the Lord is the beginning of knowledge?

Proverbs 1:7

> *The fear of the LORD is the beginning of knowledge: but fools despise wisdom and instruction.*

Psalm 33:8

> *Let all the earth fear the LORD: let all the inhabitants of the world stand in awe of him.*

Psalm 34:9

> *O fear the LORD, ye his saints: for there is no want to them that fear him.*

Ecclesiastes 12:13-14

> [13] *Let us hear the conclusion of the whole matter: Fear God, and keep his commandments: for this is the whole duty of man.*
> [14] *For God shall bring every work into judgment, with every secret thing, whether it be good, or whether it be evil.*

These other verses tell us that **we are to fear the Lord**. If we fear the Lord, we will **come to him asking forgiveness and repenting,** and as we give ourselves to the Lord, **we learn the love of the Lord**. If you believe these liberal preachers and teachers who twist, change, and rewrite the gospel message to the degree that nothing is sin and that there is no hell, and that everybody goes to heaven, **you will stand before God with no answer to the question as to why you lived the life you did**.

You may ask why these liberals have decided to preach such a message. They do this to **placate (appease, conciliate) those who are around them**. To put it in the terms of the world, **you do not bite the hand that feeds you**. The only true message these liberals are saying is, **I do not love you enough to tell you the truth**.

I was taught by my dad that if **something sounds too good to be true then it usually is**. I have found this to be true. Anything worth having is worth working for. Salvation is the same. **It is freely given, but you have to work at it to keep it.**

The second part of the problem is the **believer's ability to understand the deep things of God's Word**. The best way I can express what I am saying is to **talk to you about finding gold**. When the gold fields of the United States were first discovered, **men found gold nuggets lying openly upon the ground**. To find more gold, men began panning for gold in streams and creeks, what we call prospecting. Then they **began looking for gold in the ground**. When it was found, **they began digging for it, mining deep into the earth**.

Searching God's Word is the same as looking for gold. We read the Word of God and behold, we find **precious nuggets of truth seemingly lying upon the surface**. The more we read and study, the more we pan from the truth of God's Word. As we begin to get hungrier for all that God has for us, we begin to mine for it, **digging deep into the Word to reveal the truth**, the presence of all that God has for us. However, no matter how long we study, we can **never reach the true fullness of God**.

Peter speaks of Paul's writings to the saints, and here Peter tells them that **some of the things Paul has written are going to be hard for them to understand**. Why? The two reasons Peter gives are because **some are unlearned in the Word and some are unstable in what they believe**.

The unstable person is a person who **does not know what they truly believe**. They are always second-guessing themselves and questioning whether they did the right thing or they said the right thing. Sadly, this type of person **will have a hard time making it into heaven**. The Word tells us to **learn the scriptures to stand on the scriptures, to accept what they say as fact**. If you are settled in the Word of God, you will not be unstable, but steadfast.

People who are unstable **are never happy for long**. The devil is always causing something to happen to keep them upset; their minds are in turmoil. Do not let the devil play with your mind. When trouble arises, **put it in God's hands and keep your hands out of it**. When we try to fill in for God, we make matters worse. We think we know what should be done; however, we do not. We need to **let God take care of it, and all will be well**.

Why will an unstable person have a hard time making heaven? Because **to serve God we must be of a settled mind** when it comes to God's Word. Those who are unstable **let the devil bring torment into their minds and hearts**. They become filled with fear; fear hath torments; and **fear will cause you to not trust in God**. The only way to have peace is to have our minds rooted and grounded upon the Word of God. **We must first and foremost put the Lord in total control.** When we totally surrender control to the Lord, we can, with confidence, **bring all our trials, burdens, and cares to the Lord knowing that God knows how to handle all our cares**. Scripture tells us to submit ourselves unto the Lord; to rebuke the devil and **he will flee from us**.

James 4:7-8

> *⁷ Submit yourselves therefore to God. Resist the devil, and he will flee from you.*
> *⁸ Draw nigh to God, and he will draw nigh to you. Cleanse your hands, ye sinners; and purify your hearts, ye double minded.*

Peter was trying to tell the saints that they would find things in the scriptures which would be hard to understand. Paul taught upon things that they would not understand without searching the scriptures.

The John Phillips Commentary Series – Exploring the Epistles of Peter:

> Paul, by contrast, was wise enough to see that Christianity had little to do with Old Testament Judaism and nothing to do with rabbinic Judaism. Imposing Jewish ritual laws, Sabbath laws, and dietary laws on Gentiles would choke the church then and there. No! The church was much bigger than such things. It was universal, different in kind and character from Judaism, far bigger than James and his company could ever imagine. It was rooted in eternity; spread out through all the earth; at home in the heavenlies; spiritual in character, calling, and career; guided by principles, not by legalistic rules; united with a triumphant, ascended Christ on high;

and terrible to its foes as an army with banners. Paul, in his wisdom, saw all of that. He preached it, wrote about it, fought for it, and, in the end, died for it. Peter had come to appreciate Paul's genius.

Paul wrote deep things in the Lord, things that dealt with a Christian's everyday life. Yet as we study Paul's writings, we find things that are hard to comprehend. This is what Peter is writing about, people not being able to understand the truth, so they **go off into their own assumptions of what they want the Word to say**; assumptions that **lead them away from God to their own destruction**.

Paul wrote on spiritual things that deal with how a person is to conduct themselves before God and the wickedness of this world. We are to live a **Christ-like life before this present world so they can see the peace and joy that serving God can give**. Paul wrote on such things as the gifts of the spirit.

1 Corinthians 12:1-12

[1] Now concerning spiritual gifts, brethren, I would not have you ignorant.

[2] Ye know that ye were Gentiles, carried away unto these dumb idols, even as ye were led.

[3] Wherefore I give you to understand, that no man speaking by the Spirit of God calleth Jesus accursed: and that no man can say that Jesus is the Lord, but by the Holy Ghost. are diversities of gifts, but the same Spirit.

[5] And there are differences of administrations, but the same Lord.

[6] And there are diversities of operations, but it is the same

God which worketh all in all.

[7] But the manifestation of the Spirit is given to every man to profit withal.

[8] For to one is given by the Spirit the word of wisdom; to another the word of knowledge by the same Spirit;

[9] To another faith by the same Spirit; to another the gifts of healing by the same Spirit;

[10] To another the working of miracles; to another prophecy; to another discerning of spirits; to another divers kinds of tongues; to another the interpretation of tongues:

[11] But all these worketh that one and the selfsame Spirit, dividing to every man severally as he will.

[12] For as the body is one, and hath many members, and all the members of that one body, being many, are one body: so also is Christ.

Next, we have Paul's writings on marriage.

1 Corinthians 7:1-40

[1] Now concerning the things whereof ye wrote unto me: It is good for a man not to touch a woman.

[2] Nevertheless, to avoid fornication, let every man have his own wife, and let every woman have her own husband.

[3] Let the husband render unto the wife due benevolence: and likewise also the wife unto the husband.

[4] The wife hath not power of her own body, but the husband: and likewise also the husband hath not power of his own body, but the wife.

[5] Defraud ye not one the other, except it be with consent for a time, that ye may give yourselves to fasting and prayer;

and come together again, that Satan tempt you not for your incontinency.

⁶ But I speak this by permission, and not of commandment.

⁷ For I would that all men were even as I myself. But every man hath his proper gift of God, one after this manner, and another after that.

⁸ I say therefore to the unmarried and widows, It is good for them if they abide even as I.

⁹ But if they cannot contain, let them marry: for it is better to marry than to burn.

¹⁰ And unto the married I command, yet not I, but the Lord, Let not the wife depart from her husband:

¹¹ But and if she depart, let her remain unmarried, or be reconciled to her husband: and let not the husband put away his wife.

¹² But to the rest speak I, not the Lord: If any brother hath a wife that believeth not, and she be pleased to dwell with him, let him not put her away.

¹³ And the woman which hath an husband that believeth not, and if he be pleased to dwell with her, let her not leave him.

¹⁴ For the unbelieving husband is sanctified by the wife, and the unbelieving wife is sanctified by the husband: else were your children unclean; but now are they holy.

¹⁵ But if the unbelieving depart, let him depart. A brother or a sister is not under bondage in such cases: but God hath called us to peace.

¹⁶ For what knowest thou, O wife, whether thou shalt save thy husband? or how knowest thou, O man, whether thou shalt save thy wife?

¹⁷ But as God hath distributed to every man, as the Lord hath called every one, so let him walk. And so ordain I in

all churches.

¹⁸ *Is any man called being circumcised? let him not become uncircumcised. Is any called in uncircumcision? let him not be circumcised.*

¹⁹ *Circumcision is nothing, and uncircumcision is nothing, but the keeping of the commandments of God.*

²⁰ *Let every man abide in the same calling wherein he was called.*

²¹ *Art thou called being a servant? care not for it: but if thou mayest be made free, use it rather.*

²² *For he that is called in the Lord, being a servant, is the Lord's freeman: likewise also he that is called, being free, is Christ's servant.*

²³ *Ye are bought with a price; be not ye the servants of men.*

²⁴ *Brethren, let every man, wherein he is called, therein abide with God.*

²⁵ *Now concerning virgins I have no commandment of the Lord: yet I give my judgment, as one that hath obtained mercy of the Lord to be faithful.*

²⁶ *I suppose therefore that this is good for the present distress, I say, that it is good for a man so to be.*

²⁷ *Art thou bound unto a wife? seek not to be loosed. Art thou loosed from a wife? seek not a wife.*

²⁸ *But and if thou marry, thou hast not sinned; and if a virgin marry, she hath not sinned. Nevertheless such shall have trouble in the flesh: but I spare you.*

²⁹ *But this I say, brethren, the time is short: it remaineth, that both they that have wives be as though they had none;*

³⁰ *And they that weep, as though they wept not; and they that rejoice, as though they rejoiced not; and they that buy, as though they possessed not;*

31 And they that use this world, as not abusing it: for the fashion of this world passeth away.

32 But I would have you without carefulness. He that is unmarried careth for the things that belong to the Lord, how he may please the Lord:

33 But he that is married careth for the things that are of the world, how he may please his wife.

34 There is difference also between a wife and a virgin. The unmarried woman careth for the things of the Lord, that she may be holy both in body and in spirit: but she that is married careth for the things of the world, how she may please her husband.

35 And this I speak for your own profit; not that I may cast a snare upon you, but for that which is comely, and that ye may attend upon the Lord without distraction.

36 But if any man think that he behaveth himself uncomely toward his virgin, if she pass the flower of her age, and need so require, let him do what he will, he sinneth not: let them marry.

37 Nevertheless he that standeth stedfast in his heart, having no necessity, but hath power over his own will, and hath so decreed in his heart that he will keep his virgin, doeth well.

38 So then he that giveth her in marriage doeth well; but he that giveth her not in marriage doeth better.

39 The wife is bound by the law as long as her husband liveth; but if her husband be dead, she is at liberty to be married to whom she will; only in the Lord.

40 But she is happier if she so abide, after my judgment: and I think also that I have the Spirit of God.

Paul wrote on people's everyday lives and what God

demanded of them. These teachings are teachings that **need to be studied by searching the scriptures**, for they **hold the key to living an overcoming life for Jesus**.

We must, and again I say we must be careful **to seek out the truth of the scriptures**, for proper interpretation is a must. The scriptures **should be interpreted literally**. We must be careful of grammar and the culture of the times. It is vital for correct interpretation that **we never take the scriptures out of context**.

Paul's writings covered the known world at the time, because **his writings were spread to all the churches of that time**. His teachings were to enlighten not only the hearts of believers everywhere but **also how they were to live**. Herein is part of the problem Peter was talking about. Many new believers were not able to discern the truths that Paul was writing about. Even today **many who call themselves Bible scholars have a hard time discerning some of Paul's writings**. To the new believer, **pray and trust God, and He will never let you down**.

2 Peter 3:17-18

¹⁷ Ye therefore, beloved, seeing ye know these things before, beware lest ye also, being led away with the error of the wicked, fall from your own stedfastness.
¹⁸ But grow in grace, and in the knowledge of our Lord and Saviour Jesus Christ. To him be glory both now and for ever. Amen.

Peter concludes his epistle with these two verses. In verse seventeen, Peter gives a warning that we all should take great care to heed. **Our greatest possession is our salvation, and the enemy is out to steal that away from us.** Every day we see people who are being led away from the truth unto fables, "having a form of godliness but denying the power thereof."

2 Timothy 3:5

Having a form of godliness, but denying the power thereof: from such turn away.

Also, this verse finishes with these words, "from such turn away," which means **those who have a form but differ from the true word**. Do not listen to or follow after them. Remember that **Satan appears as an angel of light to deceive and to destroy**.

As we have studied in 2 Peter, there are four main statements we want to bring to your memory, and I like the way they are listed by *Wiersby*.

Wiersby Bible Commentary NT:

1. Beloved . . . be mindful (3:1-2)
2. Beloved, be not ignorant (3:8)
3. Beloved . . . be diligent (3:14)
4. Beloved . . . beware (3:17)

We are to beware of anything that differs from the Word. I was in a church service not long ago, and the minister made this statement: "We all sin every day. I know I do." When I began to think about what he was saying, he was saying that **the power of God was not strong enough to keep us from sin.**

What is wrong with this modern church world? When I first came to the Lord, our pastor preached that the God who saved our souls and washed them clean in the blood of the Lamb **is able to**

356

keep us from sin as we live for Him. Jesus come into my heart and set up His abode, and **there He lives this Christian life through me**. The message that we have to sin every day is a lie to mislead people. It is only an excuse **to try to cover up the true reason that people sin, and that is because they desire to do so**. My pastor preached the Word, and he preached it straight and true. He preached **the soul that sinneth it shall die**.

Ezekiel 18:24

But when the righteous turneth away from his righteousness, and committeth iniquity, and doeth according to all the abominations that the wicked man doeth, shall he live? All his righteousness that he hath done shall not be mentioned: in his trespass that he hath trespassed, and in his sin that he hath sinned, in them shall he die.

The scripture teaches that no man can serve two masters.

Matthew 6:24

No man can serve two masters: for either he will hate the one, and love the other; or else he will hold to the one, and despise the other. Ye cannot serve God and mammon.

James tells us that **no fountain can bring forth good water and bad**.

James 3:12

Can the fig tree, my brethren, bear olive berries? either a

357

vine, figs? so can no fountain both yield salt water and fresh.

What do these verses tell us? They tell us that **if you sin every day, then you are a sinner.** You cannot be a saved sinner. Either you are saved, or you are a sinner; you cannot be both, not according to the Word. **We are saved by the blood of Jesus Christ.** Water baptism will not save us, and church membership will not save us. **Only the blood can save.** Peter tells us to beware lest we let men deceive us with the error of the wicked, **lest we fall from our steadfastness back into a world of sin and lose our souls.** Beware, beware, beware, lest in that day we be weighed in the balances and are found wanting in the sight of our Lord and God.

Daniel 5:27

TEKEL; Thou art weighed in the balances, and art found wanting.

Beware and again I say beware for the enemy is out to destroy you. Beware!

Wiersby Bible Commentary NT:

One of the great tragedies of evangelism is bringing "spiritual babies" into the world and then failing to feed them, nature them, and help them develop. The apostates prey on young believers who have "very recently escaped" from the ways of error (2 Peter 2:18). New believers need to be taught the

358

basic doctrines of the Word of God; otherwise, they will be in danger of being "led away with the errors of the lawless."

There must be a steady rate of growth for the child of God. To those who are willing to follow Jesus, you will find that **God's grace is sufficient for every problem and everything that Satan can throw at us**. Remember, it is by grace that we are saved, the amazing grace of God, and the blood of His dear Son that washes away our sins.

The John Phillips Commentary Series – Exploring the Epistles of Peter:

> Think, too, of God's *sufficient* grace. Come demons, disease, or death, Jesus has conquered them all. Peter watched Him do it! What needs do we have? Are they spiritual, physical, mental, financial, or circumstantial needs? There is abundant grace for all saints, for all situations, and for all sins. God's grace flows into our lives like a mighty river. Paul could say, "[His] grace is sufficient for [me]," having learned the lesson directly from God in a trying circumstance of life (2 Cor. 12:7-10). Peter had learned that God's grace was sufficient when, on the resurrection morn, after his threefold denial of Christ, the Lord sought him out to restore him to the fold. And now he was anticipating death, a cruel death, death on a Roman cross. Was God's grace enough for that? Oh yes! There was sufficient grace!

That grace covers a multitude of sins. It is a grace that gives strength when there is no mortal strength, **a grace that will take us home to be with the Lord**. A child of God grows in grace. **Grow in the grace of Almighty God**; it makes all the difference in our lives. Above all, grow in grace.

Chapter 3 Review Questions

1. Why did Peter write his second epistle?

   _____

   _____

2. What does Satan forget? _____

   _____

3. Of the two opinions on Peter 3:5-7, what is the opinion most

   commonly accepted? _____

   _____

4. What is the second opinion on these scriptures?

   _____

   _____

5. This world, Earth, will be destroyed by

   _____.

6. Once again, I ask the question, where did sin originate?

   _____

7. It is God's will that all men _____

   _____.

8. What does the word rapture mean?

_____

9. The child of God has been given a promise. What is that

promise? _____

_____

10. Is everyone going to live forever?

_____

11. Peter wrote in the 15th verse; "account _____

_____ is salvation.

12. What vital lesson must the child of God learn?

_____

_____

13. Why do you think the Lord has waited so long to return?

_____

_____

14. The person who is ignorant of the gospel of the Lord will in

the end _____

_____.

15. Why do liberal scholars say that Jesus and the apostles did not believe the same thing?

_____

_____

16. In Proverbs 1:7 we read an important truth what is it?

_____

_____

17. What two reasons does Peter give why people have a hard time understanding some of Paul's writings?

_____

_____

18. What is vital to us in understanding the word of God?

_____

_____

19. In verse seventeen, Peter gives us a dire warning that we all should heed. Salvation is our greatest possession and we need to guard it because?

_____

20. Many are the people who have a form of godliness but deny

_____ .

21. There are four statements that we need to remember and they

are:

a) _____

b) _____

c) _____

d) _____

22. The God who is able to cleanse you, to make you clean and

whole through the blood of the Lamb is able to?

_____

_____

23. At salvation Jesus comes into our hearts and sets up His abode

and there He

_____ .

24. In verse eighteen, Peter leaves us this important message, and

it is to?

_____

Bibliography

I would like to express my thanks and appreciation to the following authors for their tireless work in bringing the scriptures to life for the average person. Without their labor in making the meaning of the scriptures come to light, this Bible Study would not have happened, and many people would never hear of these men and women. They may never read their works, but it is their loss. I recommend these works to anyone who desires a deeper knowledge of the Word of God.

2 Timothy 2:15

> *Study to shew thyself approved unto God, a workman that needeth not to be ashamed, rightly dividing the word of truth.*

Rev. Matthew Henry
    Matthew Henry's Commentary on the Whole Bible
    Hendrickson Publishers Inc.
    Fifth printing – May 1998
    Copyright 1991

Rev. Albert Barnes

      Barnes Notes on the New Testament
      Baker Book House Company
      Grand Rapids, Michigan
      Reprinted 2005
      Reprinted from the 1847 edition published by
          Blackie & Son, London

Rev. Finis Jennings Dake

      The Dake Annotated Reference Bible KJV
      Dake Bible Sales Inc.
      Lawrenceville, Georgia
      Twenty-seventh printing – April 1998
      Copyright 1963, 1991

Rev. Warren W. Wiersbe

      The Wiersbe Bible Commentary: New Testament
      Published by David C. Cook
      Colorado Springs, Colorado
      Second Edition 2007

Rev. John Phillips

      Exploring the Epistles of Peter
      The John Phillips Commentary Series
      Kregel Publications
      Grand Rapids, Michigan
      Published 2001

Rev. Elizabeth Williams, D. D,

      Prevision of History
      Part One - The Book of Daniel
      Part Two - The Book of Revelation

Messenger Publishing House
Copyright 1974

Mark Water
    Compiled by
    The New Encyclopedia of Christian Martyrs
    Baker Books
    Grand Rapids, Michigan

Rev. Marvin R. Vincent, D.D.
    Vincent's Word Studies in the New Testament
    Hendrickson Publishers
    Peabody, Maine

W. E. Vine, M. A. (1873 – 1949)
Merrill F. Unger, Th.M., Th.D., Ph.D. (1909 – 1980)
William White Jr., Th.M., Ph.D.
    Vines Complete Expository Dictionary of Old and
        New Testament Words
    Thomas Nelson Publishers
    Nashville, Tennessee
    Published 1985
    Copyright 1984

Webster's New World College Dictionary
    IDG Books Worldwide Inc.
    An International Data Group Company
    Foster City, California
    Fourth Edition
    Copyright 2000

Jay P. Green Sr.
>   General Editor and Translator
>   *The Interlinear Bible*
>   Hebrew, Greek, English
>   Sovereign Grace Publishers
>   Second Edition Copyrighted 1986

Joseph S. Exell
>   *The Biblical Illustrator*
>   Baker Book House
>   Grand Rapids, Michigan
>   Third Printing May 1977

Songs We Sing Complete
>   Re-Compiled and Edited By
>   Arthur Watson
>   ArtWorks Etcetera
>   Arlington, Texas

Answers to Review Questions

I Peter

Chapter 1 (page 69)

1. An Apostle is one who is sent on a mission by the Lord.
2. Three
3. Brings glory and honor to God
4. The Book of Acts
5. Only ourselves
6. Sanctification means to make holy, to set apart as holy, consecrate, to make free from sin, purify
7. For God's people to give up and have no hope
8. Because it is reserved for you
9. Not according to Peter
10. Hebrews 11:1 states: *Now faith is the substance of things hoped for, the evidence of things not seen.*
11. It is because of that personal experience we have with Jesus at Salvation
12. "Ye must be born again."
13. Through the name of Jesus
14. They were written for the purpose of learning
15. The Old Testament scriptures
16. Just to simply let Jesus live through us.
17. Oh God, less of me and more of you.
18. God judges us without respect of persons.
19. A slave, a wife and land
20. A near kinsman, being able to pay the price and be willing to pay that price

Chapter 2 (page 104)

1. The sincere milk of the word.
2. To be entertained
3. Yield to the temptation and do what the devil has tempted us with.
4. A nursery, to give them the sincere milk of the word
5. And do not the things which I say?
6. Exodus 19:5-6
7. Shall die
8. A city whose builder and maker is God.
9. Like the son of God
10. Ignorance of foolish men
11. King Nebuchadnezzar
12. Darius
13. We must be born again
14. Free indeed
15. One more night with the frogs
16. Pilate
17. Isaiah 53
18. Sheep

Chapter 3 (page 144)

1. In subjection to their husbands
2. 1 Peter 3:3 Whose adorning let it not be that outward *adorning* of plaiting the hair, and of wearing of gold, or of putting on of apparel;
3. Sara later to be known as Sarah
4. Colossians 3:19 Husbands, love *your* wives, and be not bitter against them.

5. 1 Peter 3:8 Finally, *be ye* all of one mind, having compassion one of another, love as brethren, *be* pitiful, *be* courteous:
6. Members
7. The shed blood of Jesus Christ
8. Matthew 5:48; Be ye therefore perfect, even as your Father which is in heaven is perfect.
9. A Perfect and upright man
10. Blessing
11. Evil
12. His tongue from evil
13. The Bible does not name her.
14. Righteous
15. Numbered
16. An answer to every man that asked you
17. Conscience
18. The spirits in prison
19. Eight souls
20. Sitting on the right hand of God
21. The souls of those who died before the flood

Chapter 4 (page 182)

1. With the mind of Christ
2. To believe in Christ strong enough that we are willing to suffer pain and torment in the flesh, then we have ceased from sin or else we would not have suffered
3. No
4. Do evil
5. The prize
6. A lack of restraint, indecency, wanton behavior, shameless.

7. The sinners
8. There is no wrong answer
9. No
10. Yes
11. Love
12. Salvation
13. The oracle of God
14. Fiery trial which is to try you
15. Partakers
16. Murder, or as a thief, or as an evildoer, or as a busybody
17. Ashamed
18. At the house of God
19. Saved, ungodly, sinners
20. Our souls

Chapter 5 (page 202)

1. The elders which are among you
2. The flock of God
3. Ensamples or Examples
4. Jesus Christ
5. Submit
6. Humility
7. Proud, Humble
8. Cares, cares for us
9. As a Roaring Lion
10. Whom he may devour
11. Resist
12. They are
   a. A Roaring Lion in 1 Peter 5:8
   b. A Ravening Wolf in Matthew 7:15
   c. An Angel of Light in 2 Corinthians 11:14

13. I John 4:4
14. By the grace of God, through the blood of Jesus
15. Babylon
16. Silas
17. With a kiss of charity (love)

2 Peter

Chapter 1 (page 252)

1. Peter calls himself a servant.
2. A prisoner of Jesus Christ.
3. To those who had obtained the same precious faith.
4. Every battle and every trial that we go through.
5. Exceeding great and precious promises.
6. All of God's promises are conditional on whether we live for God or not.
7. What keeps us connected to God is prayer, studying God's Word and fasting.
8. The promises of God, for even salvation is a promise.
9. To satisfy self.
10. God's arithmetic is to add to what we already have.
11. Behaves itself.
12. Moral excellence.
13. To virtue add knowledge.
14. Faith and learning by experience.
15. Here temperance means self control.
16. It is the ability to wait for God to have His way in our hearts and lives. And we get it by trials and much tribulation.
17. Job and Joseph.
18. Pantheism believes that God and the universe are all one,

and embraces all religions and all gods.

19. Charity means love.

Chapter 2 (page 321)

1. Counterfeit
2. False teachers
3. That they would become as gods
4. Basis with our Lord Jesus.
5. Polytheism is the belief of many gods.
6. Tell a lie loud enough and long enough and it becomes the truth in people's minds.
7. Sin is anything that comes between you and God.
8. Sins originally occurred in heaven when Satan and his angels rebelled against God.
9. One third.
10. Admah, Lasha and Zeboim.
11. To have control over our mouth and tongue.
12. Having eyes full of adultery and cannot cease from sin.
13. By surrendering their lives to Jesus Christ through repentance.
14. The Laodicean church age.
15. Shadow.
16. That they are wrong.
17. The fear of the Lord is the beginning of wisdom.
18. Masters.
19. That once you are saved you are forever saved. That there is no way whatever that a man can lose his salvation.
20. *"All his righteousness that he hath done shall not be mentioned: in his trespass that he hath trespassed and in his sin that he hath sinned in them shall he die."*
21. No

22. Yes
23. Our first love is that pure love we find when we come to Jesus and ask his forgiveness of our sins. And there we invite Him into our heart and life.
24. Yes.
25. **Revelation 3:16** – *So then because thou art lukewarm, and neither cold nor hot, I will spue thee out of my mouth.*
26. Answers may vary.

Chapter 3 (page 361)

1. Because it is needful for us to be put in remembrance from time to time of the things that are important to us.
2. That God will always have a remnant that will serve Him.
3. That Peter is referring to the creation as recorded in the Book of Genesis.
4. That there was a pre-Adamite world.
5. Fire.
6. In heaven.
7. Should be saved .
8. The catching away of Christ's Bride.
9. That we will inherit a new home in heaven.
10. Yes, but the question is where.
11. "that the longsuffering of our Lord"
12. We must learn to be patient before God, knowing that God hears and answers prayer in His time, not ours.
13. It may be to give more souls the opportunity to find Him as their personal savior.
14. Fall prey to the devil.
15. So that they can denounce what the apostles wrote as untrue.
16. That the fear of the Lord is the beginning of knowledge.

17. Because some are unlearned in the Word and because some are unstable in their beliefs.
18. Never ever take scripture out of context
19. Satan desires to lead us astray through the error of the wicked. Beware.
20. The power thereof and from such turn away.
21. 1. Beloved . . . be mindful (3:1-2) 2. Beloved, be not ignorant (3:8) 3. Beloved . . . be diligent (3:14) 4. Beloved . . . beware (3:17).
22. Keep you from sin.
23. Lives this Christian life through us.
24. Grow in grace, and in the knowledge of our Lord and Savior Jesus Christ.

Available Now!

A Study on the Book of James

Introduction

There is much conflict about who James really was. Some believe that he was James the elder, the brother of John the son of Zebedee. Others believe that he is James the less, the son of Alphaeus. Still others believe that he is James the Just, the brother of our Lord and Saviour Jesus Christ. To be truthful it really makes no difference as to his pedigree or genealogy.

We know that James, the brother of Jesus, lived in Jerusalem. Paul records in Galatians that he went to Jerusalem to see Peter and stayed with him for fifteen days. While there, he saw James, the brother of our Lord.

Galatians 1:18-20

> *18 Then after three years I went up to Jerusalem to see Peter, and abode with him fifteen day.*
> *19 But other of the apostles saw I none, save James the Lord's brother.*
> *20 Now the things which I write unto you, behold, before God, I lie not.*

It is common belief that James was not a believer in Jesus being the promised redeemer until after His death and resurrection from the dead. Paul states that Jesus was seen of about five hundred souls at one time and after that, He went and showed Himself to

James, His brother.

1 Corinthians 15:6-8

> *⁶ After that, he was seen of above five hundred brethren at once; of whom the greater part remain unto this present, but some are fallen asleep.*
> *⁷ After that, he was seen of James; then of all the apostles.*
> *⁸ And last of all he was seen of me also, as of one born out of due time.*

Whereupon James believed that Jesus was the Lord and Saviour, just as He had said.

After seeing Jesus, James devoted his life to the service of our Lord. James grew in the service of the Lord and His church to the point that he became the head of the Jerusalem Christian Church. James' life was a witness and an example of righteousness and holiness before God. It is reported that James continually gave himself to prayer before God for the people, that God would forgive their sins and save them.

As we know from the Word, James, though a Christian, was still very closely tied to the Jewish Law and customs. Paul, at one time, had to persuade James that the Gentiles could be saved and their sins forgiven through Jesus' blood, that the Gentiles did not, and in fact could not live for God if they had to abide by Jewish Law and dietary customs, which were in direct opposition to their way of life. After this meeting, the Gentile church grew and spread rapidly. The thing that Paul stressed to James was that the Gentiles' salvation was based upon living for God according to the teachings of the Gospel and not Jewish Traditions. Even though James relented to Paul on the matter of the Gentile Christians, he did not intend to give up his Jewish ways of living.

Paul was as much a Jew as James and far more educated in the Jewish laws and customs, but Paul's calling was to the Gentiles, whereas James had the calling to the Jewish Christians in and around Jerusalem. From papers that were written about James by the early church fathers, we can tell a lot about James. He was strongly tied to the legalism of the Jewish faith, yet at the same time, he was a very practical and moral man. James loved the church, and this love of the Christian church is what led to his death; he was killed by the Jews, beaten to death at the age of ninety-four.

You will want your own copy of this exciting new study coming soon at www.ParadiseGospelPress.com.

www.ingramcontent.com/pod-product-compliance
Lightning Source LLC
Chambersburg PA
CBHW062154270326
41930CB00009B/1531